Teacher Collaboration and Talk
in Multilingual Classrooms

BILINGUAL EDUCATION AND BILINGUALISM
Series Editors: Professor Colin Baker, *University of Wales, Bangor, Wales, Great Britain* and Professor Nancy H. Hornberger, *University of Pennsylvania, Philadelphia, USA*

Recent Books in the Series

For more details of these or any other of our publications, please contact:
Multilingual Matters, Frankfurt Lodge, Clevedon Hall,
Victoria Road, Clevedon, BS21 7HH, England
http://www.multilingual-matters.com

BILINGUAL EDUCATION AND BILINGUALISM 51
Series Editors: Colin Baker and Nancy H. Hornberger

Teacher Collaboration and Talk in Multilingual Classrooms

Angela Creese

MULTILINGUAL MATTERS LTD
Clevedon • Buffalo • Toronto

For Ida and Barbara

Library of Congress Cataloging in Publication Data
Creese, Angela.
Teacher Collaboration and Talk in Multilingual Classrooms / Angela Creese.
Bilingual Education and Bilingualism: 51
Includes bibliographical references.
1. Native language and education–England–London–Case studies.
2. Education, Bilingual–England–London–Case studies.
3. Children of immigrants–Education (Secondary)–England–London–Case studies.
4. Language policy–England–London–Case studies. I. Title. II. Series.
LC201.7.G7C74 2005
371.14'8–dc22   2004028649

British Library Cataloguing in Publication Data
A catalogue entry for this book is available from the British Library.

ISBN 1-85359-822-4 (hbk)
ISBN 1-85359-821-6 (pbk)
ISBN 1-85359-823-2 (electronic)

Multilingual Matters Ltd
UK: Frankfurt Lodge, Clevedon Hall, Victoria Road, Clevedon BS21 7HH.
USA: UTP, 2250 Military Road, Tonawanda, NY 14150, USA.
Canada: UTP, 5201 Dufferin Street, North York, Ontario M3H 5T8, Canada.

Typeset by Florence Production Ltd.
Printed and bound in Great Britain by the Cromwell Press Ltd.

Contents

Acknowledgements

This project has developed over many years and has involved the help and encouragement of many people: the teachers and students at three London secondary schools, my own university teachers and supervisors, my colleagues, friends and family.

To the staff and students at the three schools, I am indebted. Throughout this book their names have been changed, but during the production process participants have come to recognize their assigned pseudonyms and in some cases even complained about them. I am particularly grateful to Noreen, Irene and Unal, heads of EAL at each of the three schools. I hope I have done them justice in the trust they showed me during my visits to their schools.

The University of Pennsylvania, its past and present staff and students have played an important part in improving my understanding of linguistic and social processes. I would like to thank Cathrine Berg, Kristine Billmyer, Cathy Doughty, Fred Erickson, John Lucy, Alison Mackey, Ellen Sylvester-Skilton and Nessa Wolfson. I am particularly grateful to Tere Pica and Euan Reid who supported me with ideas and encouragement during this research. I owe a very great debt indeed to Nancy Hornberger for her teachings, research and supervision. She has been an inspiration, not only to me, but to many many others.

My colleagues have made many insightful comments during the life of this research in direct and indirect ways. I would like to thank Sophie Arkoudis, Jo Arthur, Richard Barwell, Arvind Bhatt, Jill Bourne, Harry Daniels, Chris Davies, Sheena Gardner, Valerie Hey, Constant Leung, Deirdre Martin, Marilyn Martin-Jones, Janet Maybin, Brahm Norwich, Ben Rampton, Hugh South and Karin Tusting. Adrian Blackledge patiently read a draft of earlier work and provided helpful and insightful feedback. I would also like to thank Peter Martin and Stephanie Taylor for their critical engagement with my ideas and for their friendship.

My thanks to my family: my dad, the late Douglas Creese, and my brother Billy and sister Joanna. To my mum, Barbara Creese, I am ever indebted. She is, and always will be, the tall woman in my life. My final and biggest debt of gratitude and thanks are for Ida and Nathan.

I would like to thank all the staff at Multilingual Matters for their guidance and good humour.

A Note on Terminology

Although there are many parallels between the educational issues presented by language minorities in English-dominant countries there are also many differences in the language policies that have evolved to deal with them. This book, although not attempting to be explicitly comparative, will draw on the policy experience of several countries in order, as fully as possible, to discuss the educational practice of linguistic minority students. However, the data presented here comes from an English context and the terminology used to describe the schools and their participants will, therefore, be that used by British educationalists.

Sometimes the same terms have different connotations across national contexts (Edwards & Redfern, 1992: 4). In Britain, the term 'bilingual' is used to describe students learning and using English as an additional language (EAL); 'thereby stressing children's accomplishments rather than their lack of fluency in English' (Levine, 1990: 5). The definition does not make 'any judgement of range or quality of linguistic skills, but stands for the alternate use of two languages in the same individual' (Bourne, 1989: 1–2). In the United States, 'English as a secondary language' (ESL) is the term probably most in use to describe children learning English while going through the education system (Adamson, 1993), although 'bilingual' is also used along with a plethora of other terms ('limited English proficient', etc.). Similarly, the term 'LOTE', is in current use in Australia to describe speakers of languages other than English. In this book, both the terms 'bilingual' and 'EAL' will be used to describe teachers' and students' states and goals in the three schools that were the main sites for this book's research.

Abbreviations

CDA	critical discourse analysis
DES	Department of Education and Science
DfES	Department for Education and Skills
EAL	English as an additional language
EALT	English as an additional language teacher
EMAG	Ethnic Minority Achievement Grant
ESL	English as a second language
GCSE	General Certificate of Secondary Education
IRF	initiation, response and feedback
HOD	head of department
HOY	head of year
IS	interactional sociolinguistics
IT	Information Technology
INSET	in-service training
L1	first language
L2	second language
LEA	Local Educational Authority
MT	mother tongue
Ofsted	Office for Standards in Education
QTS	qualified teacher status
S	student
S11	Section 11 (funding stream prior to EMAG)
SEN	special educational needs
SENCO	special educational needs coordinator
SLA	second language acquisition
ST	subject teacher
TEFL	teaching English as a foreign language

Key to Symbols Used

A, B, C	schools in this study
1–4	EAL teachers. So A1 refers to an EAL teacher in school A
5–	From 5 onwards shows that the teacher is a subject teacher

Introduction

Geography teacher working with two 15-year-old students
S = student, T = teacher

S1: Miss, what have you got that for (referring to the tape recorder)?
T: Because she (referring to me) wants to record what I am saying and what Miss Smith (EAL teacher) is saying and then she can play it back and she can see if there is a difference between the two of us.
S1: There is.
S2: Yeah, I think there should be a difference.
T: Why?
S1: Miss, you're the better teacher aren't you.
S2: Like if I don't understand and Miss Smith explains to me and I still don't understand and I call you over and you tell me a different thing.
T: So we see it from two different ways you mean?
S1: But you're the proper teacher aren't you?
T: Well no. We are both proper teachers.
S1: She's like a help.
T: No, that's not true.

This book offers a critical analysis of the collaborative teaching relationship between English as an additional language (EAL) teachers and subject curriculum teachers in schools. The extract above is used to give a flavour of what will follow. It foregrounds some issues that will be developed throughout the book: how are 'real' teachers constructed; what makes a teacher 'a help'; how and why are the teachers' expertises positioned differently; what are the implications of this positioning on the way that language diversity issues are viewed within the mainstream subject-focused classroom? The book aims to show how subject teachers (STs) and EAL teachers are positioned differently within the school through the teachers' pedagogic stances and the discourses which support them. An overarching concern is to consider how issues of power impact upon the implementation of an educational policy for bilingual children and how cultural and linguistic diversity are, in turn, viewed within English schools.

In this book, issues of power are made central to understanding the structure and function of teaching partnerships and the discourses that permeate and surround them. I ask how and why particular classroom discourses come to dominate, and look at how and why the education process endorses particular knowledge hierarchies. I argue that these questions matter because the interrelationships which teachers form with one another impact on the pedagogic diversity of classroom life in ways which implicate learners directly. Fundamentally, this book is about the policy/practice interface and describes how policy is understood and interpreted locally in three diverse London secondary schools. It attempts to answer the following questions:

(1) How do EAL teachers and subject teachers in secondary schools organize their collaboration to implement the curriculum for minority linguistic and ethnic students?
(2) In what way, if any, does the fact that within teacher teams the EAL teacher is, or is not, bilingual in one of the community languages of the classroom affect classroom content and practice in secondary schools?
(3) How are wider educational issues manifested in the discourses of teachers in the classroom?

Collaborating Teachers

Teaching partnerships are a common response in different national contexts to meeting the needs of students who are learning a subject curriculum through a new and developing language (Bourne, 1989, 1997; Bourne & McPake, 1991; Carrasquillo & Rodriguez, 1995; Coelho, 1998; Lee, 1997; Mohan *et al.*, 2001). In countries where educational-inclusive policies support language minority children's learning in mainstream curricula classrooms, these inter-professional relationships are probably the most important single means in which the schools' structures and systems support the children's full participation in the educational process. In a very real way then these teaching relationships matter, as upon their shoulders rests the success of an educational policy.

Yet little research has been done on how teaching partnerships change the traditional classroom context as we know it. As Cohen (1981: 165) has pointed out: 'Any change which brings teachers into a working relationship where they share decision making and communicate regularly about classroom matters represents a profound change for the structure of teaching.' It is precisely because there are two teachers in the room instead of one, each with shared and differing agendas, that the situation is worth examining. We need to reach an understanding of what opportunities these relationships offer in terms of classroom pedagogy, learning possibilities and meeting the needs of linguistic and ethnic minority students.

Teacher collaboration is clearly not exclusive to those working in multilingual/multicultural primary and secondary schools and it is hoped that this book will be of interest to other educational practitioners who in their work form a variety of formal inter-professional relationships with colleagues. These might include language teachers working in immersion programmes, dual bilingual programmes and international schools. It could also include relationships between classroom teachers and (bilingual) classroom assistants, a provision found in many urban schools. From a more international perspective, the content of this book could also be of interest to modern language teachers and language assistants in contexts such as Japan (Fujimoto-Adamson, 2003), where English is taught by a Japanese teacher accompanied by an English native speaker assistant. A final group of teachers who could benefit from the focus of this book on collaborative teacher relationships and classroom pedagogy are teachers of special educational needs (SEN) (Creese *et al.*, 2000; Hanko, 1999). Although the issues of bilingualism and special educational needs are distinct, there are places where the fields overlap. One of these relates to teacher collaboration. Like EAL teachers, SEN coordinators form a variety of different classroom and school collegiate relationships which are central to their work. These relationships are crucial to the way that teachers, and their domain of expertise, are positioned within schools. It is hoped, therefore, that practitioners in different educational settings can gain from the observations and analysis of teacher collaboration as viewed from the critical perspective developed in this book.

Specifically, the focus of the book is on the strengths and weaknesses of an inclusive education policy which attempts to support bilingual children in London secondary schools through the use of teaching partnerships. It examines what such a collaborative relationship can offer teachers and students through looking at the roles teachers play in class, the relationships they form and the discourses they use to perform their daily work. The book also considers directly issues of linguistic resourcing and identity through its discussion of teaching relationships between EAL specialists who are bilingual in a community language of the classroom and those who are not, and the subject teachers with whom they team up. It is hoped that the book's concern with the possibilities of collaborative teacher relationships and their pedagogies will have relevance to all those interested in learning and teaching processes where such measures have been introduced.

Teaching Partnerships: Supporting Linguistic Diversity

Despite its prevalence in many different national and educational contexts and its implementation as a means of support for learning, the workings and discourses of teaching partnerships have not yet been fully described. This book attempts to go some way to remedying this; by describing in detail one particular national context, but with the hope that this will have relevance for a wider community. There is a small but impressive body of empirical work within applied linguistics which has begun to deal with this teaching relationship through the consideration of power within particular contexts (see Arkoudis, 2000, 2003; Gardner, in press; Lee, 1997; Martin-Jones & Saxena 1989, 1996). This work considers the roles and discourses language specialist play, their take-up within mainstream settings and the affordances these ofter them.

Marilyn Martin-Jones and Mukul Saxena (1996) looked at the discourse of bilingual teaching assistants[1] and classroom teachers in primary schools. Over three years, they documented in detail the ways in which a local bilingual assistant scheme was being implemented at school and classroom level. They achieved this through a survey of all the bilingual classroom assistants who had been appointed across five local education districts. The survey was then followed up by in-depth interviews with a sample of those surveyed. Following the survey, observation and audio/video recording of bilingual teaching/learning events in classrooms was conducted. This produced classroom transcripts showing discursive differences between the assistants and the teachers. The research found that bilingual assistants within schools could not take on any voice, but were restricted by those associated with the way they were positioned. It was the subject teacher who was able to interrupt conversation, allocate speaking turns and interpreted what was significant (i.e. on task or not). Subject teachers, therefore, generally orchestrated the enactment of the learning event by both verbal and non-verbal means. This allowed a monolingual order of discourse to be maintained through the containment of other languages and their speakers.

Sophie Arkoudis (2000), similarly, has looked at the discursive construction of power in teaching relationships. Her study is based in secondary schools and uses audio recordings of two teachers working through a series of planning meetings. She highlights the linguistic resources teachers use to evaluate one another's work. The work is essentially a discourse analysis of a series of teacher-to-teacher conversations and does not include wider ethnographic contextualization of teachers' classroom practices and how these are conceptualized by the students and teachers themselves. Arkoudis argues that different forms of knowledge have different statuses in schools and receive differential organizational support. She shows how the language specialist has to recontextualize her own subject knowledge in terms of curriculum knowledge, and in doing so creates a discourse of learning support that maintains established knowledge hierarchies. Arkoudis is concerned with the positioning of English as a second language (ESL) as a methodology and the implications of this for an EAL curriculum within subject-disciplinary centred schools.

Arkoudis goes on to describe the difficulty of achieving successful teaching partnerships in an Australian context:

> The notion of working with mainstream teachers has been problematic as ESL teachers have found it difficult to teach English language development within the mainstream curriculum. (Arkoudis, 1994)

> Defining the role of the ESL teacher and the ESL curriculum in this context has been difficult in secondary schools where subject disciplines operate as separate areas within the school. Each subject area has clearly defined knowledge and content. (Arkoudis, 2003: 165)

Arkoudis (2003) argues that subject and EAL teachers have different epistemological authority within their schools linked to their different subject-specific discourses. She claims that certain epistemological positions have more status than others. For example, science has a more powerful position than ESL, with the latter often being conceptualized as a general skill that any teacher possesses intuitively. My work has similarly shown how ESL/EAL teachers become constructed into lower status positions within the school through their discourse patterns. My argument is that societal and institutional discourses on education view the work done by EAL teachers and subject teachers differently. Whereas subject teachers are linked to the transmission of subject knowledge to the many, EAL teachers are considered to be delivering support and facilitation for the few. EAL work can wrongly become positioned within schools as generic and with no subject-specific knowledge of its own (Creese, 2000, 2002b; Creese & Leung, 2003; Lee, 1997; Leung, 2001; Leung & Franson, 2001a, 2001b; NALDIC, 1999).

Fieldwork, Methods and Methodology

The methodologies and analytical frameworks used in this research can be grouped broadly under the heading of linguistic ethnography. The ethnography of communication and interactional sociolinguistics are the two primary approaches used (Gumperz, 1982, 1999; Hornberger, 1989, 1993, 1996; Hymes, 1968, 1974), although other related approaches are also taken up. These are more fully explored in Chapter 1. Specifically, the ethnography of communication and interactional sociolinguistics is used in this study to look at how an ideology of inclusion is played out through the teachers' classroom discourses and pedagogic actions.

A particular set of tools used for the discourse analysis of teacher talk in the classroom and central to the ethnography of communication will be explored. This involves combining an interest in languages' ability to index social context (Gumperz, 1982; Peirce, 1955; Silverstein, 2003; Silverstein & Urban, 1996) and its capacity to foreground particular social functions within a social context (Hymes, 1968; Jakobson, 1971). This functional approach to discourse analysis identifies the components of a speech context and the hierarchizing of functions within it. In the study discussed here a functional analysis shows how teachers discursively foreground a variety of functions within the classroom and how these position the teachers differently within the class. Language use indexes wider debates in education, so that students are able to infer who are 'real teachers' and who are there to 'help'.

Data Context

Three London secondary schools are the context for this study. The schools were approached through the head of EAL to ask whether they would be willing to take part. The schools which became part of this study all shared three criteria: first, they were in a geographic area which was linguistically and ethnically diverse;

second, the schools described themselves as operating different forms of teacher collaboration; third, the largest linguistic minority were Turkish-speaking.[2]

The three schools in this study are in economically poor and richly diverse parts of London. The schools are a lively mixture of ethnicities, cultures and languages. Between 35–65% of the students across the three schools were listed as having English as an additional language (EAL). School B (Sinchester school) is a single-sex school, while school A (Skonnington school) and school C (Soldingstoke school) were mixed. At the time of data collection all three schools were at the bottom of the nationally collected statistics for academic achievement, but they reflected average attainment for their own local areas. The students' ages ranged from 11 to 16 and it was possible for an EAL teacher to teach across the full age and subject range depending on how the school and its teachers decided to deploy their EAL resources.

Three Schools

The information on the three schools given below comes from several sources. For schools A and C government reports existed which gave uniform information as part of the inspection process. School B had at the time of data collection not been inspected in this way. Other sources include documents/information/statistics given by the schools themselves.

School A: Sinchester school

This school is a comprehensive mixed-sex school in an outer London borough. The students at school A were described by the English government's inspectorate body for schools – the Office for Standards in Education (Ofsted) – as representing,

> the whole ability range though some experience socio-economic disadvantages. There are 30% of students for whom English is the second language and support is available for these bilingual learners. Additional support is also available within an on-site unit for students with learning and behavioural difficulties. A number of students are physically impaired. The LEA has made statements of special educational needs for four students. Twenty-one per cent of the school population is entitled to free school meals. (Ofsted, 1993: 1)

There were 60.8 equivalent full-time teachers for around 950 students. Ofsted described classroom support as effective. However, the school was criticized for not publicly acknowledging the many languages spoken by the students at the school.

> Students at [. . .] School come from a very wide range of cultural and linguistic backgrounds and currently these are not adequately acknowledged or reflected in the general environment of the school or in the school's documentation. More opportunities should be sought to explore the potential of this culturally diverse community. (Ofsted, 1993: 1)

These Ofsted findings were also reflected in the head teacher's attitude to bilingual students in the school, which he spoke about in an interview I had with him. Although proud of the diversity of the school the head teacher was also keen not to promote differences in any way. At one stage in the interview he said that he intentionally did not know the breakdown of different ethnic groups in the school. He also felt that the use of the first language was appropriate for subject-learning but should not be encouraged otherwise within the school. Moreover, he felt that international evenings had to be handled with care because newly arrived communities did not always feel comfortable about sharing their cultures in the school. Since trying one such evening four years ago, the school had not organized any further similar events.

During the data collection phase at the school there were two full-time EAL teachers, who had travelled widely and were themselves multilingual (although not in terms of the largest minority languages in the school, which were Turkish and Greek). These two teachers worked with two departments in a partnership mode of collaboration. Additional funding also provided the school with a bilingual Turkish-speaking instructor (who was training for qualified teacher's status (QTS) during my fieldwork period). The school itself also employed a Turkish bilingual teacher to teach Turkish for the General Certificate of Secondary Education (GCSE). These classes were held during lunch hours.

School B: Skonnington school

This school is a single-sex girls comprehensive school with 822 pupils and 70 full-time equivalent teachers at the time of data collection. It is situated in an inner London borough. It employed two full-time EAL teachers, one of whom was bilingual in Turkish and English. The other was white and non-bilingual. Additional funding was also used to employ three part-time teachers, one of whom was Turkish-speaking. The team were based in the language and learning service and aimed to target as many students as possible, rather than working in close partnership situations with fewer teachers and fewer students. The school is multi-ethnic with the largest group being Turkish-speaking. Of the 822 students, 593 were listed as EAL students.

School C: Soldingstoke

This school is a mixed-sex comprehensive school in an inner London borough. It had 884 students and 53 full-time equivalent teachers. The government's Ofsted report gives the following background information on the school, which is worth reporting in some detail:

> [School C] is situated in the London Borough of [. . .], one of the most economically and socially deprived areas of the country, although with pockets of middle class settlement. 56.1% of the school population is eligible for free school meals, much higher than the national average.

> There is a very diverse ethnic population within the school. 58% are white, although this includes 24% who are Turkish/Kurdish, 13% are African Caribbean, 9% Bangladeshi, 8% Indian, 5% Black African, 4% Chinese, 1% Pakistani and 2% are from other groups. Its profile is changing, however. The number of Bangladeshi pupils is decreasing, and there is a significant and increasing number of pupils who are Turkish/Kurdish. Many of these pupils are from families who are political refugees and who live in temporary accommodation. Over 33 different first languages are spoken and half of the pupils come from homes where English is the second language. 65% are eligible for Section 11 support.
>
> The school receives pupils across the ability range, with reading ages at intake, for example, ranging from 5 to complete fluency. There is a higher proportion of average to less-able students. Many pupils are reported as having limited cognitive skills, and social, emotional and behavioural difficulties. 21 pupils have a statement of special educational needs. 19 boys and two girls.
>
> The school takes a large number of mid-term entrants, many of whom are non-English speakers, have learning difficulties or have had difficulties in other schools. In a recent 15 month period more than 150 pupils joined the school as mid-term entrants, of whom approximately half were stage 1 ESL learners and more than 50 had either been expelled from their last school or had left to avoid expulsion. (Ofsted, 1994: 1)

Of note here was the high mobility of the school population. Also of importance is the comment regarding the high number of early bilingual/EAL students at the time of data collection. In contrast to school A, this school was described by the inspectorate as a 'very caring community which values the cultural and linguistic diversity of its pupils'. Indeed, on visiting the school the celebration of cultural diversity was more apparent, with various poster and display boards prominently using different languages. Moreover, the school did much to promote the arts and culture of different groups particularly in terms of music and drama. This was singled out by the Ofsted report, 'the school makes considerable efforts to widen pupils' cultural knowledge ... positive examples of pupils exhibiting aspects of their cultural heritage are particularly evident within the Turkish bilingual population' (Ofsted, 1994: 11). During my fieldwork stage there were 6.8 EAL staff, who were described as having 'clearly defined roles and responsibilities and a good profile in the school' (Ofsted, 1994: 28). One of these was a bilingual Turkish speaker. In addition to these EAL teachers, the school also employed a teacher to provide Turkish GCSE. Turkish was offered on the regular timetable, although this arrangement was under threat. The Turkish teacher had started to spend more of his time supporting pupils in other curriculum subjects.

EAL teachers had worked at this school since it first opened in the 1970s. At least one member of the team has been there since that time and had herself seen and developed many new initiatives in language support including the movement from withdrawal to mainstreaming. The school was well known for its work in language support and in particular its work with bilingual Turkish-speaking pupils. The EAL department in the school advocated partnership teaching.

Data Obtained

I spent, on average, one 10-week term in each school – approximately 460 hours of observation in total. Twenty-six teachers were observed and interviewed using semi-structured and ethnographic approaches. Twelve of these were language specialists and the remaining 14 were subject specialists (teaching across the whole curriculum range). In two of the schools (B and C), two EAL language specialists were bilingual in a classroom community language (Turkish) and two were not. In school A, there was one bilingual community language teacher, teaching Turkish at GCSE, and one bilingual Turkish-speaking classroom assistant working towards qualified teacher status.

Procedures of Data Collection

Entry to the research site was through the permission of the head of EAL support. I then shadowed the language specialists through their working day. I spent just over two weeks with each EAL teacher and the teachers with whom s/he worked. The collection of field notes involved a mixture of participant and semi-participant observations. At times I was fully engaged in 'working' in the classroom and played the role of EAL teacher. In such cases, notes were made whenever a spare moment allowed during the school day and afterwards. At other times, I observed in the class and took a backseat from teaching. Observations continued beyond the classroom, to the staffroom and any other public domain in which the EAL teachers were engaged.

Classroom audio recordings were achieved through asking both the subject teachers and EAL teachers to wear a personal walkman with microphone. Teachers were recorded once or twice in consecutive lessons. All six of the non-bilingual EAL teachers and their collaborating subject teachers agreed to be recorded in this way. The six bilingual EAL teachers requested not to be audio recorded while teaching.[3] Classroom data from audio recordings therefore comes from 20 teachers none of whom were bilingual EAL teachers. Permission to record was agreed during the data collection process and depended on the goodwill of the teachers.

Interviews were held with all 26 teachers towards the end of the data collection period in each school. The EAL teachers were interviewed first. The subject teachers who I had observed working with the EAL teachers were then also interviewed. The interviews were conducted during teachers' study periods and lasted for approximately one hour.

Presenting Data in this Book

Throughout this book, I use alphabetical and numerical codes to indicate which school and teacher the information has come from. Examples can be seen in parentheses after each interview or classroom transcript, e.g. A4, B7, C3. The letter shows which school the information has been taken from and the number shows whether it is an EAL or subject teacher. Numbers 1–4 indicate that the teacher concerned is an EAL teacher, while number 5 and onwards denotes that it is a subject teacher. For the most part, I have also included additional information regarding the subject specialism of the subject teacher and the year groups being taught in the case of classroom transcripts. The decision to use codes rather than school and teachers' names was made because of the relatively large number of teachers involved. I have made two exceptions to this strategy. First, when teachers refer to other colleagues in their transcripts I have used pseudonyms to replace their real names rather than use codes; second, in Chapters 9 and 10 where the focus is on bilingual teachers. These chapter present a specific case study of bilingual teachers and personalizes their identities through the use of pseudonyms.

The Chapters of this Book

The chapters of this book are weighted to various degrees upon data, policy and theory. Chapter 1 sets the theoretical and methodological framework. Chapter 2 gives the policy context. Chapters 3 to 10 are data focused chapters, while Chapter 11 summarizes the overall findings discussed throughout the book.

The research presented in this book is multidisciplinary and I draw on many literatures within education and applied linguistics to make my arguments. Rather than presenting all the literature up-front, as is the more usual format for a book of this kind, each data chapter starts with a literature review relevant to the theme and the data presented in that specific chapter.

My overarching theoretical framework comes from linguistic ethnography and anthropological linguistics, and while this is not always made explicit in explaining the different findings presented in each individual chapter, it is implicit in the overall design of the study and the views of language and social life presented throughout the book.

The rest of the book is organized in the following way:

- *Chapter 1*: this chapter summarizes the underlying linguistic and social theoretical framework shaping this research. It outlines the theoretical and methodological tools of the ethnography of communication and interactional sociolinguistics. These traditions share a view of language and culture as inseparable.
- *Chapter 2*: this chapter is about the educational and language policies of partnership teaching and mainstreaming. The purpose of this chapter is to consider

the ideological basis of mainstreaming. The chapter discusses the inclusive paradigm and its manifestation into policy. The chapter gives an overview of policy development within EAL and argues for a local interpretation of policy.

- *Chapter 3*: this chapter looks at the ways in which teachers describe themselves and their partner teachers' roles and positions within the classroom and school in enacting an inclusive mainstream policy. The chapter develops two main themes. The first looks at the contradictions teachers face in implementing an inclusive policy within a competitive standards-driven educational climate. The second considers how hierarchies become established around EAL and subject teaching. We will look at how the pedagogies of transmission and facilitation become attached to subject and EAL teachers, and how their enactment positions the two kinds of teachers differently within the secondary school classroom.
- *Chapter 4*: this chapter analyses the language use of subject and EAL teachers in the classroom. It shows how, discursively, EAL teachers and STs use different kinds of classroom discourse. These discourses, or ways of speaking, are associated with different pedagogic styles. The analysis of teacher talk is conducted within two speech events: STs and EAL teachers engaged in whole-class teaching and in one-to-one or small-group interactions.
- *Chapter 5*: this chapter builds on the analysis of the previous chapter. It again looks at teachers' interaction patterns in the classroom. However, whereas the previous chapter focused mainly on more micro teacher/student classroom-based interaction, this chapter takes a wider look at how STs' and EALs' language use is linked to wider societal discourses on education and diversity.
- *Chapters 6 and 7*: these chapters looks at various configurations of teacher collaboration between EAL teachers and STs when working in support, withdrawal and partnership modes. It describes how these relationships impact on teachers' and students' views of diversity within the school. Chapters 6 and 7 suggest that our understanding of teaching relationships is important in creating effective teaching and learning opportunities in mainstream classrooms. It is argued that partnership teaching relationships provide the best opportunities for the transformation of the mainstream classroom. This is because such partnerships work within established institutional structures. This is not the fault of the support mode itself, but rather the prestige attributed to transmission pedagogies and their discourses in the current climate of market-driven approaches to education.
- *Chapter 8*: this chapter considers the possibilities of the mainstream secondary school classroom in terms of the opportunities it provides for the acquisition of English and the learning of subject content. It looks at how STs and EAL teachers use various resources to deliver on the dual and overlapping aims of language-learning and cognitive development. Specifically, it looks at the possibilities of a focus on language, form and meaning within the mainstream subject classroom.

- *Chapter 9*: the focus of this chapter is twofold. The first aim is to concentrate specifically on Turkish-speaking bilingual EAL teachers. The importance and distinctiveness of their work is described. The second aim is to look at attitudes towards the use of Turkish across the three schools. There are two positive arguments made about bilingualism in this chapter. The first concerns bilingual teachers' ability, through their use of their first language, to extend their role beyond that of providing support to teachers of subject curriculum content. The second is that the use of the first language has a higher profile than might otherwise be expected in a secondary school classroom, mostly because of the support given to it by STs due to its usefulness in building up scientific concepts connected to content areas.

- *Chapter 10*: this chapter presents a mini case study illustrating how bilingual EAL teachers, employed by one of the three London schools, dealt with one particular event which disrupted the school over several days. This chapter differs from previous ones in that it draws on data from only one school. It offers an account of one particular incident to illustrate the kinds of work bilingual EAL teachers do in mediating between participants in and beyond the school environment. It shows how important other languages and bilingual staff are to the school. The incident involves an accusation of racism made by one group of Turkish-speaking Kurdish background students against the school. The students accused the school of treating its students from different ethnicities differently and unjustly. This chapter looks at how different languages were used in the school by the head teacher to refute these accusations and also the role the Turkish-speaking bilingual EAL teachers played in mediating the school's message.

- *Chapter 11*: this chapter gives a summary of the findings from the previous data chapters. It also looks for ways forward and considers issues of diversity, EAL and educational policy.

In summary, the book works to achieve the following:

(1) Recognize the reflexive and creative capacity of language and its ability to entextualize as well as reflect contexts.
(2) Work within a theory of language in which language is seen as culturally constructed and therefore influenced by the rules or patterns of language use.
(3) View the school as a speech community in which participants behave in ways meaningful to them. The participants are viewed as knowledgeable and purposeful agents.
(4) Look at how the wider belief systems captured in government- and school-policy documents influence the interactions of teachers in the speech situation of the classroom. Also look at how 'macro' affects 'micro' (i.e. how policy affects classroom practice) and how 'micro' affects 'macro' (i.e. how teachers' work impacts on policy).

(5) Reveal the systematic use of speech in the speech events of class-fronted and small-group teaching by STs and language support teachers. Focus on such speech events to show how teachers construct and present their identities and how this maintains or transforms wider belief systems.
(6) Show how the kind of working relationships teachers form with one another affects the delivery of policy. Investigate the possibilities of language and subject-learning in the mainstream classroom, given the current climate.
(7) Use the methodological tools of ethnography of communication, microethnography and interactional sociolinguistics to understand the fluidity of the speech event and how meaning is negotiated between participants.

Notes

1. Bilingual teaching assistants do not have qualified teacher status (QTS).
2. The focus on Turkish-speaking EAL teachers and the Turkish-speaking student population was a methodological decision. It allowed me to follow interactions between the bilingual teachers and students.
3. It was not clear why this should be so, but there was a certain amount of ambiguity and at worse, hostility within the schools to the use of first languages for teaching the curriculum (see Chapters 9 and 10). The bilingual teachers may have wished not to have their use of first languages within the classroom captured on tape.

Chapter 1

Theoretical and Methodological Frameworks

Introduction

This chapter presents views of language and culture which have shaped the research discussed in this book. There are two main approaches described, both stemming from linguistic anthropology; the ethnography of communication (Hymes, 1968, 1974, 1980) and interactional sociolinguistics (Gumperz, 1972, 1982, 1999). The ethnography of communication and interactional sociolinguistics share an overlapping theoretical background in studying the role language plays in social life. Their combination provides the tools to make connections between the micro interactions of the classroom and the macro socio-political discourses surrounding inclusion. In this chapter I will briefly review these two theoretical and methodological frameworks with the intention of making clear to the reader their impact on the research discussed throughout this book. Both the ethnography of communication and interactional sociolinguistics are compatible with other approaches concerned with the interaction of language and social life and I will make these links explicit during this chapter.

Views of Language

Three views of language are presented very briefly below. They are worth describing because they are at the heart of the ethnography of communication and interactional sociolinguistics and have shaped the way information has been collected and analysed throughout this book.

The first view is taken from Charles Peirce (1839–1914) and his writings on meaning-making. Peirce recognized the meaning of the sign is not contained within it but rather arises in its interpretation. That is, meaning is not transmitted to us – we actively create it according to a complex interplay of codes or conventions of which we are normally unaware. According to Peirce's concept of the sign:

> A Sign . . . [in the form of a representamen] is something which stands to somebody for something in some respect or capacity. It addresses somebody, that is, creates in the mind of that person an equivalent sign or perhaps a more

developed sign. That sign which it creates I call the interpretant of the first sign. The sign stands for something, its object. It stands for that object, not in all respects, but in reference to a sort of idea, which I have sometimes called the ground of the representamen. (Peirce, 1955: 2.228)

Peirce argued that the meaning of a representation can be nothing but a representation itself. Meaning-making is therefore always in motion. In his concept of the sign, Peirce described three main types: iconic, indexical and symbolic.

- Icon/iconic: the sign vehicle resembles its object – being similar in that it possesses some of its qualities e.g. sound effects in radio drama, onomatopoeia, map.
- Index/indexical: the sign vehicle is contiguous with the object. The signifier is not arbitrary but is directly connected in some way to the object e.g. a footprint, pronouns (such as I, you, that, this), accents, code-switching, the choice of words. An index has a dynamic relationship with the object it represents.
- Symbol/symbolic: the sign vehicle stands for the object only because of laws of convention.

In terms of this study, I have drawn on Peirce's work in three ways. First, the concept of indexicality has been crucial towards making my arguments surrounding discourse and power. Indexicality is language's ability – through the sign – to call up social knowledge and association in an immediate and local context. Meaning is made through interpreting these signs and deciding which presuppositions are at work (Gumperz, 1999; Silverstein, 2003). Because signs index social life while also creating new meanings, the concept of indexicality has been useful in this book to look across macro and micro social orders in order to focus on how multilingual students are discursively constructed both in policy documents and secondary-school classrooms. We will see which meta-pragmatic (Silverstein, 2003) and 'big' discourses (Gee, 1999) on education come to dominate, and how these appear in classroom interactions. Here, Gee's position on the interaction between discourses is useful:

> It is sometimes helpful to think about social and political issues as if it is not just us humans who are talking and interacting with each other, but rather, the Discourses we represent and enact, and for which we are 'carriers'. The Discourses we enact existed long before each of us came on the scene and most of them will exist long after we have left the scene. Discourses, throughout words and deeds, carry on conversations with each other through history, and, in doing so, form human history. (Gee, 1999: 18)

I shall be arguing that EAL teachers and STs index various 'big' discourses predominantly through their pedagogic actions and stances. An example of such indexicality is the different ways that EAL and subject teachers use the personal pronoun 'I' to interact with the whole class (see Chapters 4 and 5). 'I' is indexical in the sense that its meaning is contiguous with its object. That is, it is not possible to understand 'I' without its context. However, EAL and subject teachers' use of 'I' indexes different discourses. Whereas subject teachers use 'I' to link their discourse to the student's actions and curriculum-learning, EAL teachers, while at the front of the class, use 'I' to define a place for themselves in the mainstream classroom (see Chapters 4 and 5).

Another relevant element of Peirce's work within this book is the notion that we are always creating meaning anew. Contexts are fluid and speech communities change. In this study I have attempted to portray the teachers in the three schools in complex ways. I try to show that teachers are not 'stuck' in their institutional roles and discourses but can create new contexts and communities through their relationships and interactions. An example of this would be teachers working in a partnership mode, breaking down the boundaries which often spring up around subject disciplines in secondary schools (see Chapters 6 and 7).

The final way in which Peirce's work has been influential upon this study, is in the distinction he makes between sign types. The symbolic function of language is often privileged over its other uses in education. This is because of the role language plays in concept formation (see Chapter 8). Throughout this book, I shall argue that we need to look at meaning-making beyond the transmission of subject content if we are to understand what inclusion means to the participants in schools.

The second view of language and culture which has shaped this book is contained in the writings of Edward Sapir (1921, 1949), whose study of language greatly influenced the ethnography of communication. Sapir viewed language as a cultural symbol. He believed that language is a way of communicating ideas, emotions and desires by means of voluntarily produced symbols (1921). For Sapir, the ability of language (as a system of symbols) to represent something psychological – separate from the purely physical actions of man – is what makes language 'stand aloof'. In making the distinction between the physiological and the psychological, he showed that sounds have different values. Sapir argued that some sounds are more 'psychologically real' to the speaker than others, just as some social actions are (see the discussion of emic on p. 24). Thus, it is not the physical properties themselves that make up language but the symbolic and indexical meanings that these sounds are able to carry. As such, language can perform a variety of functions, all of which define it as a cultural artefact that has its foundations in the organization of humankind and its culture. Sapir puts it best when he says: 'Language does not exist apart from culture, that is, from the socially inherited assemblage of practices and beliefs that determines the textures of our lives' (Sapir, 1921: 207).

Thus, Sapir views language as a social action, most particularly as a communicative action (Lucy, 1991). This view of language and culture shaped Hyme's concept of speech community which we will look at on p. 23. What is of relevance from Sapir's work in this book is his arguments surrounding the fundamental role language plays in organizing our social lives. Throughout this study, I shall argue that all teachers need an understanding of how language functions in teaching and learning, and in identity and community creation and maintenance. Without such an understanding of the role language plays in a school's community, any response to diversity will be incomplete (Creese, 2003).

The third view of language comes from the work of Roman Jakobson (1960, 1971) and his writings on how participants use language within a speech community to privilege particular functions over others. Jakobson called for the investigation of language in all its various functions (1960: 352), and went about characterizing these functions. He started with identifying the significant components of a speech situation and describing these six parts (see Figure 1). Jakobson then associated each of these components with a function (See Figure 2).

Importantly, Jakobson draws together and shows the interplay of these functions, speech-situation components and the language forms which represent them. According to Jakobson, the most important of all these functions is the referential. This is concerned with referring to and/or predicating upon something within a given context. Structurally, it is centred on the third person pronominal form and it receives formal recognition in the indicative mode (Lucy, 1991: 19).[1] Second is the emotive, which is concerned with the expressive purpose of a language. This

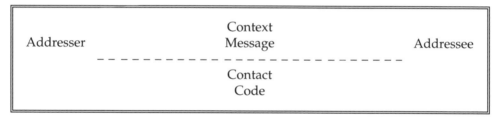

Figure 1 Components of speech situations

Source: Jakobson, 1960: 353

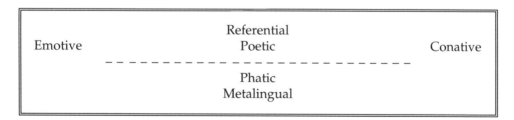

Figure 2 Associated language functions

Source: Jakobson, 1960: 357

function is concerned with language's ability to show the addresser's attitude and feelings towards what is being spoken about. Centred on first person pronouns, it receives formal recognition in interjections and the conditional mode.[2] Third is the conative function, which relates to language's capacity to affect addressees and make them act. This is centred upon the imperative mode.[3] Fourth is the metalingual function, which comments on the structure of a language. Any language-learning activity will draw on this function heavily.[4] Fifth is the poetic function, which corresponds to forms that communicate about the message itself. The poetic function is not the sole purpose of verbal art, but it is the dominant, determining one.[5] It is concerned with indispensable features of poetry and verbal art, such as the selection and combination of sounds and meanings. The final function is the phatic, which relates to the contact component. Put simply, it is our ability to open channels of communication.[6]

I will use Jakobson's theory of functions throughout this book. In particular, I will be looking at interplay between the emotive, directive and referential functions in teacher discourse (see Chapters 4 and 5). I shall also describe how the metalingual function is put into use in the secondary-school context. I will show that, despite attempts by EAL teachers to foreground the metalingual within the subject-focused lesson, the referential function relating to subject knowledge dominates (see Chapter 8). As such, it is very difficult for the metalinguistic function to gain priority in the subject-based classroom, despite EAL teachers' attempts.

Jakobson's work is important not only because he did so much to define language and its functions and to relate it to speech situations, but also because he looked at the interface between function and form; which was something little considered by linguists at the time. Jakobson (1971: 130) characterized all utterances as consisting of messages (M) and codes (C).

> A message sent by its addresser must be adequately perceived by its receiver. Any message is encoded by its sender and is to be decoded by its addressee. The more closely the addressee approximates the code used by the addresser, the higher is the amount of information obtained. Both the message (M) and the underlying code (C) are vehicles of linguistic communication, but both of them function in a duplex manner; they may be at once utilized and referred to. Thus a message may refer to the code or to another message, and on the other hand, the general meaning of a code unit may imply a reference to the code or to the message. Accordingly four DUPLEX types must be distinguished: 1) two kinds of CIRCULARITY – message referring to message (M/M) and code referring to code (C/C); 2) two kinds of OVERLAPPING – message referring to code (M/C) and code referring to message (C/M).

Examples of these include:

- Message about the message (M/M), e.g. the use of reported speech, in which language is used to comment on language.

- Code about the code (C/C), e.g. proper names, such as 'Tom', which are conventional assignments and have no general definition without a reference to the code. That is, whereas 'pup' has the general definition of 'a young dog' and can be indicated with abstractions like 'puppyhood', 'Fido' cannot be qualified in this way.
- Message about the code (M/C), e.g. comments on the regularities of language; for instance, 'get' is an irregular verb.
- Code about the message (C/M), e.g. markers of tenses and 'shifters' (such as personal pronouns). These direct the listener to attend to some aspect of the present speech event in order to deduce the full meaning.

Throughout this book, the concept of the duality of language has been applied. In particular, the analysis I shall present makes use of studying the code to understand the message. I have done this through analysing the use of the personal pronoun 'I' in teacher discourse at the front of the class, in which teachers direct students towards enacting a teaching/learning task. I have also examined teacher discourse for the messages teachers can send out about the code itself. That is, how the teachers focus on the metalingual function to refer students to aspects of the linguistic code or grammar of the language (see Chapters 4, 5 and 8).

Peirce, Sapir and Jakobson's work can be applied to a focus on language use; on how language reflects and constitutes social life and how social life affects language use. All three scholars have influenced the ethnography of communication and interactional sociolinguistics.

Ethnography of Communication

> ... it is not linguistics, but ethnography, not language, but communication, which must provide the frame of reference within which the place of language in culture and society is to be assessed ... (Hymes, 1974: 4)

> The ethnography of speaking is concerned with the situations and uses, the patterns and functions, of speaking as an activity in its own right. (Hymes, 1968: 101)

The ethnography of communication has been shaped by theories of language, while the methodological principles of ethnography have developed from anthropology. Along with others, I would characterize this approach as embedded in linguistic anthropology and ethnography (Hornberger, 2003; UKLEF, 2004). Dell Hymes draws on the work of Sapir and Jakobson in his development of the ethnography of speaking/communication, and in doing so unites Sapir's concern for language as a creative cultural process with Jakobson's concern for the mechanics of functional and structural analysis. Hymes makes the primary base of his analysis the speech event, which he places between the broader speech situation and the smaller speech act. He explains a speech event as:

[activities] that are directly governed by rules or norms for the use of speech. An event may consist of a single speech act, but will often comprise several ... It is of speech events and speech acts that one writes formal rules for their occurrence and characteristics. (Hymes, 1974: 52)

Hymes is concerned with how patterns of communication interrelate in a systematic way with – and derive meaning from – other aspects of culture. Drawing on Jakobson, Hymes (1974: 53–61) goes on to shape the constituents of a speech situation into the mnemonic device of SPEAKING: Setting; Participants; Ends (the purpose and goal of the event); Act sequence (the message form and message content); Key (tone and manner); Instrumentalities (channels of speech: oral or written); Norms of interaction (the social structure and relationships in a community) and interpretation (the belief system of a community); and Genre (categories such as the poem, myth, etc.).

Hymes took a paradigmatic approach to the study of language in context. He was interested in discovering the dimensions of contrast within communities, rather than revealing the sequence of cultural interaction as found in the work of ethnomethodologists (Schegloff & Sacks, 1973) whose syntagmatic approach was more concerned with the position in a sequence (such as the sequence of a telephone conversation). Hymes argued that a paradigmatic approach to co-occurrence and contrast meant that researchers could discover the rules of appropriateness for a person or group. This concept of appropriateness will be important within this book. I will show how classroom participants come to expect particular discursive routines. When teachers break these routines or create new and different ones, they do not go unnoticed by students. However, the participant structures which grow up around these discursive routines are also open to change. A theory of meaning-making which can capture this fluidity is, therefore, necessary.

It is in the nature of meanings to be subject to change, reinterpretation, re-creation. One has to think of people, not as the intersection of vectors of age, sex, race, class, income and occupation alone, but also as beings making sense out of the disparate experiences, using reason to maintain a sphere of integrity in an immediate world. (Hymes, 1980: 94)

As such, Hymes recognizes meaning-making as fluid with many interpretations. The ethnography of communication and interactional sociolinguistics sets about describing both the patterns of language use within a social context and also how participants of an interaction use language to contextualize their activities (Gumperz, 1999; Hanks, 1996; Hymes, 1968, 1980; Ochs, 1996; Wortham, 2003).

I have used all these features of Hymes' work in this book. In particular, the notion of a speech event has been central. The teacher-fronted introduction of tasks and the individual teacher–student interactions have been viewed as two such different speech events. In Chapters 4 and 5 I demonstrate the patterned nature of these speech events and show that students come to expect such patterning. This is achieved through applying a paradigmatic approach, in which contrasts are drawn between different members of the speech community. One finding is that EAL teachers and STs use language differently at the front of the class; for instance, in the giving of answers, in reference to the examination system and in ownership of teaching tasks. I also show that there are qualitative and quantitative differences in the ways that the two kinds of teacher work with small groups and individual students; in the way for example, teachers ask questions and scaffolded interaction.

Interactional Sociolinguistics and Microethnography

Interactional sociolinguistics (IS), like the ethnography of communication, is grounded in earlier linguistic anthropological work. According to Gumperz,

> Interactional sociolinguistics (IS) focuses on communicative practice as the real world site where societal and interactive forces merge. The goal is to show how individuals participating in exchanges use talk to achieve their communicative goals in real life situations by concentrating on the meaning making processes and the taken-for-granted background assumptions that underlie the negotiation of shared interpretations. (Gumperz, 1999: 453–4)

Within IS, the interpretive assessment of interactors is always built on locally- or context-specific background knowledge, which takes the form of presuppositions that shift in the course of an encounter. The researcher attempts to describe how meanings are made through an analysis of the exchanges between participants. Any inferential interpretation of particular interactions can be demonstrated through ethnographically informed detail. In this book, IS has allowed for an analysis of the micro interactions of teacher/teacher talk and teacher/student talk. It is through the study of local interaction that researchers – using the ethnography of communication and IS frameworks – seek to capture the emic perspectives of participants as they are played out inter-discursively. My aim in combining the ethnography of communication and IS is to bring together the 'macro' and the 'micro'. Silverstein (2003: 202) describes the interplay between the 'macro' and 'micro' as:

> the macro-sociological is really a projective order from within a complex, and ever changing, configuration of interdiscursivities in micro-contextual orders, some of which, it turns out, at any given moment of macro-order diachrony asymmetrically determine others.

An aim of both IS and the ethnography of communication is to understand how linguistic signs come to have meaning in both cultural and interactional contexts. Work on indexicality has been important in pursuing this question. Gumperz and others (Ochs, 1996; Wortham, 2003) have argued that indexicality is central to understanding the conversational involvement of speakers. Wortham describes this well when he comments, 'competent hearers identify members of their own linguistic community and make sense of utterances by attending to cues that are used in appropriate contexts' (2003: 13). IS attempts to understand how language is creative in constituting contexts. As Peirce argued, the sign is creative. Indexicality might anchor you to the here and now, but it also creates new symbols. The magic of language is that it weaves the indexical and symbolic together. As such, indexicality is very important in the context of this book. One example of its significance is in finding that teachers combine language functions in particular ways that index their roles in relation to the curriculum and students' actions. Moreover, EAL teachers and STs, through their language use, come to index and embody wider societal metadiscourses of what counts as knowledge in the secondary-school classroom.

Closely related to IS is Erickson's microethnography (1975, 1990, 1996). Hornberger summarizes this concept as:

> Microethnography with its emphasis on the importance of situationally emergent social identity and co-membership, suggests that, no matter what the social and cultural givens in an interaction, there is always the possibility of communication which builds up rather than breaking down participants' learning. Taken together, these approaches provide educators with a truly powerful set of insights and tools for implementing change in our schools. (Hornberger, 1996: 246)

Through his research, Erickson argues that people react to one another's communications in response to the local frame of a particular social situation. Within this frame, the social situation is constructed by the participants, who in turn shape the conditions for their language use. Erickson's work is about dynamic and emergent speech in context. Much of his research is concerned with the importance of social factors – such as ethnicity, class, sex, age, etc. – in determining the success of vital gatekeeping interviews for the participants involved. Erickson also illustrates how we use speech to move beyond the boundaries of such socially defining factors (Erickson, 1975; Erickson & Shultz, 1982):

> What happens in a given situation may be powerfully influenced by general societal processes – the economy, the labor market, and the class position of participants in the situational race, ethnic, and gender relations, religious identification and beliefs, broad patterns of language and culture in the society at large. But these factors do not totally determine what happens when particular people interact in a social situation. When we look very closely at what people actually do in situations, we realize that there is some 'wiggle room' there, some room for improvisation. Interaction in a social situation, then, although not totally independent from societal rules, patterns, and interests, can be seen as not so much rule governed as rule influenced. (Erickson, 1996: 283)

> We are not just typecast by a single category of social identity throughout an entire encounter. Our social identity is situated in the interaction at hand; we perform it as we go along and we do so conjointly with the other interactional partners. . . . Culture and language style differences, in other words, sometimes made a big difference for the way interaction happened, and sometimes it did not. (Erickson, 1996: 295)

All these approaches have shaped the research discussed in this book. Their analytical tools enable movement between the 'micro' context of people interacting, the 'meso' level of a school as a community and the 'macro' discourses of policy.

Speech Communities

A speech community can be defined as 'a community sharing knowledge of rules for the conduct and interpretation of speech. Such sharing comprises knowledge of a least one form of speech, and knowledge also of its patterns of use.' (Hymes, 1974: 51) Similarly Gumperz describes it as 'a group of speakers who share rules and norms for the use of language' (1982: 24). Although there has been a recent softening of the phrase 'rules of language use' to 'patterns of language use' (see Erickson, 1990, 1996), ethnographers of communication continue to use Hymes and Gumperz's work to look for continuities and patterns in how a community is shaped by language use and how language use shapes a community. This is achieved by approaching the study of community as inherently complex:

> If one analyses the language of a community as if it should be homogenous, its diversity trips one up around the edges. If one starts with the analysis of the diversity, one can isolate the homogeneity that is truly there. (Hymes, 1972: 276)

In Hymes and Gumperz's work on speech community the study of communication is culturally framed and communicatively constituted. It is the speech activity of a community which is the primary object of attention. Rampton (1998: 3) points out that for Hymes and Gumperz speech community functions as an ontological marker, 'a necessary primary term in that it postulates the basis of description as a social, rather than a linguistic entity'. Indeed, Hymes' concern with the social in linguistics has led to his other key analytical tools, such as communicative competence, speech situations, events and acts. As such, the speech community provided the starting point for Hymes to look at ways of speaking within it: 'The ethnography of speaking is concerned with the situations and uses, the patterns and functions, of speaking as an activity in its own right' (Hymes, 1968: 101). 'The descriptive focus in the speech economy of a community' (Hymes, 1968: 107).

Others have pointed out the problems of making the 'speech community' operational (Eckert & McConnel-Ginnet, 1998; Irvine, 1986 in Wolfson, 1989; Wolfson, 1989). For instance, Irvine asks:

> What are the social characteristics of a social unit? I would suggest that the concept of the speech community is still an abstracted, idealized notion that runs into practical problems when you try to opertionalise it in conducting fieldwork. (1986, in Wolfson, 1989: 51)

Eckert and McConnel-Ginnet (1998: 490) argue that by choosing a location to study rather than practice as social engagement we fall into the danger of defining communities in terms of abstracted characteristics, such as age, gender, ethnicity and social class: 'We are then forced into reconstructing the social practice from which the characteristics and linguistic behaviour in question have been abstracted.' Wolfson summarizes Hymes as arguing that, 'The simplest answer is to begin by looking for groups that have some sort of pre-existing definition apart from speech usage' (Wolfson, 1989: 50–2). What Hymes is suggesting then for his speech community is an already socially organized unit formed around location and/or (non-linguistic) social practice and activity. Thus, for Hymes, humankind 'cannot be understood apart from the evolution and maintenance of its ethnographic diversity' (1974: 33). What was required, therefore, was a general theory and body of knowledge within which the diversity of speech, repertoires and ways of speaking could take primacy as the basis for analysis.

In this book, I have defined each school as a speech community. This is illustrated most clearly in Chapter 10 where the concept of a school speech community is fully applied in the case study of one school. Here the school's speech community is viewed as conflictual as well as communal.

Emic Perspectives

The emic is a central concept in ethnography, particularly the ethnography of communication (Hymes, 1968, 1974) and interactional sociolinguistics (Gumperz, 1982). Hymes explains its origins as,

> Pike generalized the endings of the linguistic terms 'phonetic' and 'phonemic' to obtain names of these three moments of inquiry. The general framework with which one begins analysis of a given case he called 'etic'. The analysis of the actual system he called 'emic'. The reconsideration of the general framework in the light of the analysis he called 'etic'. (Hymes, 1980: 93)

'Etic' – which stems from 'phonetic' – denotes all the possible factors significant to describing language use in a social context. In contrast, 'emic' – which stems from 'phonemic' – signifies those factors which are fundamental to the participants themselves in their language use in particular localized contexts. What the concept of emic attempts to describe, therefore, is the status of social action within a system in order to understand the system.

The ethnography of communication combines an emic focus – which aims to describe and understand the local meaning-making processes of participants' language-in-use – with an etic focus – consisting of a list of universal components and functions constituting speech events, which are used to guide the researcher as aide-mémoire in the field. It is in the contrast between emic and etic that the emic takes on its significance. It is the emic perspective which defines the ethnography of communication as a departure from earlier normative and functionalist models of language use (Creese, in press).

In this book, the aim is to interpret participants' discourses and actions emically. That is, the interpretation process looks to represent the participants' meaning-making as purposeful and always within given contexts. In these emic interpretations, it is important to present the participants and, indeed, the speech communities themselves as highly complex, with contradictions and inconsistencies as well continuities. Hymes has warned against creating false dichotomies, as these 'fail to capture the nature and complexity of the problem' (1980: 148). In recognizing such complexity, Hymes argues for the continued development of models or theories which show the interaction of language and social life. He looked for ways in which the ethnography of communication, '[. . .] partly links, but partly cuts across, partly builds between the ordinary practices of the disciplines [linguistics, anthropology, sociology, psychology] to answer new questions . . .' (Hymes, 1974: 32).

Hymes points to the role that linguistic ethnography can play in understanding social life across a number of different disciplines. Indeed, I have used the ethnography of communication and its theoretical and methodological frameworks to hold together the rather disparate education literatures which introduce each chapter in this book. These texts incorporate teacher change, teacher support, classroom interaction, orders and levels of discourse, second language acquisition, content-based language teaching, language planning and policy, and multilingualism. It is the linguistic–anthropological theories of language and social life introduced in this chapter which overarch these various literatures. In the next section I discuss several additional theories which have also shaped this research.

Language and Power

Deborah Cameron has argued that we never stop becoming who we are (1997). While Rampton reminds us that, 'individuals form complicated and often contradictory patterns of solidarity and opposition across a range of category memberships' (1995: 8). Indeed, at the centre of this argument is the belief that subjectivity is socially constructed, highly contextualized, fluid and variable (Johnson, 1997; MacLure, 2003). This means that we need not view society purely in hegemonic terms. As human agents, we are able to bring into play multiple, alternative social roles and identities in any speech situation, which need not be governed only by our gender, class, ethnicity or role (Hornberger, 1996). This all points to the necessity of a view of the social actor as mobile and performative. Here, Giddens is helpful: 'To be a human being is to be a purposive agent, who both has reasons for his or her activities and is able, if asked, to elaborate discursively upon these reasons . . .' (1993: 89).

This sociological perspective encourages us to view actors as drawing on their knowledge of social structures (including language) in their constitution of social relations. As Giddens points out:

> To be an agent is to have the capability of 'making a difference', of intervening in the world so as to influence events which occur in that world. To be a human agent is to be highly knowledgeable and skilled individual, who applies that knowledgeability in securing autonomy of action in the course of day-to-day life. (1993: 257)

Giddens' work shows that there is no such thing as a societal totality (1993: 89), but rather social practices, which are structured across space and time. Giddens' view of human beings as purposive agents is linked to his theory of power:

> Power is part of action. Action or agency implies the intervention (or refraining) of an individual in a course of events in the world, of which it would be true to say that 'he could have done otherwise'. Defined in this way, action involves the application of 'means' to secure outcomes, these outcomes constituting the intervention in the on-going course of events. . . . Power in this broad sense is equivalent to the transformative capacity of human action: the capability of human beings to intervene in a series of events so as to alter their course. . . . It is precisely the concept of interest that is most immediately linked to those of conflict and solidarity. The use of power is frequently accompanied by struggle; this is not because of a logical relation between the two, but because of a lack of coincidence of actors' interests in circumstances of the application of power. (1993: 227)

This definition of power is useful as it gives a purpose agency to all research participants, who Giddens argues are 'never wholly dependent and are often adept at converting whatever resources they possess into some degree of control over their conditions' (1993: 243).

Giddens (1993: 157) suggests the following tenets are important in the description and analysis of social behaviour:

(1) The need to avoid impoverished descriptions of agents' knowledgeability; the agents are seen as active not passive recipients.
(2) A sophisticated account of the motivation: the idea that social action is purposeful, although it may result in unintended consequences. Participants

behave as they do because they know a great deal about society even if they have an imprecise awareness of aspects of the wider society that influence the contexts of their own activity. They partially understand their position in society and this may have unintended consequences.

(3) An interpretation of the dialectic of control: participants may be deeply opposed in their interpretations of reality.

Throughout this book power is a central issue. I will argue that teachers are both shaped by and shape their own discourses. I will show that there are not only wider discourses which support the different work EAL and subject teachers do within their schools, but also how the teachers' discourses themselves can create particular statuses. In addition, I have looked at ways in which teachers can transform these more entrenched discourses through their partnership work. Giddens' work is helpful here as it provides a theory of power and teacher agency which fits well with the theories of language and social life I presented earlier in this chapter. I have shown that language use is both patterned and transformational: social life becomes patterned, structured and entrenched but it can also be shifted and transformed by people. This concept of purposive agency also fits with the notion of the emic, which views research participants as purposeful in their meaning-making.

Schools may play their part in endorsing particular ideologies and their discourses in education, but teachers can actively transform their contexts. As Hornberger and Skilton-Sylvester (2000: 100) have argued:

> In looking at the ways in which power is constructed through language and in interaction, actors can begin to see themselves as agents who have the power to transform practices and not merely as recipients of already decided upon norms.

Chapter Summary

This chapter has looked at the theories of language use embedded within anthropological linguistics that have shaped this book. These theories view language use as patterned, while also flexible and dynamic. The notion of a speech community is embedded in a theory of language use which allows the researcher to capture the patterns and heterogeneity of language use.

I have argued that the ethnography of communication and interactional sociolinguistics provides the tools of analysis for the understanding of speech communities. Through the use of analytical tools found within the ethnography of communication and interactional sociolinguistics – such as speech event/act, language function, sign type and emic perspectives – we can determine an explanation of how participants interact and negotiate their various positions within events and how particular discourses come to dominate.

Notes

1. An example of the referential function: 'New towns sprang up in England after the war.'
2. An example of the emotive function: 'I think that's awful.'
3. An example of the conative function: 'Open that bag, would you?'
4. An example of the metalingual function in the English language: *in reported speech, the present tense verb changes to the past tense.*
5. An example of the poetic function: 'Workers of the world unite.'
6. An example of the phatic function: 'Hiya!'

Chapter 2

Policy into Practice

The case for honest perplexity in the face of a worrying future is also a case for scaling down our pretensions, not trumpeting certainties we do not truly feel, and not claiming that there are always solutions to every malaise and difficulty. The reality is more ambiguous and demands humility. (Woollacott, 1995: 26)

Introduction

This chapter is about the educational and language policies of partnership teaching and mainstreaming. 'Policy' is interpreted generally here to refer to government reports and guidance. This includes reports sponsored by the national and local governments and published in their name whether they have statutory power or not. The purpose of this chapter is to consider the ideological basis of mainstreaming and its aims and to set up a framework for evaluating these against the interpretation and implementation of policy-into-practice in the three London secondary schools.

The chapter is organized around three broad themes. The first discusses the ideological basis of inclusive and multicultural education. The second goes on to look at how mainstreaming and partnership teaching have emerged from this paradigm and considers bilingualism and multilingualism in the mainstream classroom. The third theme discusses the current changes in provision for bilingual students in English schools and discusses the relevance of these changes to this research.

Educational Paradigms and their Discourses

In recent years we have equipped ourselves with more refined tools for analysing the role language plays in upholding and contesting ideological positions (Ball, 1997; Blackledge, 2001; Fairclough, 1995; Van Dijk, 1993). The link between educational ideologies and language policies has been made explicit in various studies (May 2001; Ricento 1998, 2000a, 2000b). Within language planning and policy literature there is a recognition that concepts such as inclusion, bilingualism and multilingualism are conceptually complex and ideologically laden, and that language planning is not a neutral problem-solving process. Moreover, ideologies of language are not only about language but are linked to other ideologies. Gal and Woolard (1995) show that ideologies that appear to be about language are often about political systems, while ideologies that seem to be about political theory are often implicitly about linguistic practices and beliefs. Educational paradigms therefore cannot be viewed purely as classification devices, which allow us to describe and interpret the complexities of the social world in a neutral impartial way, rather they are ideologically laden. Education is full of conflicting paradigms: inclusive and exclusive education and assimilationist and pluralistic approaches to linguistic difference represent examples of conflicting paradigms within education. We will consider these in this chapter.

Inclusion as Ideology

The inclusion movement started in the 1960s (Vislie, 1995: 42) and was part of a general movement to empower and give equal rights to those groups in society which had been denied them. These changes came about in times of economic revival and an improvement in the standard of living.

In Britain the ideas behind inclusive education are now captured in a combination of legislation, government reports and through the practice of teachers in schools. The move towards inclusive education is one that sees the diversity of students' learning and behaviour characteristics as normal and healthy. As Ballard (1995: 1) points out,

> An inclusive school defines 'differentness' as an ordinary part of human experience, to be valued and organized for. Schools that practice exclusion define differentness as not ordinary, as outside their area of responsibility and, by implication, as not as valuable as 'ordinariness'.

Mainstreaming of bilingual pupils is an example of policy that stems from the principles expressed in the paradigm of inclusive education. It contrasts with a policy of withdrawal in which children are taken either from the class or from the school and placed in a situation in which they are given the 'special' education that they are seen to need. Withdrawal is seen to fit into the paradigm of excluding education. In England, mainstreaming of bilingual students was a response to the kinds of issues described by Reid (1988: 187):

> [bilingual students were] separated from their English-speaking peers ostensibly so that they could be taught English to a level which would allow them to join classes in ordinary schools, but also, of course, to satisfy majority parents that their children would not be 'held back' by the presence of large numbers of immigrant children in the same classes.

Within the education literature dualities of this kind, for example, between mainstreaming and withdrawal, are often found, with one paradigm supported by teachers over another. Often, the ambiguities of practice can get stripped away in the support of the preferred paradigm. The choice then becomes simple and teachers and educators are asked to sign up for one paradigm over another. In reality, teachers face many dilemmas in education in their support and contestation of different paradigms. This is because ideological discourses are always changing along with the identification positionings which individuals take up around them. So, teachers may find themselves agreeing with inclusive policies, but arguing for withdrawal for particular reasons within the school day or organizing for withdrawal to meet particular needs. These tensions are what Billig *et al.* (1988) refer to as ideological dilemmas. They are a usual and purposeful part of daily life and they contribute to what Billig *et al.* call a 'thinking society'. These dilemmas are explored more fully in Chapter 3.

We can expect some ambiguity from teachers in their discourses and practice around inclusion. Creese and Leung (2003: 5) argue that: 'In more or less liberal democracies we can expect a huge variability of views in the ways teachers talk about and respond to the notions of inclusion, diversity and difference.' They go on to argue that the belief that it is possible to 'deliver' a strategy or a policy in the public arena in a straightforward way is increasingly being called into question. As Yanow (1996) observes, the relationship between policy and implementation outcome is not necessarily linear or straightforwardly top-down. And Ball (1997: 270) argues that we need a much more localized understanding of how policy works:

> The prevailing, but normally implicit view is that policy is something that is 'done' to people. As first-order recipients 'they' 'implement' policy, as second-order recipients 'they' are advantaged or disadvantaged by it. I take a different view . . . That is, as noted earlier, policies pose problems to their subjects, problems that must be solved in context. Solutions to the problems posed by policy texts will be localised and should be expected to display 'ad hocery' and messiness. Responses indeed must be 'creative'. Policies do not normally tell you what to do; they create circumstances in which the range of options available in deciding what to do is narrowed or changed or particular goals or outcomes are set. A response must still be put together, constructed in context, offset against or balanced by other expectations. All of this involves creative social action of some kind.

Ball's point above is that policy is an interpretive and potentially messy process. Creese and Leung agree,

> Thus, individually and collectively teachers within their school communities will operate policy according to their local contexts, experiences and values, even where there is a strong element of statutory compliance. They will interact with policy not in a one-to-one reading of what 'is required' but in an interactive frame which involves their own interpretation within localised communities of practice. (Creese & Leung, 2003: 5)

The above quote makes the point that schools and teachers will make sense of policy locally and this will result in different ideological positions taken up around policy guidance and statements. In the next section we consider other paradigms which teachers face in their daily practice in relation to their bilingual students: those of assimilation, pluralism and multiculturalism.

Ideologies of assimilation, pluralism and multiculturalism

Assimilation deals with student bilingualism by rejecting it. The bilingual student is expected to learn the new language and culture as quickly as possible. Assimilation aims for a single homogenizing common culture by merging different groups and their heritages into a single culture core. It requires minorities to take on the traits, practices and behaviours of the dominant majority. Loyalty to traditions are expected to decline as immigrants and their children negotiate upward mobility (Kottak & Kozaitis, 1999). Cultural differences are minimized in favour of the majority's culture which is hostile to cultural expressions different from its own (Feinberg, 1996).

Pluralism views student bilingualism as different but equal. Pluralism allows cultural differences to thrive and tolerates diversity. It recognizes that right of people to express their differences and treats these differences as equal in the common public sphere. Unlike the assimilation position, pluralism does not attempt to actively destroy heritages and cultural diversity. However, pluralism has been criticized for its benign approach to cultural maintenance. Feinberg (1996) argues that identities can be allowed to dissolve if insufficient numbers of individuals choose not to pursue their heritages. That is, pluralism does not play an active part in maintaining difference. Kottak and Kozaitis (1999) argue that pluralism is only tolerated as long as minority cultures do not threaten the dominant culture. A further criticism is that pluralism fixes boundaries creating a monolithic image and ignoring diversity within the group.

Multiculturalism, like pluralism, also conceptualizes student bilingualism as 'different but equal'. However, unlike pluralism it is more active in its validation and support for difference (Feinberg, 1996):

> Unlike pluralists, multiculturalists do not envisage even the possibility of a culturally neutral public sphere. Their ideal of cultural fairness is not to maintain a wall of separation between culture and public, but to assure that no group dominates the public sphere in a way that serves to exclude from it the bearers of other cultural forms. Hence, the public sphere is viewed as an arena for cultural negotiation where the goal is inclusion, culture and all. ... In other words, benign neglect is not sufficient for the multiculturalist.

Within this paradigm, society is not seen as having clearly demarcated traditions which blend into distinct heritages but as the coexistence of many heritages and newly invented traditions within a single nation-state (Kottak & Kozaitis, 1999). The emphasis is on fluidity and new combinations and crossings (Rampton, 1995) and heterogeneity prevails.

In England, the two paradigms of inclusion and multiculturalism are probably the dominant ideologies found in the discourses of practicing teachers speaking about bilingual students and so it is worth considering the two paradigms alongside each other for a moment. Both come from the same source, liberal political and educational theory. And in many ways, the two paradigms complement one another. That is, they both adopt a view of 'difference' as usual and complex and are active in supporting it rather than attempting to eradicate it. The inclusive and multicultural educational paradigms aim to provide all children with access to the full and rich curriculum of the mainstream classroom rather than the potentially impoverished curriculum of the withdrawal classroom. As we have seen above, both inclusion and multiculturalism are presented as progressive policies and as social contracts in the making. However, as others have argued, inclusive and multicultural approaches must be viewed in conjunction with other ideologies within education, such as what counts as success (Benjamin, 2002) and what counts as linguistic capital within the classroom and beyond (Blommaert & Verschueren, 1998; Creese & Martin, 2003; Heller, 1999; Heller & Martin-Jones, 2001; Pavlenko & Blackledge, 2004). Benjamin (2002), for example, shows the difficulties children with special educational needs face in the mainstream classroom when success is measured predominantly through standardized curriculum and assessment procedures and classroom and school cultures do not and cannot adapt to meet their students' needs. The result is a rhetoric of inclusion where difference is celebrated but where practice is not changed.

In this book I attempt to show what happens to these liberal philosophical orientations when they are played out in practice in the particular contexts of three large London secondary schools. What the data show are in fact contradictions and oppositions to these orientations. So, on the one hand we hear some teachers speak of the importance of inclusion and multiculturalism in their interview transcripts and on the other hand we sometimes see opposition or difficulty in managing 'difference' in their classroom practices. Across the interview transcripts, classroom interactional and observational data, we will see how teachers try to reconcile these conflicting educational pressures and dilemmas in creating teaching and learning opportunities for bilingual children.

Interestingly, debates around the ideologies of inclusion, assimilation, pluralism and multiculturalism often make little reference directly to linguistic difference and, instead, focus their discussion on culture. This means that linguistic diversity becomes hidden behind a discussion of 'cultural heritage' which can be in danger of simplification and essentialization (Atkinson, 1999; Holliday, 1999; Kramsch, 1998). Blackledge (in press: 47) states that:

> Very often, multilingual societies which apparently tolerate or promote heterogeneity in fact undervalue or appear to ignore the linguistic diversity of their

populace. A liberal orientation to equality of opportunity for all may mask an ideological drive towards homogeneity, a drive which potentially marginalizes or excludes those who either refuse, or are unwilling, to conform.

Later in this chapter we will consider how an ideology of monolingualism continues to prevail within the multicultural and inclusive paradigm adopted within English schools. But for now, we turn to look more specifically at mainstreaming in the English context as a means of supporting minority linguistic and ethnic students.

Mainstreaming and Partnership Teaching

Mainstreaming in England developed as a progressive educational policy and is intended to be inclusive. Previous provision had tended to exclude bilingual children from mainstream classes until they were 'proficient enough' in English to join their peers. This was viewed as having the effect of exacerbating prejudices rather than recognizing and valuing diversity. Mainstreaming was intended to challenge the monolingual status quo while remaining solidly anti-assimilationist (Bourne, 1989). The purpose of this section is to interpret in detail one core piece of policy that established the principles of partnership teaching in the implementation of inclusion for bilingual students.[1]

The rationale behind the current mainstreaming/integrationist provision for bilingual students can be explained by grouping the various objectives in a key government document on bilingual pupils in English schools, known as the Swann report and published in 1985 (DES, 1985). Despite the age of this document it continues to be the most in-depth document in which an overall educational strategy for bilingual children is outlined. It has been several decades since a report making schooling for bilingual students its centrepiece has been produced. This is despite major changes in the English education system. An excellent account of policy changes relating to bilingual students since Swann is given in Barwell (2004). Barwell shows how piecemeal the legislation has been with regard to bilingual children's educational needs since Swann. Some of this policy is dealt with later in this chapter. Given that Swann continues to set the tone for provision for bilingual students, I look briefly at this report below. I have grouped the arguments made in Swann and related education documents for mainstreaming bilingual students under four different headings: second-language learning, cognitive development, meeting students' affective needs, and societal planning.

Second-language learning: From a language-learning point of view mainstreaming is believed to provide contextualized opportunities for real communicative purposes and thus, for language-learning:

> The needs of English as a second language learners should be met by provisions within the mainstream school as part of a comprehensive programme of language education for all children (DES, 1985: 426)

Cognitive development: In organizing the classroom so that inquiry-based activities through student group collaboration are predominant, the mainstream classroom is believed to provide the best opportunity for access to the curriculum and thus, to cognitive development. Transitional bilingual support, one form of language support, is seen as one possible aid to enhancing cognitive development:

> [Because bilingual pupils] should not be offered materials with a reduced cognitive demand ... there may be a need for bilingual teaching support and for books and other written materials to be available in the pupils' mother tongues until such time as they are competent in English. (DES, 1989)

Meeting students' affective needs: Students' affective needs are met in the multicultural, multilingual mainstream classroom because it is a place where children learn about language diversity and where this diversity is valued:

> As a basis for an appreciation of linguistic diversity it is clear that all pupils need to have an insight into the nature of language and its role in our society as well as some knowledge of different forms of language. (DES, 1985: 420)

Societal planning: This can be seen in policy statements regarding the role of education in shaping Britain through the 1980s and beyond. Since the Bullock report (DES, 1975), and continuing to the Swann report (DES, 1985), government reports on education, reacting to grass-roots opinion (Bourne, 1989; Levine, 1990), had argued against withdrawal classes for bilingual students because segregating students can deepen further the racist ideas already prevalent in British society:

> We also see education as having a major role to play in countering the racism which still persists in Britain today and which we believe constitutes one of the chief obstacles to the realization of a truly pluralistic society. We recognize that some people may feel that it is expecting a great deal of education to take a lead in seeking to remedy what can be seen as a social problem. Nevertheless we believe that the education system and teachers in particular are uniquely placed to influence the attitudes of all young people in a positive manner. (DES, 1985: 319)

Withdrawing minority students from mainstream classes has been seen as an example of institutional racism in that 'it denies an individual child access to the full range of educational opportunities available' (DES, 1985: 389). It is the equal opportunity arguments which come out ahead here with the emphasis on shared needs and equality of opportunity. However, these shared needs, according to Swann, can only be met through English, which provides access to equality of opportunity:

> We believe that essential to equality of opportunity, to academic success and, more broadly, to participation on equal terms as a full member of society, is a good command of English and that first priority in language learning by all pupils must therefore be given to the learning of English. (DES, 1985: 426)

What is noticeable from this quote and elsewhere in the document is how little attention is paid to explaining how English will be learned through the mainstream curricula. It appears it will happen through immersion in an English-speaking environment. However, without some attention to how languages can be learned in this particular context, the policy amounts to a submersion policy which also has as its overall outcome, if not its goal, assimilation. Also noticeable is the absence of the role of other languages for learning. The report fails to give a place to the use of other languages for learning in the mainstream except as a transition to the eventual use of English only. It is certainly true that the Swann report with its emphasis on multicultural education or 'education for all' was against programmes of bilingual education. Chapter 7 of the report, entitled 'Language and Language Education', begins with: 'The English language is a central unifying factor in "being British", and is the key to participation on equal terms as a full member of this society' (DES, 1985: 385). Later the report argues:

> We find we cannot support the arguments put forward for the introduction of programmes of bilingual education in maintained schools in this country. Similarly we would regard mother tongue maintenance, although an important educational function, as best achieved within the ethnic minority communities themselves rather than within mainstream schools, but with considerable support from and liaison with the latter. (DES, 1985: 406)

The place for the other languages of the bilingual students in the mainstream classroom is limited to the following, as listed by Swann:

- a resource to help with the transitional needs of a non-English-speaking child starting school (DES, 1985: 407);
- a resource so that all students become aware of the linguistic diversity of British society and develop an understanding of the role and function of language in all its forms (DES, 1985: 427);
- a subject on the secondary school curriculum (DES, 1985: 428).

The Swann report reflects a prevailing drive towards homogeneity and monolingualism. Community languages other than English are seen to be outside the domain of schooled instruction, except in the case of the third point above where some provision is made for students to take qualifications in the language or literature of selective community languages in some schools. The notion of a language ecology in the classroom is not a consideration for Swann (Creese & Martin, 2003). The use of other languages for learning and the identity work that goes with learning is not a route that the Swann report supports except for transitional purposes. There is continuity in this position in government policy. Bilingualism is presented as a 'resource' in the mainstream classroom but only until the student's English is proficient enough for the processes of teaching and learning in English. As Swann clearly states above, there is no consideration given to any kind of mainstream bilingual education within English schools. And as Baetens Beardsmore (2003: 10) argues, there continues to be a 'deep-seated and widespread fear of

Table 1 The development of EAL methodology in UK schools

Time periods	*English learning*	*Bilingualism*	*Ideology*	*Curriculum*	*Funding*
1950s–1960s	Modified EFL. Separate provision or 'they will pick it up'.	Mother tongue (MT) not relevant, or worse – a problem. Home-use of MT discouraged.	Assimilationist.	Little response. English customs and traditions to be explained.	No accountability to the home office.
1970s	Wide range of practices. Separate provision for English and other curriculum areas. What about mainstream?	Beginning to be support for 'MT maintenance'. Specific classes. Two separate strands of language development. Provision within the community.	Pluralist and inclusive.	Multicultural Broaden and Relate.	Tug of war. Devolved expenditure v. LEA-controlled.
1980s	Exclusive or main focus = *mainstream.* Withdrawal = discrimination.	Bilingual development good for learning English.	Multicultural and anti-racist. Equal opportunities and inclusion.	Anti-racist. Don't just describe difference – explain inequality.	LEA accountability – detailed requirements. Target success criteria.
1990s	Measurement/target setting. Value added.	Opportunities reduced. Squeezed by other priorities.	As above.	'Broad and Balanced'. Centrally defined and monitored. Entitlement.	
2000–onwards	Movement towards content-based language teaching and EAL specialism?	Recognition of role community languages can play in educational achievement?	As above.	As above.	Further movement towards devolved budgets.

Source: Adapted from White, 1999

bilingualism. Moreover, there is an all-pervading tendency to couple the notion of "problems" to that of bilingualism'.

This position continues to hold firm even within inclusive and multicultural approaches to education and despite others' attempts to show the 'normalness' of bilingualism and multilingualism (Edwards, 1995; Dewaele *et al.*, 2003; Martin *et al.*, in press).

> To be bilingual or multilingual is not the aberration supposed by many (particularly, perhaps, by people in Europe and North America who speak a 'big' language); it is, rather, a normal and unremarkable necessity for the majority in the world today ... A monolingual perspective is often, unfortunately, a consequence of possession of a powerful 'language of wider communication', as English, French, German, Spanish and other such languages are sometimes styled. This linguistic myopia is sometimes accompanied by a narrow cultural awareness and is reinforced by state policies which, in the main, elevate only one language to official status. (Edwards, 1995: 1)

Some of these discussions are depicted in Table 1, which shows the approaches to EAL and community languages over the last 50 years or so. This table outlines the major developments in the provision for bilingual students since the early 1960s. It shows how the policy of mainstreaming has become well established. The nature of EAL provision has never been secure. There have been constant changes in funding structures which have directly impacted on the professionalism of EAL. In turn, the lack of financial security around EAL has directly impacted on what schools and LEAs have been able to provide and consequently on the professional training possibilities for teachers as specialists.

EAL teachers

In educational policy documents, EAL teachers have historically been subsumed under a generic category. So, for example, no distinction has been made between those EAL teachers who are bilingual in a community language (bilingual EAL teachers) and those who are not (non-bilingual EAL teachers).[2] They are described as doing the same work. However, in this book, a distinction is made. A particular interest in what the bilingual EAL teacher brings to the classroom and the school will be referenced throughout the book, especially in Chapters 9 and 10. In those chapters, I explore how bilingual EAL teachers develop additional roles in mainstream classrooms through their bilingual pedagogies and explore the importance of first languages in the learning process.

In addition, it is important to point out that EAL teachers are in fact 'subject teachers'. In England and Wales, it is not possible to specialize in EAL or make language issues central in initial teacher training. EAL teachers are therefore subject-trained in a secondary school curriculum area. Moreover, all teachers, regardless of their specialism, receive very little input on EAL and bilingualism issues during their initial training. EAL teachers' specialization comes through practice and continuing professional development courses run through their local government services and university courses or through membership of professional forums.

The National Association for Language Development in the Curriculum (NALDIC) (www.naldic.org.uk/) provides a professional forum for EAL teachers. It describes the distinctiveness of EAL.

> EAL pedagogy is the set of systematic teaching approaches which have evolved from classroom based practices in conjunction with the development of knowledge through theoretical and research perspectives. These approaches meet the language and learning needs of pupils for whom English is an additional language. They can be used in a wide range of different teaching contexts.
>
> Teachers who have acquired expertise in EAL, whether they are specialists or class/subject teachers, will:
>
> - understand progression in second/additional language learning;
> - be able to assess pupils' understanding of curriculum content and use this information in their planning;
> - draw on pupils' bicultural and bilingual knowledge and experience;
> - incorporate first language knowledge and use appropriate staff resources where available;
> - take account of the variables that apply in different contexts, and capitalise on the potential for working in partnership with their mainstream/specialist colleagues.
>
> (www.naldic.org.uk/ittseal/issues/Pedagogy.cfm, visited July 2004)

This list outlines particular expertises in addition to the subject curriculum knowledge which teachers will have gained through their earlier studies. However, it is only recently that there has been recognition and support from the government for a specialist qualification in EAL (DfES, 2003).

Collaborative teaching

Collaborative teaching relationships have been argued for in government documents since 1985, when Swann suggested:

> a role for a language specialist or specialists in primary and secondary schools with substantial numbers of pupils for whom English is not a first language, to work alongside teachers or subject specialists through a 'team teaching' approach. (DES, 1985: 427)

The 'team teaching approach' is an attempt to make schools and subject teachers realize that responsibility for language development must be shared equally (DES, 1985: 428). We see a continuity in endorsing collaborative teaching in the 'Teaching Standards' for initial teacher training (www.tta.gov.uk/training/qtsstandards/standards/standards1.htm, visited January 2004). Below, I have selected clauses which refer directly to teacher collaboration.

Those awarded Qualified Teacher Status must understand and uphold the professional code of the General Teaching Council for England by demonstrating all of the following:

1.6   They understand the contribution that support staff and other professionals make to teaching and learning.

3.1.3 They select and prepare resources, and plan for their safe and effective organisation, taking account of pupils' interests and their language and cultural backgrounds, with the help of support staff where appropriate.

3.1.4 They take part in, and contribute to, teaching teams, as appropriate to the school. Where applicable, they plan for the deployment of additional adults who support pupils' learning.

3.2.5 With the help of an experienced teacher, they can identify the levels of attainment of pupils learning English as an additional language. They begin to analyse the language demands and learning activities in order to provide cognitive challenge as well as language support.

Similarly, from the 'Aiming High' policy document (DfES, 2003):

2.21   We must use the knowledge, skills and expertise of specialist teachers more effectively. Many are currently funded through the Ethnic Minority Achievement Grant, and the Traveller Achievement Grant. Many provide excellent additional support for individual pupils. However, specialist teachers are too often marginalised and have little influence on the practice of their mainstream colleagues. Moreover, a recent Ofsted report found that many teachers working as English as an Additional Language specialists do not hold qualifications relevant to their specialism. We want to enhance the role of the specialist so that they can use their expertise to develop more effective partnerships with classroom teachers, to provide expert advice and lead whole school training. (DfES, 2003)

Noticeable in these more current policy documents is the recognition of teacher responsibility in working with other adults and support staff in the classroom. In these more recent policy documents, working with others in the classroom is now being seen as a skill which teachers need to develop. The lack of support for EAL teacher professional development is acknowledged and their marginalization is also mentioned.

The sharing of teacher responsibility, knowledge and skills, whatever the teacher's training, was however, recognized in the early partnership teaching literature. Back in the late 1980s and early 1990s, it was recognized that for mainstreaming to work as an inclusive education policy, changes needed to be made to the mainstream classroom. This required teachers negotiating their differing roles when working together in the classroom.

Levine (1990: 29) wrote about mainstreaming:

[it requires] a move away from bilingual pupils being seen chiefly as the responsibility for specialist language teachers, to the view of all teachers having responsibility for them . . . Further, from the point of view of bilingual learners 'taking their rightful places in "normal" classes', mainstreaming fits the principles of an entitlement curriculum, along with mixed ability grouping and with interactive teaching practices.

The idea of an entitlement curriculum (mentioned by Levine above) suggests that the secondary school subject classroom must make changes so that all children have equal access to learning opportunities. Similarly, Bourne (1989) has argued that mainstreaming is more than an assimilationist approach: that it warrants a separate category:

> This paradigm might be called 'multilingual education', where it is accepted that classrooms are linguistically diverse, where all children are encouraged to draw on their full range of linguistic resources in communication and learning in the classroom in an informal way and with the aid of multilingual personnel and resources, but within which flexible small group strategies can be developed to bring pupils together to develop literacy in languages other than English whenever this is both practically feasible and supported by pupils and parents. (Bourne, 1989: 13–14)

Teacher collaboration between EAL and STs required an understanding of multiple teaching and learning agendas. Teaching partnerships therefore aimed to change the mainstream classroom to a place where different expertises were brought together to benefit the diverse learning needs found there. The complexities of this task is fully explored in Chapters 6 and 7 where a full consideration of different modes of collaboration is given. In these chapters I show how teacher support can be divided into three broad categories each with many subdivisions and each with overlaps. However, the point to be made here is that the responsibility for multilingual education has been placed on the shoulders of partner teachers without relevant teacher training in the areas of teacher collaboration or bilingual/multilingual pedagogies and this has been the case for several decades.

Change in Provision

One of the recurring themes of domestic politics in contemporary Britain has been concerned with the need to find a way of living with ethno-linguistic diversity. Creese and Leung (2003) argue that over the last two decades there has been a fairly consistent policy direction, which celebrates diversity but does little to uphold the distinctiveness of EAL as a subject specialism or encourage the use of other languages for curriculum-learning. There is continuity in policy statements about the inclusion of minority communities but there is also continuity in presenting an under-defined and unproblematically imagined educational mainstream in which all students are to benefit equally. We can see this 'majority–minority coming together' view of society reflected in the education policy documents below:

Many children in English schools regularly speak a language other than English and about 200 different languages are used by pupils in the classroom. Such linguistic diversity is an asset. It provides an opportunity for pupils to gain first-hand experience, knowledge and understanding of other cultures and perspectives. It also helps to prepare pupils for life in a multicultural society by promoting respect for all forms of language. Variety of language is a rich resource which schools should use as they implement the National Curriculum. (NCC, 1991: 1)

The National Curriculum recognises that variety of language is a rich resource which can support learning in English. Where appropriate, pupils should be encouraged to make use of their understanding and skills in other languages in learning English. (SCAA, 1996: 2)

In the above quotes we see a celebration of other languages not only to show the rich diversity of English society but also to be used as a transition to the full use of English for learning. However, there is increasing criticism of this 'rich resource' view of other languages because it does little more than 'celebrate' bilingualism to indicate moral and social approval (Bourne, 2001; Martin-Jones & Saxena, 2003). It is rarely translated into systematic curriculum action. The point made is that minority languages are, as a rule, not used in the classroom by teachers or students in arguably the most important of schools' aims, the guided construction of curriculum knowledge (Mercer, 1995). Therefore, the marginal use, if there is any one at all, of minority languages can function in ways which lower their status within the school setting. The inclusive rhetoric of government policy towards linguistic difference, then, is held at the level of a celebratory discourse without any real bite. However, a recent policy document does, for the first time to my knowledge, reference the possible benefits to be gained from complementary schooling and the teaching of community languages in terms of the value added that such schooling brings to achievement across educational domains (DfES, 2003):

> **2.36**   Successful schools reach out to their communities. They often make premises available for community use, which can build bridges and develop dialogue. Many pupils have also benefited greatly from out-of-school-hours learning in community-run initiatives such as supplementary schools. Some supplementary schools focus on the curriculum, others on cultural, mother tongue or religious faith instruction. Attendance can enhance pupils' respect, promote self-discipline and inspire pupils to have high aspirations to succeed. (DfES, 2003)

This is a forward-looking statement and recognizes the important role complementary schooling plays (see also Martin *et al.*, 2004, for an account of the role complementary schooling plays in bilingualism, identity, learning and community cohesion and extension). However, despite such an endorsement, education policy still sees provision for community languages teaching and maintenance mainly beyond the remit of state schooling.

Creese and Leung (2003) have argued that mainstream curriculum and educational practices are selectively inclusive and ambiguously exclusive at the same time. They are inclusive in the sense that all students are welcome in the classroom. However, they are exclusive in the sense that government fails to supports EAL as a legitimate cross-curriculum discipline (see also NALDIC, 1999) or to endorse the use of community languages for extended curriculum-learning. Creese and Leung are careful not to suggest that mainstreaming is a 'failed' policy in the sense that the key tenets of this policy are wrong-headed or ill-conceived. Rather they argue that it is necessary to look at how policy is implemented locally to understand what inclusion might mean for its recipients: students and teachers:

> What we are suggesting is that if we are to understand what a policy means, and how it works out, we need to pay attention to the ways policy meanings are understood and taken up by practitioners/teachers. The implementation of a policy clearly does not entirely depend upon individual teacher interpretations and responses. However, for an educational policy to be something that teachers can work with productively, and not just a requirement to be carried out as a kind of 'performativity', then it has to resonate well with teachers' perceptions and concerns. This means that policy makers and planners may have to take note of the ways the rational and the cognitively known elements of policy interact with teacher values, and local practices and concerns. (Creese & Leung, 2003: 17)

This is exactly what this book attempts to do. It looks at how policy for bilingual students is delivered through teaching partnerships. It makes central prevailing teacher values and institutional practices as teachers collaborate with one another. It looks at their discourses through interview transcripts, their interactions with students and their interactions with one another, and their practices through observational vignettes. It does this by placing particular school contexts in its socio-political context.

Chapter Summary

I started this chapter with a quote from a newspaper article which called for a recognition of the complexities and tensions we all have to deal with in daily life. I have tried to argue that although paradigms of opposing views are useful in helping us take up positions in the work we do, they are never clear-cut when put into practice. There are dangers in adopting inclusion and exclusion as absolutist positions. Such positions encourage hostility and guilt. Mainstreaming and team teaching, which should help to transform the traditional classroom, presents teachers with daily dilemmas which they must try to deal with in fair and reasonable ways. Transforming the mainstream classroom is an ongoing action; as social life and policy changes, so does our understanding and enactments of policy. Teachers are attempting to maintain a precarious equilibrium which must take account of social policy, institutional and individual values. It is in this spirit that I look at the work of the teachers in this book. This chapter, therefore, ends as it was started, with two statements suggesting the need for supporting humility.

> But it is whimsical to suppose that, under present world conditions, a dogged insistence upon the notion of 'absolute value' will make the uncertainties go away. All one can hope for is a viable pluralism braced by a willingness to negotiate differences in world-view. . . . I take open-mindedness to be a willingness to construe knowledge and values from multiple perspectives without loss of commitment to one's own values. . . . I take the constructivism of cultural psychology to be a profound expression of democratic culture. It demands that we be conscious of how we come to our knowledge and as conscious as we can be about the values that lead us to our perspectives. But it does not insist that there is only one way of constructing meaning, or one right way. It is based upon values that, I believe, fit it best to deal with the changes and disruptions that have become so much a feature of modern life. (Bruner, 1990: 30)

> My position is that values in society generally, and in education specifically, are in tension, that there is no clear overall and coherent set of values which can justify policy and practice at all levels in education. Because of these tensions and the dilemmas which arise, there is no ideological purity in education, no single value or principle, whether it be equality or individuality or social inclusion, that can encompass what is commonly considered to be worthwhile. My call is therefore for appreciating the benefits of ideological impurity and living hopefully with it. . . . From my perspective, ideological impurity means recognizing the tension in principle, and in practically fulfilling the values of individuality and distinctiveness, equality, connectedness and inclusion. (Norwich, 1996: 3–4)

Notes

1. Readers are referred to Leung and Franson (2001a) and Rampton *et al.* (1999) for a historical account of development in EAL teaching.
2. The government has started to support training programmes for bilingual classroom assistants. Bilingual classroom assistants are not qualified teachers.

Chapter 3

Teachers in Multilingual Mainstream Classrooms: Enacting Inclusion

Introduction

This is the first of the data chapters. In this chapter, we look at the ways teachers describe themselves and their partner teachers' roles and positions within the school and classroom. The purpose of analysing teachers' role descriptions is to investigate the success of mainstreaming as an inclusive educational policy. My specific angle is to analyse policy through an exploration of the collaborative teaching relationship of EAL and subject teachers. I show that what counts as knowledge in the secondary school classroom stratifies the two types of teachers and helps to explain the dialogue with which this book started. I look at the interface of how local institutional and classroom discourses interact with larger societal discourses on what counts as knowledge. The power relationship between EAL and subject teachers is necessary to understand because we will see that this power is linked to wider educational debates that support the teachers differently in their teaching practices. These educational hierarchies impact on the possibilities of these teaching relationships, which in turn influence the extent to which policy aims of inclusion can be achieved.

This chapter develops two main themes. The first looks at the contradictions teachers face in implementing an inclusive policy within a competitive standard-driven educational climate. This is achieved through looking at teacher interview data on the possibilities of mainstreaming. Through an analysis of this information, a distinction can be made between what constitutes support and advice. The data shows that both STs and EAL teachers experience contradictions between their intellectual and lived ideologies. Intellectually, STs support policies of inclusion, while finding it difficult to meet individual needs in practice. Intellectually, EAL teachers highlight their advisory role in bringing about change in the mainstream, while in practice compensating for this lack of change by doing individual support work. Both STs and EAL teachers recompense for weaknesses in policy by complementing one another's work in balancing different pedagogies in the classroom. The second theme looks at how hierarchies become established around EAL and subject teaching. We will look at how the pedagogies of transmission and facilitation become attached to subject and EAL teachers and how their enactment positions the two kinds of teachers differently in the secondary school classroom.

This chapter is structured along the following lines: first, a discussion of the ideological basis of dilemmas and how teachers reconcile these around inclusion and exclusion; second, a discussion about the nature of support and advisory teaching within the mainstream, which is returned to in Chapters 6 and 7; third, interview data from STs and EAL teachers is presented, which is broadly focused upon describing their roles, pedagogy and positioning within the classroom.

Educational Dilemmas

> [Teachers] have to accomplish the practical task of teaching which requires getting the job done through whatever conceptions and methods work best . . . But these practical considerations, inevitably have ideological bases, which define what 'the job' actually is, how to do it, how to assess its outcomes, how to react to is successes and failures, how to talk and interact with pupils, how many can be taught or talked to at once. (Billig, 1988: 46)

Billig's point in the above quote is that the most practical of considerations have an ideological basis. He makes a distinction between intellectual ideologies, which are consistent, and lived (or common sense) ideologies, which are inconsistent and variable. Support for equal opportunities would be an example of an intellectual ideology, while deciding not to allow all students to finish off a task before moving on would be an example of a lived ideology. Teachers face such dilemmas on a day-to-day basis. Billig argues that these dilemmas are not to be seen as something negative, but rather as actually facilitating a 'thinking society' (Billig *et al.*, 1988: 1). Dilemmas arise because people share values, norms and social expectations. Moreover, it is not merely that bits and pieces of social knowledge are shared socially, but that those which are shared are conflicting. We will see some of these 'conflictual bits and pieces' reflected in the teachers' interview transcripts as they describe their roles in the classroom. In order to do this I make use of an eclectic range of educational literature. Specifically, I draw on the inclusion literature of special educational needs, pedagogic literature and discussions about advisory and support teaching. I bring all these literatures to bear on the EAL teacher and ST's collaboration. I see the discussion around EAL teaching and bilingualism as distinctive. Therefore, in referring to SEN and pedagogy literature I am not attempting to conflate these fields or iron out crucial differences between the needs of a bilingual child and those of a child with special educational needs. My belief here is that the ideologies of inclusion and particular pedagogies have impacted on how EAL children are taught in the classroom and in turn, have presented particular dilemmas for teachers. It is helpful, therefore, to learn from the SEN's literature of inclusion.

Within inclusive education an ongoing dilemma for teachers is that between providing equality of opportunity for all pupils and catering for children with individual needs. Clark *et al.* (1995) found that there were two perspectives operating in schools. The first of these tended to be advocated by senior managers and reflected the *dominant* perspective of current thinking in the organizational model (Clark *et al.*, 1995), which highlights a whole school, problem-solving, collaborative equal opportunities approach to dealing with issues concerning the mainstreaming of children with special educational needs. The second perspective they termed *subordinate* (Clark *et al.*, 1995: 84). This view tended to be held by classroom teachers who felt that the dominant perspective was only a piece of rhetoric that had little meaning in dealing with the needs of individual children in the mainstream of a busy school. These teachers were primarily interested in making sure that individual children who were seen as struggling were given support in some way.

Clark *et al.* provide a good example of how teachers struggle with the discourse of an ideology to which they see themselves broadly supporting, but which does not resonate comfortably with them in their localized practice. These teachers do not see their withdrawal work as excluding children, but as providing for their individual needs. It is an example of how large ideological discourses are also in flux as debates within them extend and narrow what inclusion means. The dilemma of how to best cater for difference is summarized by Norwich (1994: 296):

> This can be seen as posing a dilemma in education over how difference is taken into account – whether to recognize differences as relevant to individual needs by offering different provision, but that doing so could reinforce unjustified inequalities and is associated with devaluation; or whether to offer a common and valued provision for all but with the risk of not providing what is relevant to individual needs.

Norwich distinguishes between individual and common needs and argues for an interactionist model. In the interview transcripts which follow, we will see that both STs and EAL teachers struggle with reaching this balance. On the one hand we will hear the teachers voice intellectual ideologies which are consistently in favour of inclusive education and common needs, while on the other hand they refer to common sense ideologies that stress the difficulties of providing for individual students. This juxtaposition of individual and common needs is important here because not only is this balancing act linked to the difficulties that teachers must face and reconcile, but also fulfilling individual and common needs are linked to different kinds of pedagogy. I will show how these pedagogies are hierarchized in terms of importance in the mainstream classroom. Facilitative pedagogies become associated with working with the few, meeting individual needs and are linked to the EAL teacher, while transmission pedagogies become associated with teaching the many and are connected to the ST.

Pedagogies of Transmission and Facilitation

Clearly, meeting both common and individual needs is what teachers do on a daily basis. However, perhaps what is not so obvious is how addressing common and individual needs becomes linked with particular pedagogies and particular teachers. We will see that these pedagogies associated with transmission to the many are determined as having a higher and more important profile than facilitation pedagogies of working with the few.

Within education these two pedagogic positions of transmission and facilitation are often discussed. On the one hand, teachers can be viewed as 'technicians' whose task is simply to deliver the national curriculum (Woods, 1993: 3), and on the other, teachers are viewed as 'facilitators', 'reflective practitioners' (Pollard, 1988 in Woods, 1993), 'extended professionals' (Hoyle, 1989 in Woods, 1993), or 'teacher-researchers' (Cochran-Smith & Lytle, 1993; Stenhouse, 1975, in Woods, 1993).

Teachers as technicians are viewed as the source of 'knowledge' and their communication is expected to dominate proceedings. They are free to direct pupils to maximize their 'learning' and must be allowed to present the curriculum in an 'orderly' fashion (summarized from Hammersley, 1984: 22). The teacher as a facilitator, however, is seen as only part of the learning process, albeit a very important one. Here the emphasis is placed on the teacher's ability to encourage the child to experience and discover, as in the learning constructivist theories of Vygotsky (1986) and Bruner (1990):

> Learning awakens a variety of developmental processes that are able to operate only when the child is interacting with people in his environment and in co-operation with peers. Once these processes are internalized they become part of the child's development achievement. (Vygotsky, 1978: 90)

Despite what appears to be two totally opposing views on the role of teachers in the learning process, it is clear that the teachers themselves rarely adopt only one position. Billig summarizes this well:

> Supporters of traditional, transmission-oriented teaching are unlikely in all contexts to insist that pupils must remain passive recipients of the received wisdom, that education is always one-way traffic, an unchanging reproduction of all that has gone before. Similarly, the advocates of child-centered, autonomous learning will not insist that children are taught nothing, that the acquisition of a largely ready-made culture of knowledge and understanding is not, in however child-centered a way it is achieved, an important goal of education. (Billig *et al.*, 1988: 45)

Instead, teachers draw on a variety of pedagogies in their classrooms. They juggle the dilemmas of daily practice within the trajectories of policy document guidelines which are underpinned by ideologies of what teaching and learning should be. Teachers are working within layers of discourse, which includes their own voices, their schools, and wider educational, government and media institutions, of what teaching and learning should be. This chapter places teachers' self-descriptions within their local and wider contexts to show how different pedagogies are valued differently, making an inclusive policy difficult to implement. Although EAL and subject teachers can and do draw on the full range of pedagogies available to them in teaching bilingual/EAL students, I will show that the teachers themselves tend to privilege particular pedagogies over others when they describe the work they do. These descriptions and actual practices have implications for their own status in the mainstream and, more importantly, for the students they work with.

Support and Advisory Teaching in Mainstream Settings

Throughout research and policy literature there is a tendency to refer to EAL teachers as 'language support teachers'. In my own work I prefer the terms 'language specialists' and 'EAL teachers' in order to move away from notions of support and to highlight the specialist knowledge that goes with educational linguistics in mainstream settings (Creese, 2002a, 2002b; NALDIC, 1999).

Jill Bourne (1989) refers to EAL teachers as advisory teachers doing in-class language support. She includes the two core elements of EAL work in her definition: support and advisory. However, even a cursory glance at the words 'support' and 'advisory' suggest very different practices in the classroom. If we take each word as a verb we find across a variety of dictionaries that *to support* means: to hold up, to sustain, to maintain, to back up, to nourish; while *to advise* means: to counsel, to recommend, to inform, to announce, to guide. Moreover, *supporter* (follower, backer) is very different from *adviser* (mentor, director, counsellor). And whereas *advisory* exists as an adjective to describe a noun – in this case an *advisory* teacher – the adjective for support, *supportive*, cannot be used to describe the same noun. A *supportive teacher* is obviously what every teacher should be, whereas the compound noun 'support teacher' clearly has a specific institutional role. Overall the word *supporter* has the connotation of a follower, a backer, whereas *adviser* has the connotation of a knower, a doer.

Biott (1991: 71) defines the difference between support and advisory teaching as a matter of who is being targeted:

> [T]he former [support teachers] are primarily there to supplement the teaching given to the students, while the latter [advisory] are primarily there to support the professional development of the teacher. In either case, the establishment of a supportive working relationship with the teacher is crucially important.

Biott does not dwell on how 'support' and 'advisory' get played out in practice in schools. His last sentence in the above quote speaks of how important relationships are between teachers whether working in a support or advisory capacity. He appears to give the two concepts equal importance. Biott is not concerned with the power dynamics of support and advisory teaching in particular contexts. His work focuses helpfully on describing the different kinds of collaborative work teachers can do with one another (see also Chapter 6).

However, Biott's definition of support work as a supplement to teaching is of interest. It would suggest that EAL teachers are there to supplement something missing from the mainstream classroom. MacLure (2003: 124–5) argues that a *supplement* always points to a flaw in the thing that it supplements:

> The supplement never merely adds some (minor or contingent) element: precisely by adding something, it also replaces something that is not present, and so takes away from the self-sufficiency and intactness of the original . . . As Derrida notes, if the supplement did not have this usurping function, if it really did leave the original untouched, then the supplement would be entirely useless.

The argument here is that if support teaching supplements other teaching, something is missing in the mainstream. In the following section of this chapter we look at how teachers describe the possibilities of mainstreaming. We will see the importance that STs given to of the concept of support teaching for supplementing something which is missing from their classrooms. We will also see the importance given to advisory teaching by EAL teachers as a way to make the mainstream classroom more adaptable to diversity.

In the remainder of this chapter we begin to look at interview data from 26 teachers across three London schools. A profile of each school is given in the Introductory chapter of this book. The reader is reminded that schools are given an alphabetical code of A, B or C. The numbers following this letter show whether the teacher is an EAL teacher or ST: numbers 1–4 are EAL teachers; numbers 5 and above are STs.

The Possibilities of Mainstreaming: Policy into Practice

In semi-structured interviews, subject teachers were asked the question: do you think that mainstreaming bilingual children is the best means of providing for their needs? Eleven of the subject teachers replied to this question and all except one were in favour of mainstreaming EAL/bilingual students as a preferred policy for bilingual children as long as support teaching was available:

1   I think if the child gets support in every lesson, then support has to be the best way because they actually feel part of the class, they get to know the teachers so there is so many plus points to that. If they only get a support teacher in a classroom infrequently, you know I think there is a question over which is better in that case because I think they lose the string of things quite quickly when there isn't someone there in the room giving the support. (A7)

2   I think it [mainstreaming] totally depends on how much support you get. If you've got good support when you need it, then it seems to me that the children should be in the mainstream and learn along with everyone else.

Oh yes, if support is there, keep them in the classroom, excellent. . . . If you have got support in there with you and support helping you prepare the lessons and things like that, then I can't see any reasons why they should be taken out at all, but without the support it seems to disadvantage a lot of the other kids in there and because it does take so much time and you have got to modify the lessons so much . . . to keep these kids going that it doesn't seem to be cost effective. (C5)

In Quotes 1 and 2, we can see support for the policy of mainstreaming as long as it is supplemented by an EAL or support teacher. The teachers in these first two quotes highlight the role support teachers play in not only addressing the needs of bilingual students, but also indirectly the needs of non EAL children as it allows STs to keep the group more cohesive. The work the EAL teacher does allows all the children to progress more quickly. However, as the following quotes show, teachers also saw a place for withdrawal when support was not available:

3   But with the limited resources and limited support that we get often I wonder whether it might be best to take those children and teach them English or the basic English and then put them back. (C5)

4   I don't think withdrawal for everything but I think, but I think to just back up the language, just to back up what they are doing, not complete withdrawal but just to give them that little bit of extra help. . . . I wouldn't like them to be taken out and miss out but then again you want them to get the help they should have. So more support really, more support. (A9)

5   Well, I think, this is my personal opinion. I think that in school we have got so many Turkish and Kurdish children, that having them in the classroom, and the idea is that they learn almost by osmosis [laughs], it doesn't work, because there are a lot of children here who go five years through school and they still can't speak any English. I think it works when you have got one or two children. Like one of my tutor group student's is a Portuguese speaker who didn't have any English when he got here, but he is fluent, orally fluent, because he had nobody else to speak to so he had to speak English to survive, but it is not true of the Turkish children here and um I think just putting them in the first year does a real disservice to them. And is completely against the notion of equal opportunities because they don't have the opportunity to learn English or to understand any of their subjects. So I would withdraw them and teach them English. (C8)

What is interesting about these teachers' comments is that despite broadly endorsing the inclusive, progressive policy designed to meet the needs of the bilingual children, they appear to feel little responsibility for meeting language/ learning needs of individual students. Indeed, in Quote 5, the teacher refers to the policy as if it were a sink-or-swim submersion policy rather than an inclusion policy. That is, she sees the children as being just left there to survive. This, of course, is also indicative of how she regards her own role in providing for the language-learning needs of bilingual children. Only those children who are already of a certain level of English should be in her class, because she does not see herself making provisions for language-learning to occur there.

The subject teachers involved in this study were supportive of the ideas behind inclusive education, but recognized the dilemma they faced in balancing the individual needs of students with the demands of a national curriculum. Here we can see one of the many dilemmas described by Billig earlier in this chapter. Teachers are supportive of the intellectual ideology of inclusive education and mainstreaming in particular, while also recognizing the difficulty of making it work in practice. They adopt the position that mainstream classes should be inclusive of all their students but recognize that they have problems meeting individual needs without additional support from EAL teachers. STs explain this concern through a focus on lack of time for meeting individual needs:

6   I feel I don't give enough attention to the pupils, period. Not just the bilingual pupils and to be quite frank I don't know who the bilingual pupils are. I have seen the pupils I am teaching currently, I have seen them five times. I don't know who the bilingual pupils are, the low ability or the high ability. So I tend not to target anybody. I tend to target the whole class. . . . But I never really spend a lot of time in a class of 31 with any individuals other than if they put their hands up for help and I would go round as I walk periodically around the class as well, but I would never identify any pupils. (A6)

7   I don't think as a class teacher you can cope with bilingualism as well as controlling 30 children. . . . I find I haven't got the time to sit with them and they need you to sit with them and explain things again and you haven't got the time to explain every activity again and to read through the text with them, you just haven't got that time when you have got 20 or so other kids who might need some help as well. (A9)

8   It depends on their language ability. Where we have complete and utter beginners, no I don't think they should be in the classroom. There are just so demanding in terms of time, you either teach them or you don't and if you teach them nobody else gets a look in, or the amount of time they have from me is so minimal that it is not fair on anybody. . . . Yes, I am always conscious that they want more time. . . . On the other hand you are aware that the lesson is coming to an end in 5 minutes time, you want to do an overall summary for everybody and often it is much quicker to say well, that is the answer, and do it for them. (B5)

9   Because sometimes a new member joins us and she just can't speak English at all. And for me that is very difficult because there is absolutely no way I can communicate with that student and because the supporting staff come

only once or twice a week I think the child is suffering from that and I am not helping the child at all, and having said that if I spend ten minutes with her that means I have to spend ten minutes less with somebody else and sometimes that creates a rift in the class room, as is happening at the moment and I think that issue needs to be addressed quite clearly. (B6)

10   I don't have the time nor the personal resources to cater for everyone in my classroom when you've got classes of 30, particularly um when you have got children with really specific needs, often I don't even know how to help them, . . . so it is really really helpful to have support there to do those things that I can't do. (C7)

11   A lot of the time some kids flounder terribly and it takes so much of the teachers time just to keep them in touch with the rest of the group that I think probably it [mainstreaming] is not the best way to do it. (C5)

These quotes taken from interview data show how pushed for time STs are and what kinds of dilemmas they face in sharing this scarce resource around. In Quotes 6–11, we see the subject teachers highlighting the individual needs of students over the commonalities of equal opportunities and intellectual ideologies of inclusive education. Although on one hand we can react against the subject teachers' construction of bilingual/EAL students as taking too much of their time, their comments are a declaration that, without the assistance of the EAL teacher, individual children are being ignored. The subject teachers' interview extracts make for uncomfortable reading, but give a view of how policy might be implemented in context. Let us now contrast this with how EAL teachers describe the possibilities of mainstreaming. Like the STs, they were asked the same question, Do you think that mainstreaming bilingual children is the best means of providing for their needs?

12   I think mainstreaming is preferable to withdrawal, for the simple fact that their not speaking a language is enough without being kept in separate rooms. Because if you think that, you can join in the camaraderie that is going on in a classroom, I mean, a lot of children who don't speak English have still got friends and have many friends and are aware of what is happening. They are not these people on the outskirts of the school society, which I think is what would happen if there were withdrawal only. (C2)

13   But I think you've got to provide a context for meaningful use of target language and the mainstream classroom does that every time. If it's properly organized and if classroom control is good, and there is a proper context for what is being done in the classroom, I mean that is what children would normally be doing. Why can't they do it just because it's another language? (A1)

14   Withdrawal is a poor impoverished resource, impoverished accommodation. There is very little idea of what is it for, what are we doing here,

who is doing it and why? You get little cohorts together, then you think about what the hell you're going to do with them. (A1)

In the above quotes we see that EAL teachers are particularly concerned with meeting bilingual/EAL children's social and emotional needs in the classroom. The EAL teachers comment on the importance of the socialization process in children becoming part of the school's community. The extracts clearly highlight the importance, in terms of learning and teaching, of fitting in with others and experiencing commonalities. The EAL teachers, in contrast to the STs, are focusing on inclusion and the social connectiveness of children's common needs. At first glance, it is curious that EAL teachers highlight the importance of educational inclusion, while STs highlight individual needs. But on reflection, we will see that this is not so surprising. It is the EAL teachers who work with individual EAL children mostly in addressing their language and learning needs. From the EAL teachers' perspective, the subject teachers are not doing enough to include these students into the mainstream. From the subject teachers' point of view, on the other hand, the ideology of inclusion is sacrificing the individual needs of learners. Without the EAL teacher, the STs claim they cannot meet the individual needs of bilingual/EAL children. EAL teachers in the classroom allow STs to support the intellectual ideology of inclusive policy. Now let us turn to looking at how different pedagogies become associated with addressing individual and common needs.

Specific Knowledge and Generic Skills

In the following extracts from STs, we will see that they lay claim to owning a subject-specific expertise while constructing EAL teacher knowledge as generic. The EAL teacher is presented as simplifying language and, by implication, simplifying the curriculum. Alison Lee has argued that language teachers working in a school or university disciplinary setting are often seen as possessing a generic knowledge not bounded by a subject curriculum. This kind of knowledge is associated with the general and generalizable. This is subordinated to a second kind of knowledge, disciplinary knowledge, which is presented as contextualized and specialized (Lee, 1997).

In the following extracts we see subject teachers describe their own work in relation to the EAL teacher:

15 If it is technical language, I think it comes down to me, like technical words like designing briefs, like ergonomics and things, but often the basic language and the simplification of language, is done by the support teacher. (C5)

16 Well, I have expertise in terms of the curriculum, the syllabus and so I am directing what we are going to study next and plan that in relation to the curriculum. (B5)

17 [I] tend to have more responsibility in the instruction. (A5)

18 I am responsible for the skills they have got to learn in history. I am mainly responsible for that and Lucy is mainly responsible for providing the extra support for the bilingual students. I would say our major responsibility is different but that within the classroom you can cross over in that I'd be responsible for saying which skills they should learn and Lucy might come up with ideas to make the skills more accessible to them, due to her experience in bilingual learning, but I would say our responsibility is different. (A8)

In these interview transcripts we can see that the subject teachers describe ownership and responsibility for the curriculum. The subject teachers think primarily in terms of the 'what of' in a lesson. In this sense they are topic-centred. Their main focus is on the transmission of knowledge, not the methodology of how to do this. This does not mean that the teachers do not consider such things, only that in terms of working with an EAL teacher they distinguish their roles by foregrounding their part in the teaching of content. In contrast, when STs talk of the EAL teachers' role in the classroom they highlight these teachers' skill in relation to the 'how to' of the lesson:

19 She seems to pick up on two groups . . . one who have language difficulties and she explains the more complex technical language that we use, therefore the kids can access the work. Particularly in year 11 when they are doing exams, they don't understand the questions a lot of the time and she can explain that and also she picks up on kids who haven't done homework for various reasons. Sometimes it is because they haven't understood it, sometimes it is because they find difficulty doing it because everything seems to be hard for them so she can go through it slowly and carefully with them and that is very useful as well. (C5)

20 Well, I'd do like a lesson plan and then I'd say this is what I was going to do, and I'd ask her, it would probably be about only half an hour before we went into the classroom, sort of, you know, what do you think? And then she might give ideas of how to present something in a more accessible way. And she would say to me, well, do you want me to do that and that, you know that part of the lesson and so she just looks through and decides which bits she quite fancies doing and you know how to make some of the other stuff more accessible, as she is more experienced in bilingualism. So I would really ask her advice really, being a new teacher. (A9)

21 They do overview things and they do see things in educational terms rather than the hammer and nails. Because it is so valuable because you can lose it. (A7)

STs view the EAL teacher as accessing concepts, being creative with ideas and simplifying language. Because the subject teachers are topic-focused, they think primarily in terms of the 'what of' in a lesson (the 'hammer and nails'), followed by the 'how to'. The STs see the role of EAL teachers as being the reverse of this. The EAL role is seen as being activity-centred. By this I mean that EAL teachers are assumed to have skills in making the topic interesting and relevant to students, not knowledge of the subject itself. These access and simplification skills are applied across the full curriculum range. Instead of stemming from the 'objective' knowledge base of what is tested in school exams and prescribed by the curriculum, the language teachers' strengths are seen to lie in the creativity of coming up with suggestions. Quote 21 reminds us that pedagogic creativity can become lost among the 'hammer and nails' of curriculum content. Pedagogic creativity benefits not only students but teachers too. STs made the following comments:

> 22 They [EAL teachers] are very good at telling you where you are going wrong on board work. Because I mean there are good techniques for good board presentation and that can be illustrated by a good support teacher from the perspective of the less able children or the bilingual. (C5)

> 23 Basically she would rework what I had been using for the past three years, or provide extra resources to go on top of what I would have done anyway. (A6)

> 24 Graham is extremely good at just adapting, you will see him pick up a topic that you are doing. Write a few words, and photocopy it and come back with it. (B5)

In these examples we can again see how subject teachers view the work of EAL teachers as activity-focused, where skills that emphasize creativity and spontaneity are valued. This is true whether the EAL teachers are playing a support role in terms of accessing the curriculum for students, or an advisory role in showing STs how they can make their classes more accessible.

Subject teachers describe EAL support as at its best when the support provided is continuous and allows the ST to keep the students grouped together in terms of achieving content-based aims:

> 25 I suppose support at its best is when it is bringing children who are very difficult to reach because of their language and learning problems, it is keeping them with the rest of the group and often without support those kids are very difficult to keep up with the rest of the group and support will bring them along and keep them going. (C5)

> 26 It needs a continuous support in every lesson. If a child, a bilingual student, goes into a class with no support, they are not going to get what they should out of that lesson. They will probably end up only understanding half of it maybe, depending on their level of, you know, depending on how long they have been in the country or whatever. (A9)

> 27 If there are two of us, I think it is a lot easier to achieve that aim because you can help them quicker. And also the support teacher will guide the

weaker pupils a lot more and I will just be there for general queries but they will probably help the weaker child a lot more. (B5)

In these quotes the subject teachers recognize the work EAL teachers do in keeping the class cohesive in terms of subject-learning. EAL teachers provide for the individual needs of children, which allows subject teachers to pursue the curricular subject-based aims of instruction. Keeping the students together as much as possible obviously makes the job of delivering the curriculum easier for the subject teachers. The individual help that EAL teachers provide allows STs to endorse ideologies of inclusion and equal opportunities. Teachers are always faced with a dilemma of how best to allocate teaching time and skill across instructional objectives and students. Gerber and Semmel (1985) have argued that teachers aim to raise average outcomes for the whole class, while minimizing class variance. There was evidence of this in my study. To this end, teachers were just as anxious about the 'quick' students as they were about the 'slower' ones. In one class in which I observed, a group of girls had been working very hard. They were completing the material, which had been rewritten by the EAL teacher for the ST to use with the students so that it was more task-based. For making such progress they were praised by the ST, but in a backhanded way, which the girls picked up on:

ST: You have really been rushing ahead haven't you!
S: Rushing ahead sir?
ST: I mean you have been working hard. (B5)

EAL teachers played an important role in assisting the ST in keeping the class more closely grouped together. However, what was curious was how EAL facilitative work became positioned as less important than transmission teaching. We see this taken up below:

28 The support teacher doesn't have half these things to do – half their time is free – they haven't got reports to write, they haven't got to talk to parents, they haven't got this to do, they haven't got that to do, therefore they have got all that chunk of time you can occupy them with something else. I mean standing up in front of 20 to 30 children, delivering and teaching is a very arduous job and I don't think anybody else does that sort of work, whether you be a support teacher or a whether you be a headmaster. The nature of the job is very demanding. I think you just have to see support teaching as a different job. I think their role is totally different. They can work with a few kids who have special needs and problems and they can sort those through, which is not the same as teaching 30 children en masse hour after hour after hour. I mean that has got its demands. And it is not the same, it is a different job altogether. They get the same wage structure and things like that which perhaps they shouldn't, perhaps they should be seen as a separate entity, with different wage structures, different scales and things like that. (C5)

This subject teacher sees the 'arduous' work as delivering the curriculum to the many and the easier work as sorting through problems with the few. The whole-class teaching of the subject is seen as more important and difficult than providing for the individual needs of children who need the curriculum to be differentiated. The teacher in Quote 28 talks about the support teacher 'sorting through' the special needs and problems of a few children. Starting with the needs of the individual child is not seen as being as 'arduous' as teaching the subject matter to the whole class. For the subject teacher, 'arduous' here means teaching the subject while the easier work means being pedagogically aware of the needs of individuals and their place within the community of the class. In this transcript we see the transmission of knowledge versus facilitation of learning argument constructed. The subject teacher is there for curriculum transmission, but not to get involved with the one-to-one support work. He discursively removes himself from the particularities of one-to-one support. The absence of a curriculum subject to teach positions the EAL teacher's work as a generic skill and less important than the subject teacher's task:

29   I mean usually the support teachers are usually much brighter than the average teacher as far as I can see, that is why they have got such a cushy number. (C5)

30   There is a perception of those special needs and ESL, that they are just a handy number, you know, and I mean I don't think there is an awful lot going on here to kind of defuse that kind of prejudice. (C6)

31   The job of ESL staff is to support the kids whose first language is not English at whatever level in the classroom. It is also to make resources more appropriate. This only happens on an ad hoc basis. There is a feeling that ESL staff have an easy life. (Head of Year, school B)

EAL teachers working in support relationships rather than partnerships had a different institutional status than the subject teachers they worked with (see Chapters 6 and 7). They were seen as helpers to others' more important agendas. Part of the difference in institutional status was constructed around the pedagogies the teachers used. The subject teachers projected a transmission pedagogy based on specific curriculum knowledge. The teaching of the many, the management of the syllabus, classroom discipline and routines made up their daily routines. While it might be easy to look negatively on the ST for not adapting the transmission pedagogy nor working with more individuals and small groups of students, we need to view this in a climate where the ST is under heavy pressure to transmit an outcomes-orientated curriculum in classes of 30 or more students. Certain aspects need to be covered, information needs to be exchanged and the children need to pass exams. Talking to the many appears potentially more satisfying and successful than working with the few. The majority of STs did not see their work in terms of a language focus or working with individual students. They had little interest in the relationship between language and subject teaching and providing opportunities for second-language learning. However, they were persistently worried about how individual children were at risk from the force of the dominant transmission pedagogy. Their hope was that EAL teachers would make amends for this. Let us now turn to how the EAL teachers describe their own and their collaborating teachers' roles in class.

EAL teachers' description of their role in the classroom can be grouped under the following headings: teaching participant structures, advocate, scaffolder of the curriculum and language teacher. Let us take each of these in turn.

Teaching participant structures: The first of these is the teaching of participant structures to newly arrived bilingual/EAL children. The teacher in the following quote is referring to refugee children whose education before arrival has been disrupted:

> 32   These are children who have had very little schooling so they haven't learned the classroom skills, and so many of these things, that I used to think of as petty and unnecessary, you realize with our beginners are essential. They become unnecessary and petty when people don't have to be reminded and do them. But our pupils, just getting them into a classroom, organized, sitting down, knowing that when the teacher is there, waiting to start, that they should also be ready to start, and it's hard to teach our pupils that. So we are launching them really ... at the same time trying to encourage them to participate in the school diary system and folder system, um and build up the relationship with those and they can come back and talk and ask for help and feel that there are teachers around they can turn to if they need to. So that is part of the purpose of the induction. (C1)

Here we can see that the bilingual students are spoken of as 'our pupils' and they need special assistance in helping them to find their place in the school. The EAL teacher is aware the bilingual/EAL students need to be taught the school's participant structures explicitly so that they may take part in the daily routines as quickly as possible. Related to this role is that of being an advocate for the bilingual pupils' needs with the subject teacher.

Advocate:

> 33   If I think the pupil is capable of understanding half of the words that are coming at them, then I will leave them there [mainstream classroom], because that is one of the ways that you learn. If I think a pupil is understanding less than that, I will pull them out and work through the materials with them. (B3)

The EAL teacher represents the bilingual/EAL student. They can be an activist for students in many different ways. They may argue to take the child out from the class. They may work with the ST to improve learning opportunities for the student. As in Quote 33, we see that the EAL teacher takes on responsibility for individual students in class. Another role is that of scaffolder of the curriculum.

Scaffolder of the curriculum:

> 34 I mean when I am presenting things in class I think I do look at words and forms and things, or maybe I am more aware of it than content [subject] teachers. Sometimes I think that content teachers are making it unnecessarily complicated. I think most of the time I am preparing material for the class to use, . . . perhaps because I feel that is what should be there and isn't. (A2)

> 35 Well, first of all it is to assess the demands of a particular lesson in terms of language and in terms of content, the concepts and see whether I can possibly get across a quite complex concept by simple means. (B4)

The EAL teachers speak here of one of the core professional discourses associated with EAL work in the classroom: facilitation of learning. The teachers are concerned with accessing curriculum content by considering how it can be expressed in language which the bilingual/EAL children will be able to understand. Such work is often referred to as 'support work'. Implicit in these transcripts is the notion of working out the child's level of understanding through scaffolded interaction. At the heart of this description are the ideas of recontextulisation and reconstruction which Mercer describes (1995). The teacher aims to work with the child to elicit the knowledge they share. Also in Quotes 34 and 35 we see reference to 'simplifying'. The EAL teacher is referring to the need to modify subject input so that students will be able to comprehend the message. This fundamental role of EAL teaching is explored further in the next chapter, where we look at the classroom interactions of EAL teachers and STs working with students. Another key role described by EAL teachers is their work as language teachers.

Language teacher:

> 36 I don't think you can really separate the two [content and language] because I suppose we are trying to promote language acquisition through the content. I mean I suppose I would say language, the language is more important, but maybe that is just because I am a language teacher. (A2)

> 37 I would say the most important aspects of the job were to teach English and through that, the content of the subject that we are working in. So the most important thing is to get them to learn some English, but only a fraction of a centimetre behind that would be the importance of getting them to learn the subject. But partly because the two things go hand in hand. (B3)

The EAL teachers here are referring to two levels of knowledge development: progressing subject concepts as well as developing language proficiency. We can see that the subject matter is given the highest priority by the EAL teacher. The teachers recognize their role as working within the subject content to teach English.

In addition to supporting the individual needs of bilingual/EAL children in this way, EAL teachers also aim to play an advisory role in the school. However, as can be seen in the majority of the following quotes, there is some frustration with achieving this goal:

38　What I would like to see from that is there then being um a sort of carry over effect and I find that very difficult in that I would like to see teachers thinking well, Lucy is with us for a term, we are going to work on this and this strategy so that I can do it the next term when she is not there. So that I can then successfully work with bilingual students when she is not there and I won't need her. That doesn't happen at all. I mean teachers I have worked with for a very long time and tried to work on developing strategies or materials or whatever and they still see it in terms of me supporting the students and therefore they still think they can say, 'Oh I have got six early stage bilingual', which they haven't but they think they have, 'I have got six early stage bilingual, I really need your help'. Even though I have been helping in inverted commas, you know for the last year. They don't see it as a carry over effect. They don't see it as a sort of progression. (A2)

39　But I think the main thing for me is raising awareness of the staff as to why we are operating in the way we are doing and at the moment there's a sort of negative feeling around educating bilingual beginners, there's a sort of feeling 'oh no, she doesn't speak any English'. Not 'let's find out what she's good at, let's find out what this child has contributed or can contribute'. (A1)

40　I have to say that one of the functions we could serve and the special needs group to a degree as well, is I think we could be used in the assessment, in staff assessment. Not officially, but that could be something that could be used within school. Because I could tell any teacher that I teach with something about the way they teach which is making their life harder. And if someone were watching me they could tell me exactly the same thing, The question is whether they would take it. (B4)

41　To some extent although I don't feel that we have influenced their [STs] practice, as much as I would like, but that is partly because the people from our team [EAL staff] who have worked there, have not seen it as necessarily the role, as it could be, well enough. I mean they are doing something useful, or worthwhile, but they don't see themselves as people who **influence** the practice in the [. . .] department. Rather that they are trying to **accommodate** what the [. . .] department wants from them and it is not quite the same thing. So there is a problem to some extent there, but it has improved over the years to the extent that members in the team have been able to take on a role of influencing practice and as not everyone in the team can do that, I don't think we are going to get very much further, not significantly further in that because if we can't help them to develop their practice, we can only respond to their requests, then we are not, we can't go much further. (C1)

42   I mean when I see teachers taking on board suggestions that I have made or trying out things I think it does make a difference. I mean not saying that all my suggestions are fantastic. Some of the teachers might not want to use them because they know it wouldn't work with a particular class, but I think it has made a difference. So when I sort of say to teachers that um, you know about presenting the key vocabulary before they look at the text, and they have done that. I feel that students have understood the text much more than they would have done if the teacher hadn't sort of thought about it. And it is nice when teachers sort of take things suggestions on board and you see them trying it out. (A2)

Quotes 38–42 all make the same point: that EAL teachers would like to see their role in terms of influencing the work of STs rather than just accommodating existing ideas. They see themselves as agents of change. The EAL teachers would like to see STs take on more responsibility for the needs of bilingual children in the class. In their advisory capacity, we see the EAL teachers reinforce an inclusive/equal opportunities ideology. Again, we see an ideological dilemma at work: EAL teachers are engaged in individual work despite a desire to see STs take up more of this; STs are engaged in the discourse of inclusive education despite relying on EAL teachers to include bilingual/EAL students. The inclusive policy of mainstreaming worked when EAL teachers and STs used common sense ideologies to make sense of conflicting agendas. So, in the interview extracts, the STs' preferred discourse was the importance of meeting individual needs while the EAL teachers' preferred discourse was stressing common needs. However, in the daily practice of classroom life the reverse often seemed to happen, with STs stressing common learning outcomes to the whole class and EAL teachers working to meet individual student needs. Such sharings and conflicts in intellectual and lived ideologies would not perhaps be a problem if the work EAL teachers did with individual children was seen to be of the same pedagogic importance as delivering the subject curriculum. However, this was not the case. Pedagogies of transmission had higher prestige than pedagogies of facilitation, scaffolding and accessing. It was only in partnership mode that both STs and EAL teachers swapped roles and pedagogies (see Chapter 7). For the most part, STs did not get involved in the individual language work necessary for bilingual/EAL children.

Let us now turn to EAL teachers' perceptions of STs' roles in class:

43   I think that subject teachers see themselves very much as subject content teachers, rather than language teachers. I'd be interested to hear what they

had to say. Because from what I have seen and from what I have discussed with subject teachers, I don't think they see themselves as having any sort of part in this language teaching at all. I think the subject teacher does take, in a way, does sort of have to take responsibility for the subject because that is how they are assessed or judged. I mean I think it would be very difficult for them to let go of that sort of control if you like completely, because at the end of the day they are responsible for their exam results and how the students are doing and they would have to be able to answer for that. Whereas, I don't think the EAL teacher is quite in that same position of being responsible. (A2)

The EAL teacher acknowledges the STs overall responsibility for the class of students. She recognizes that STs are evaluated on their subject teaching and the students' learning. She understands that this is where their institutional pressures apply. She also acknowledges that she is free of those same pressures. She goes on to describe the STs she works with as feeling no responsibility toward language teaching:

44   I don't think they see themselves as having any sort of part in this language teaching at all. And I think that is shown by their sort of attitude and thoughts about bilingual students. I think they do see that as being the EAL teachers' role. And I suppose they might think well if the EAL teachers are saying that is not their responsibility, then what are they there for? (A2)

Mainstreaming is built upon the premise that practice will change to accommodate difference and diversity. For bilingual/EAL students this means attention to the role language plays in learning subject content, and making subject content accessible for second-language learning to develop.

Policy Implications

This chapter started with the aim of looking at policy into practice and its successes concerning educational inclusion and the particular learning agendas of bilingual students. My argument has been that a language policy founded on inclusivity will achieve little if it does not consider how micro contexts of classroom life interact with larger discussions, discourses, debates and conversations on education policy. Mainstreaming as education policy and practice seeks to transform the secondary school subject-based classroom. It matters, therefore, what teachers working together do and say in class to create a new environment or sustain old ones.

Currently the policy is not working as envisaged. I have tried to show that this is not the 'fault' of the teachers themselves. As Norwich (1996: 37) says:

It is commonplace that the educational climate is not favourable for vulnerable children when governments are anxious about relative international educational standards and the system is designed to reward high attaining schools.

Teachers are easy targets on the frontline of policy difficulties and failure (Ball, 1997). However, I have tried to show that it is rather the discourses underpinned by ideologies at institutional and societal level that have come to endorse certain pedagogies and sideline others.

Educational policy requires STs to take full responsibility for bilingual children. The data presented in this chapter has shown this can present a contradiction for STs as they strive to work to a tightly structured syllabus while also being sensitive to the needs of students struggling to keep up. Current policy does not assist STs in helping to resolve these contradictions. We see this in the way STs speak about bilingual students and 'the time it takes to teach them'.

It is important that bilingual children have access to pedagogies that allow them to negotiate meaning in their classroom interactions. Teacher responsiveness and teacher negotiation are important skills. EAL teachers have such skills and knowledge which they use to complement subject teaching. The EAL teachers interviewed described their role in the class as having particular educational skills and knowledge which they could apply to the classroom context. These include:

- Accessing, facilitating and scaffolding discourses for teaching/learning in one-to-one interactions; the ability to come up with creative ideas across the curriculum.
- An understanding of the role language (first and additional) plays in learning and teaching and an application of this knowledge to improve learning/teaching opportunities.
- Knowledge of second-language learning processes and the ability to develop opportunities for this to progress across all skill and curriculum areas.
- Knowledge of the linguistic and cultural diversity in the class, school and wider neighbourhood.

Many of these attributes are included in a table produced by Leung (2001: 208) and NALDIC (1999) which describes EAL teacher knowledge and skills. In this chapter, I began my argument with the notion that many of these skills do not have the same status as those connected to the teaching of subject content to the many. Facilitative pedagogies need to sit equally alongside other dominant classroom discourses, such as the transmission of subject knowledge. In all three schools, EAL teaching was seen as less important than subject teaching. Such observations were made by management, STs and children. EAL teacher work – described as facilitating, accessing, scaffolding and often working with the few – was positioned as support, helping and generic. But without this EAL facilitative support work, the policy of mainstreaming would amount to little more than submersion.

Chapter Summary

In this chapter I have shown how both STs and EAL teachers view the possibilities of mainstreaming as an inclusive education policy. I have shown that the majority of STs and EAL teachers support mainstreaming despite its problems because the subject classrooms of secondary schools are felt, potentially at least, to offer a meaningful context for language acquisition and subject-learning for bilingual children. Moreover, because education is also about being socialized into a community, both EAL and subject teachers understand that placing children in the mainstream classroom provides children with a rich environment to experience majority cultures and for majorities to experience minority cultures. However, both STs and EAL teachers have misgivings about mainstreaming when appropriate adaptations to the mainstream class are not made. STs are concerned that there should be language support in the classroom because, despite their best intentions, they worry that limited resources will mean bilingual children do not receive the help they need to keep up with the curriculum aims of the class. EAL teachers also have misgivings about mainstreaming. They are concerned that it falls short of what it promises when STs do not make the necessary adaptations to the classrooms. One of their complaints is that the STs rely on them too much to do support work with individual children, rather than making fundamental changes to ensure the class and the curriculum are more appropriate for the diversity of children learning there.

To a certain extent it can be said that STs and EAL teachers are at cross purposes with one another, with STs wanting more support, and EAL teachers wanting to give more advice so that STs no longer need them. However, a closer look reveals that both kinds of teachers are actually concerned with the same goal: providing the best for their students. STs see this happening most effectively through sustained and increased support as diversity increases, and EAL teachers see this happening by STs making changes that would necessitate them being as much concerned with the language-learning needs of the bilingual students as with a subject-teaching agenda.

Chapter 4

Teachers Talking: The Discourses of Collaborating Teachers[1]

Introduction

In this chapter I will analyse the language use of subject and EAL teachers in the classroom. Particular traditions of discourse analysis will be used to understand how classroom participants use language to establish, maintain and challenge their roles and ensuing status positions. The findings presented in this chapter stem from a detailed analysis of the teachers' discourse in class. The analysis is based on audio recordings of 8 non-bilingual EAL teachers working with 14 STs. For the most part I recorded each teacher only once for an entire lesson, although I observed each teacher on average for ten lessons. This chapter is organized along the following lines. It starts with an overview of the literature on classroom interaction and introduces different analytical tools to describe and explain teachers' language use. It then goes on to look at two different kinds of interaction classroom patterns. The first is STs and EAL teachers engaged in whole-class teaching. The second is one-to-one or small group interactions. This chapter is closely related to Chapter 5, which continues to focus on how teachers' talk is linked to institutional structures of power and status.

Interaction in Two Teacher Classrooms

Studies in classroom discourse have produced some consistent findings. We know that teacher talk dominates around 60% of classroom time (Chaudron, 1988: 50). We know that discourse is patterned (Sinclair & Coulthard, 1975) and consists of complex exchanges (Hoey, 1991). Teacher questions play a central role in classroom activity. Chaudron (1988) has argued that 20–40% of classroom talk consists of teacher questions, while Tsui (1985) found that nearly 70% of classroom talk consisted of a teacher question, nomination and feedback sequence. We also know that the pattern of adult/child interaction is different at home from that of school. Wells (1986) found that children in school speak with adults much less than at home, get fewer speaking turns and ask fewer questions. Moreover, the meanings that children express at school are of a smaller range and the sentences they use are syntactically much simpler. Wells argues that this is because teachers do most of the talking in the classroom. It is they who determine the topic of talk, and initiate most of the questions and requests. This literature has been and continues to be of great importance to those of us interested in understanding the role language(s) plays in learning and teaching.

A major weakness in such literature, however, is its narrow conceptualization of the classroom and its participants. Tsui (1995: 1) defines the classroom 'as a place where more than two people gather together for the purpose of learning, with *one* having the role of teacher' (italic added). It is the conceptualization of the classroom as a place where only one teacher is interacting with a class of students with which I take issue. That is, the classroom continues to be described as if the only significant adult for interactional and learning opportunities is the classroom teacher. Tsui is not alone in making this assumption. A quick glance through any of the major publications on classroom discourse speak of *the* teacher and appear not to acknowledge the other adults working in classrooms. Instead, discussions of classroom interaction continue to conceptualize the classroom in terms of the 'one teacher, one class' model. But this model does not do justice to the variety of teaching unisons and educational provision in our schools. In many schools we find a variety of other adults in the classroom. This could include two teachers working together in partnership, ongoing visits by specialists teachers to work with groups or individual children, parent helpers, classroom assistants, bilingual assistants, educational psychologists, researchers, etc. Some of these visits are sporadic and temporary but many of them are long-term and routine. And yet, we know very little indeed about what kind of impact other adults' discourses have on classroom interactions. Valdés (2004) argues that what is missing from studies of classroom-learning is the full range of experiences and interactions that surround minority youngsters. He also argues that there needs to be increased communication between ESL and mainstream teachers so that bilingual students do not become marginalized in the ESL communicative spheres (Valdés, 2004: 119). One aim of this book is to describe and analyse teacher collaboration between EAL and mainstream teachers. It is also to consider how the marginalization of bilingual children can happen even when teachers are brought together in mainstream settings. As I have begun to argue, this happens partly because the different teachers reference different epistemological knowledge and skills which become manifest in the teacher's pedagogic identity (Arkoudis, 1999; Morgan, 2004; Varghese, 2004). Moreover, these different epistemologies have different power bases and so those who become entangled in them are also subsequently involved and positioned as particular kinds of learners. These learner identities become fostered on to bilingual learners, who might not otherwise choose such identities (Pavlenko & Blackledge, 2004).

There appears to be very little in sociolinguistic classroom interaction literature or broader educational literature that looks at discourses of learning in classrooms with either more than one teacher or with other adults also playing a teaching role. In other words, the classroom interaction literature has not kept pace with practice in interactionally complex classrooms. For example, we do not know if having more adults in the class produces even less time for student interaction or whether it doubles the numbers of questions asked by teachers. Nor do we know if having two teachers in the classroom breaks IRF/E (initiate, respond, feedback/ evaluate) routines or creates new interactional patterns. I believe that such work is important because increasingly in urban schools teaching and learning inter- actions are happening between a growing number of adult interactants and the students with whom they work. It is possible that this impacts on learning and teaching opportunities in these classrooms.

Talk Among Teachers and Learners

I will introduce three broad strands of literature to assist my analysis of data in this chapter. The first strand of research literature draws on discourse tools from education literature which views learning in teacher/student interaction as dialogic. As such, learning is a guided social activity within a zone of proximal develop- ment (Vygotsky, 1978). Through involvement in culturally organized activities, a child may 'appropriate' meaning resulting in cognitive change (Leont'ev, 1981). The second strand comes from second-language acquisition literature and stresses the importance of negotiation processes in the modification of input and output (Long, 1983; Pica, 2000; Swain, 1995). This theory sees second-language learning as furthered through opportunities for negotiation of input resulting in modifications of form. The outcome of this negotiation is comprehensive input. A third strand of literature used comes from anthropological linguistics and views language as representing and indexing social needs (Gumperz, 1999; Hymes, 1974; Jakobson, 1971; Sapir, 1921). Taken from this tradition, a semiotic functional analysis can enable an understanding of how the two different kinds of teachers privilege partic- ular views of teaching/learning in their interactions.

It is no accident that I have drawn upon these three types of literature to assist in understanding teacher/student interaction. In many ways the three literature strands combine the factors which interest me most about multilingual secondary-school classrooms. That is, how bilingual/EAL children learn subject curricula through a new language, how subject curricula can be used to teach and extend English language acquisition and, finally, possibilities of teacher collaboration in this context.

Sociocultural approaches

In attempting to guide learning, Mercer (1995) argues that teachers use talk to do three things:

(1) *Elicit relevant knowledge from students,* so that they can see what students already know and understand and so that the knowledge is seen to be 'owned' by students as well as teachers. Teachers elicit knowledge through the use of cued and direct elicitations.

(2) *Respond to things that students say*, not only so that students get feedback on their attempts but also so that the teacher can incorporate what students say into the flow of the discourse and gather students' contributions together to construct more generalized meanings. Teachers respond to what students say through the use of confirmations, rejections, repetitions, elaborations and reformulations.

(3) *Describe the classroom experiences that they share with students* in such a way that the educational significance of those joint experiences is revealed and emphasised. Teachers achieve this through the following means: 'We' statements, literal recaps and reconstructive recaps.

Mercer makes the argument that 'To be effective, any teacher needs to explore the scope of a learner's existing knowledge' (1995: 10). This is achieved through eliciting knowledge from students, responding to what students say, and describing the classroom experiences that they share. That is, teachers need to follow a student's line of thinking in order to stimulate their thinking further. At the core of this debate is an understanding of learning as dialogic. Teachers need to respond to what students say and vice versa. It is through the *response* process described above that students and teachers begin to appropriate the other's knowledge. Mercer (1994: 105) suggests appropriation can be used:

> ... to explain the pedagogic function of a particular kind of discourse event whereby one person takes up another person's remark and offers it back, modified, into the discourse ... teachers do this with children's utterances and actions, thereby offering children a re-contextualised version of their own activities which implicitly carries with it new cultural meanings ... Teachers often *paraphrase* what children say, so as to present it back to them in a form which is considered by the teacher to be more compatible with the current stream of educational discourse. They also *reconstructively recap* what has been done by the children in class, so as to represent events in ways which fit their pedagogical framework. (italics in original)

Mercer presents appropriation as a teacher opportunity to incorporate the student's ideas into the teacher's response. That is, it is through the teacher's response that meaning begins to be created and shared. In discursive terms, responding moves are the linchpin of a lesson (Brown & Wragg, 1993: 22).

Jarvis and Robinson (1997) have looked in particular at teacher response. They argue that exploring teachers' responses to pupils may give insights into how teaching and learning processes may be linked in the classroom context (1997: 215). In their paper, Jarvis and Robinson give special attention to the discursive moves of 'extend/guide' and 'extend/bridge' in which they describe a teacher extending pupils' 'yes' answers by guiding them through a use of questions to elaborate on their understanding. In their analysis, Jarvis and Robinson develop the concept of teacher *responsiveness*. Responsiveness includes the teacher's knowledge of his/her pupils and their planning and structuring of learning through decision-making in the classroom.

The teacher is responsive in the sense that through her minute-by-minute choice of contingent response to what pupils have said, she uses what the pupils say, and builds on it. Her response looks back to what the pupils have said, and forward to topic development or topic shift. In this process, fuller meanings are articulated, and alternative grammatical structures used. (Jarvis & Robinson, 1997: 219)

This quote is particularly interesting as it makes the link between the creation of meaning and the form of the message. That is, through the negotiation process not only do meanings become refined and changed, but so does the grammatical form which expresses them. This link is of interest here as in the teaching partnerships described in this chapter the remit of the teachers is not only the teaching of subject content but also the development of English language. Teachers in multilingual urban secondary schools with bilingual/EAL students have the dual aim of English-language development through the teaching of subject curriculum.

Input interactionist approaches

In addition to the cultural theories of learning already drawn upon, there is another theory of learning which is of use in this chapter. This is the input interactionist theories of language-learning (Long, 1983, 1991; Mackey *et al.*, 2000; Pica, 1991, 2000). This strand of second-language acquisition literature has looked at how language is modified in interaction in order to assist language development. It stresses the importance of negotiation between participants in reaching shared understandings. The strength of this research lies in showing how particular features of interaction assist in the second-language learning process. The emphasis is very much on understanding how interactive features help interactants reach shared meaning and progress their second-language learning.

Second-language learning classroom research has emphasized the kinds of questions asked (Chaudron, 1988; Johnson, 1995; Lynch, 1996; Tsui, 1985, 1995), these include: open/closed; factual/reasoning; display/referential. Long and Sato (1983) refer to knowledge-checking questions as 'display' questions and those to which the teacher does not have the answer as 'referential' questions. According to Tsui (1997: 28) display questions 'generate interactions that are typical of didactic discourse, whereas referential questions generate interactions typical of social communication'. The kinds of questions teachers ask have important effects on student responses and the kinds of interaction generated in terms of opportunities for second-language learning. For example, a teacher may modify the syntax from a 'wh-' question to a 'yes–no' question. This kind of modification often succeeds in getting a student response because the answer to the question is much narrower: students only have to answer 'yes' or 'no'. As Tsui cautions though, while this kind of modification helps students to produce a response, it is restrictive in terms of language production and overuse of this kind of modification deprives students of the chance to produce longer responses.

Semiotic functional approaches

The third strand of literature that can assist in this analysis views language as a social action. Jakobson called for the investigation of language in all its variety of functions (1960: 352), and went about characterizing these functions. This approach to discourse analysis identifies the components of a speech context and the hierarchizing of functions within it. A functional analysis can show how teachers discursively foreground various functions within the classroom and how this positions teachers differently within the class. For a full discussion see Chapter 1, which describes this process in detail. The functions that will become part of the analysis later on in this chapter concern the following:

- Referential: e.g. 'Rainforests have no seasons.'
- Emotive: e.g. 'I don't like the way you are doing that.'
- Conative: e.g. 'Open your book at page 3 please.'
- Metalingual: e.g. '"I" is a subject pronoun.'

Within formal schooling it is the referential function which is highlighted as having great significance, although other functions are obviously of considerable importance. Formal schooling is understood to have as one of its primary aims the imparting of scientific concepts (Scribner & Cole, 1973). The referential function of language plays an important role in achieving concept formation because this function highlights language's ability to convey symbolic meaning away from a particular setting. It allows us to talk about the world away from the 'here and now' of the classroom. The referential function of language allows teachers to transmit knowledge. The transmission of subject content is often done through the subject teacher addressing the whole class in a lecture style.

We now turn to data that comes predominantly from classroom audio recordings of STs and EAL teachers working together. The following key is provided for the interpretation of this information:

Transcription conventions

+ + +	long pause
. . .	short pause
=	speaker interrupted by listener's interjections
( )	information about the interaction
XXX	unable to transcribe interaction
yes I know	
but what do you think?	overlapping talk
italic	speaker emphasizes utterance
bold	part of transcript particularly relevant to point being made

Speaking to the Whole Class

The transmission of the subject curriculum is one of the ST's primary aims. We should not be surprised, therefore, to find substantial spoken texts where teachers lecture and direct students about subject content and learning tasks. We see one typical secondary school example below:

> 45   Now if you have a look at source E. That is the map. You will see that
>   King Harold of England actually had to fight two battles. He was in
>   London. If you can find London. He was in London and first of all he had
>   to march up to Stamford Bridge to meet Harold of Norway. He had to
>   fight Harold, once he had beaten him he then had to march all the way
>   back down to Hastings to meet William of Normandy. So can you imagine
>   they were extremely tired when they got down to Hastings. Because if
>   you have a look at the scale. If you have a look at the scale, if you have
>   a look at the scale at the bottom of E. How far did they have to march
>   back down to Hastings? How far is York to Hastings. Germane? (no pause
>   and no answer). It is almost 200 kilometres. So it was a long distance.
>   Now, I want you to do two things today. I want you to look at this work-
>   sheet, titled the Battle of Stamford Bridge and I want you to copy out this
>   paragraph filling out the correct gaps. After you have done that I want
>   you to draw source E to show the route that King Harold had to take to
>   meet both Harold Hardrada and William of Normandy. All right? So I'd
>   like you to do the writing first. Do the writing first. The date is the 18th,
>   18th of November. The title is the Battle of Stamford Bridge. (A9)

This example shows how the ST skillfully interacts with the children by inter-twining the three primary functions of emotive ('**I want you . . .**'), conative (directive function: '[I want] **you** to look at the scale . . . to copy this page . . . to draw source E . . . do the writing first') and referential (factual function: 'It is about 200 kilo-metres'). Subject content information is mingled with what the ST wants the students to do with it. The teacher gives answers and then extends these answers by adding new information: 'How far is York to Hastings. Germane? It is almost 200 kilo-metres. **So it was a long distance.** Now, I want you to do two things today.'

In the ST's discourse we see how she brings herself, her students and her subject area into interaction with one another. She uses the personal pronouns 'I' and 'you' to direct students around the learning of specific curriculum content. There are many examples of this '*I* want *you* to do/learn *something*' exchange, which I have labelled as 'TYS' (Creese, 2002b), throughout the classroom data:

> 46   If you turn to page 7 you will find out what happened. When you have
>   found the page look at source C. This explains what happens during that
>   battle and **I** want you to do what you did yesterday, **I** want you to look
>   for three things. You can write them in the back of your books. **I** want
>   you to look for the groups of the people involved, **I** want you to look for

what the source is about and I want you to look for the result. Who won in the end? So look for three things, the groups of people in involved, what the source is about and what the result was. Just have a look at source C now and find out those three things. (A8)

47   Now I want to see copies of those things. Don't tell me you have got them on file. I want to see copies of those things. And I want to see one in your file and one in your ID folder. All right? So if you have finished that go make sure you have got your book cover. And I want a proper book cover that tells the story. (C6)

48   And I want you during the day today to think up a design, for just yourself, not for the group. Just for yourself. I want you with a piece of card, to write the word technology and your name, or design and technology or DT and a personal logo if you have a personal logo because this is your folder for the next two years. (C10)

49   Now, I'd like to do practical work and I know Miss Harrington wanted you to do practical work. She was more forceful than me. What I want you to do, is make sure you have got your contents pages organized. I am going to give you until the last day of term to get your work completed and could you hand your folders in on the last day to me please, or put them in my pigeon hole. . . . Yeah but it needs to be before Christmas because I need to mark it over Christmas. Er, Christina, please. You don't go in the draws. Take those out of your mouths and start listening both of you. (A5)

Here we can see how STs are able to direct students by placing themselves at the centre of the teaching. This is achieved by combining the use of emotive, conative and referential functions. The IYS exchange is a typical classroom interaction pattern in secondary schools. It is a speech event which dominates most subject-focused classrooms, as the teacher sets up a task for the students to do. In many ways we can say it is formulaic, that students expect to hear it and teachers to use it. Let us now turn to look at EAL teachers' language use to the whole class.

The first thing notable about EAL teachers is that, generally, they do much less class-fronted instruction than STs. However, when they are involved in teacher-fronted interaction there are some similarities to STs in the way EAL teachers use speech. That is, EAL teachers also set tasks and, thus, highlight the emotive function, centring it in 'I':

50   Right, can you listen very carefully. Don't start reading it yet because there are some things I want you to do as you are reading it. There are three things I want you to think about really. And if you need to jot any notes down you can jot them in the back of your history books. The first thing, I hope everybody is looking at page 3, the first thing I want you to jot down is all the names and groups of people that there are in that passage,

OK so names and groups of people. Could you just look at me for a minute so that I know everybody is listening. The second thing I want you to think about is what is the whole page about. What is it about? OK. And the third thing I want you to do is to look at the top of it. The title that is given in the book is Conquest. You might be able to think of a different title, or even a better title than that. So, how many things have I asked you to do, how many things have I asked you to think about as you are reading the passage? (A2)

In many ways this discourse is similar to Quotes 46–9 taken from the STs. The EAL teacher uses IYS sequences to encourage students to complete the task. However, unlike Quote 45, it is not interspersed with new or reoccurring segments of subject knowledge. Instead, the EAL teacher is focused on task completion. What is interesting about this extract is that the teacher discourse around the task could be set in almost any subject-based lesson. It is only the words 'history books' and '*Conquest*' which reveal the subject area being studied. The EAL teacher is using the front of the class to teach students classification skills which are important across all curriculum areas. She uses the referential function of language to teach study skills rather than subject knowledge. In Quote 50 the EAL teacher is setting a task, the context for which has already been introduced by the ST.

It is perhaps not surprising that EAL teachers in support mode do little teacher-fronted subject-focused instruction when there is another teacher in the room who is a subject specialist. However, the front of the classroom is a powerful position, as is talk around curriculum content. For this reason, the majority of EAL teachers I observed working in mainstream classes did at some time take up this position. They did this, though, for different reasons than the STs. These included:

- to set tasks which do not refer to the subject material, thereby playing down the referential function linked to the teaching of subject curriculum;
- to collect students' answers after they have been working on a task, rather than to introduce new material;
- to position themselves as experts on non-subject-based matter – such as language/style, punctuation, study skills.

An example of the first of these reasons was given in Quote 46, in which the EAL teacher set a task, but did not mix it with new subject content. An example of the second is shown in data below, in which the EAL teacher paraphrases students' answers from a task set previously by the ST. Note that at the end of the inter-action, the EAL teacher hands the floor back to the ST for the introduction of new subject material:

51
EAL: OK. We are going to go through this now. So: People are still talking.
ST: Nicola

EAL: OK, can anyone put up their hand and tell me who was involved? Yes?

S: Earl Tostigg.

EAL: Earl Tostigg. OK. And who else?

S: King of Norway. Is that Hardrada or Harald?

EAL/ Harald
ST:

EAL: OK, King of Norway (writes on the board). Were they on the same side or on separate sides?

Ss: Same side.

EAL: Yes, they were on the same side. Right, Harald, the King of Norway, versus who?

S: The King of England.

EAL: OK. And what was his name?

Ss: Harold.

EAL: Right. Another Harold (noise level up) (writes on the board). Can you stop talking please? Right, we have got two Harolds here, we've got Harald King of Norway and Harold King of England. Slightly different spelling though. OK? So what happened? What did all these people do? Janan? Janan, what did these people do? What happened?

S: XXX

EAL: Right, you need to listen then? What happened. Somebody on this table can you tell me? There was a? What?

S: A battle.

EAL: Yes, a battle. And where was the battle? Where was the battle?

S: Stamford Bridge.

EAL: OK. So we have the Battle of Stamford Bridge (writes on board) (noise level up). Who won the battle? Who won the battle? Anyone? Was it the Norwegians?

S: No, the English.

EAL: Who won?

S: The English.

EAL: The English won. So what happened to Tostigg and the King of Norway? What happened to them? Look the same people are putting up their hands. Yes, um?

Ss: (students say her name)

S: They were killed.

EAL: Yes, they were killed. So these two were out of it. They were=

S: =slain

EAL: =They were killed, they were slain and Harold won the battle (looks at ST).

ST: Yep. Now if you have a look at source E. (A2 and A8)

This whole-class teaching follows a question–answer pattern. At first glance it seems very similar to the teaching exchanges identified by Sinclair and Coulthard

(1975) of the initiation, response, feedback (IRF) pattern. And, indeed, the utterances do contain all the elements:

EAL: Where was the battle? (*initiate*)
S: Stamford Bridge. (*respond*)
EAL: So, we have the Battle of Stamford Bridge (*feedback*)

However, what is interesting is that although they contain the follow-up move (feedback) of *accepting* the answer, the EAL does not engage in *evaluating* or *commenting* on the answer. The EAL accepts the students' answers without adding additional subject information. Thus, although EAL teachers use the IRF pattern in what seems to be a similar way to STs, there are actually subtle differences. For instance, whereas the ST is willing and able to evaluate and comment on students' answers as well as simply to accept them, the EAL has a more limited repertoire. This is obviously related to knowledge of the subject area. EAL teachers are in a complex situation within the subject-focused secondary school classroom. They realize the importance of taking a position at the front of the class. This is a powerful position within the classroom and not to occupy it sends a message about teacher status. However, in occupying this classroom space, teachers are expected to 'know'. Knowing in all areas of subject content across the school curriculum is obviously an impossibility for the EAL teacher. In the following extract we see the same teacher run into trouble in collecting answers in the same history lesson:

52
EAL: Let's go onto the second thing I asked you to do, which was just to um find out about what the whole passage was about. Just very generally what was it about? Yeah?
S: It was about Normandy and England which led to the Battle of Hastings.
EAL: + + + Right? (whispers to ST) It leads to the Battle of Hastings? (back to students) Does it **lead** to the battle of Hastings.
S: It **was** the battle of Hastings=
EAL: =It **was** the battle of Hastings, right. So it was the battle of Hastings. And finally, an alternative title for this passage instead of conquest. Did anybody come up with anything? Yes?
S: The Battle of Hastings in 1066.
EAL: The Battle of Hastings in 1066, good, yes.
S: The Bloody War (students laugh).
EAL: The Bloody War. OK. Right, good. Put your hands down. In the book it is called conquest, but who was it a conquest for? + + + Was it a conquest for the English or for the Normans?
S: The English
EAL: The English, OK. What, do you think, if this passage had been written from the point of view of the (she stops in mid sentence as the ST talks to her about the misunderstanding). Yes, who won the battle?

Ss: The Normans

EAL: The Normans won it, OK. If the English had won, if this passage had been written from the point of view of the English do you think they would have called it the conquest?

Ss: No

EAL: No? So what might they have called it? + + + So can you think of a different word, instead of conquest?

S: Defeat of the Battle of Hastings.

EAL: **Defeat** at the Battle of Hastings. Yes. (A2 and A8)

This extract shows how an EAL teacher follows the pattern of accepting students' answers, even when she is unsure of the answers herself. We see the IRF pattern with the EAL teacher mirroring the students' answers as feedback, without adding further information. In terms of Mercer's categorisation of teacher talk introduced at the beginning of this chapter (1995), EAL teachers are good at eliciting answers but are not able to respond to these answers using the full range of *confirmations*, *rejections*, *repetitions*, *elaborations* and *reformulations* for subject teaching which he describes as part of the complete range of teachers' responding moves. Moreover, because EAL teachers in support mode in secondary schools are rarely able to attend the class continuously, neither are they able to make full use of Mercer's third category of teacher talk – describing *the classroom experiences that they share with students*. Thus, EAL teachers are less likely to use *'we'* statements (*'I'* the teacher and *'you'* the students), *literal recaps* and *reconstructive recaps* of material already covered.

EAL teachers do, however, find ways to do classroom-fronted teaching. That is, they position themselves as specialists on topics other than curriculum subject matter. An example of this shows an EAL teacher focused on language style and correctness:

53

EAL: (to class) Can I just point out to you that these words here have got capital letters. Why have they got capital letters?

S: Because they are names.

EAL: Names of?

S: Places and people

EAL: Places and people. Can you check in your writing that you have put capital letters for names of places and people as well. (A2)

Such data shows the EAL teacher's willingness to take a front position in the classroom to discuss language issues. Another opportunity for the EAL teacher to take the space at the front of the class is for issues related to study skills, such as examination techniques and presentation of homework:

54 Could I intervene there? An exercise I did with the ESL group might help **all** of you, that if when you are reading through, you actually underline

the significant words, then when you read it through again you take in those bits. (C1)

55   Right, right. I won't waste everybody's time doing that now. What I am going to do when Miss Rubins comes back. She is bringing down a project on advertising which was done last year in order to show you. What I am going to do is type up for each of you a card, you know a piece of thin card, hole punched so that you can keep it in your, Nihan, please don't talk while I am doing this, otherwise we won't understand and I will list all the homeworks week by week for this project so that way if you miss one because you were absent um or for whatever reason you will have a total record of what the homeworks are and you can do them over the course of the unit. And save all this time. On it, there will also be a space for your parent or carer to sign he or she has seen your homework. The reason for that is a lot of parents have asked us would, can they, you know they want to know what you are doing in school. They want to see your work and this is what we did with the last group and it was very successful. Umm I will do that when Miss Rubins comes back and so each of you will have a yellow card which you can put in your yellow-backed folder and it is much easier than having to do it each week. And then you won't forget. OK? Umm. If those people who are going home at lunch time to get their homeworks. You know, when you get it, get them. If you would put them either in Miss Rubins tray or in mine in the staffroom, that would be very helpful. Thanks very much. (To Miss Rubins) A very good homework record this week. A couple of people blew it but mostly it is much much better than last week. (C4)

What is interesting in this extract on homework is the missing conative function. There is no mention of '*you*' (i.e. the student) engaging in any action. The emotive '*I*' is not linked to the students' action plan. Instead, the teacher uses it to define a place for himself in the mainstream class, rather than linking '*I*' directly to students' learning through the referential function.

In this section on teacher-fronted whole class instruction I have tried to show how the two kinds of teachers mark themselves out as discursively different. I am not trying to make an argument that there is anything either intrinsically good or bad about these differences in teacher talk. My intention has been to show that when two teachers work together in the same room, their discourses mark them out as playing different roles and that these discourses are linked to wider social orders of power. Such subtleties have gone unnoticed by policy planners. Classrooms, like any routine social context, come with patterns of interaction. When these patterns are changed, participants notice or 'feel' the difference. The differences in discourse markers of STs and EAL teachers may be very subtle indeed, but they play their part in the status construction of these two kinds of teachers, in class and through them to the students they work with.

Let us now turn to look at the language use of subject and EAL teachers in small group interactions with the students, as the two teachers move around the class.

Speaking to Individuals or Small Groups

The aim in this section is to analyse whether similar patterns of interaction exist when EAL teachers and STs interact in small groups or individually with students. Part of my agenda was to show, through an analysis of classroom discourse, that the facilitative, accessing and scaffolding work done by an EAL teacher requires particular skills and knowledge. I do not intend to argue that subject teachers lack this skill. Rather, that they are under different pressures within the secondary school classroom to perform different discourses. I aim to show that the work the EAL teacher does may be constructed as less important in wider institutional and educational discourses, but that without it bilingual/EAL students might not have access to interaction patterns endorsed as good practice by educational and applied linguistic literature.

In this section I make a comparison between one pairing of an EAL teacher and subject teacher working with two different individual bilingual/EAL students within a geography class. The teachers are both experienced and had worked together in this year 10 class (14–15-year-old female students) for five weeks at the time of recording. They had also worked together in different classes over several years. I have named the EAL teacher Graham, and the geography teacher Simon. Their particular collaboration has been selected for commentary because it represents a typical secondary-school teacher collaboration. The teachers described their work as in support rather than in full partnership mode (see Chapters 6 and 7) (Bourne & McPake, 1991; Creese, 2000). That is, the EAL teacher attended only some of the lessons with this class and was scheduled through his timetable to work with individual students, rather than being assigned to work with particular subject departments or teachers.

The teachers were wearing a walkman with a small microphone and were moving around the class working with individual students. The geography subject teacher (ST) had just finished giving the whole class some input and then set some individual/pair work. It is important to note that I am not attempting to generalize from these extracts. It is not my intention to argue that all subject teachers interact in one way and all EAL teachers interact in another. Teachers can use a variety of interactional patterns. Learning and teaching are highly situated, and one would expect patterns to change depending on interactants and institutional cultures. However, I do argue throughout the book that teachers with different institutional roles are under different pressures. These, along with teachers epistemological backgrounds and beliefs, lead teachers to view pedagogic knowledge and skills differently resulting in differing classroom practice (Arkoudis, 2003; Edwards, 2000).

The following extracts (56–7) record the two teachers working with two different newly arrived bilingual/EAL students. Neither of the teachers speaks Turkish, which is the first language of the students they are working with. The geography topic is 'Climate/Seasons' and the students are learning to read and interpret graphs. I present the two extracts consecutively before moving on to an analysis:

56
Geography teacher working with bilingual/EAL student)

ST: Join the dots to give a line graph. Join.

S: Yeah.

ST: Join with crosses. That is our line. It is our line graph. OK. Bars. This is a bar. A rectangle is a bar. These are all what we call a bar graph.

5   OK. You done that? Now we have got to look at the climate. Look at this and think. Seasons are winter and summer. Yes? Seasons equals winter, spring, summer, autumn.

S: Weather.

ST: Weather, yes it goes up and down. So it is a season. Winter, summer,

10   spring. We have our winter holidays, summer holidays. In England. In Turkey, it is hot in summer and cold in winter?

S: Yeah.

ST: In the rainforests, it is?

S: Cold in winter.

15 **ST:** Is it cold? (pause) It is hot all the time, isn't it? 26 degrees centigrade is hot, isn't it? We don't need sweaters and it is hot in January, February, March, April, May, June, every month. Every month it is high. 26, 27, it is always high. So we can say there is no seasons. The rainforests don't, do not, do not have seasons. We can write these

20   sentences out. The temperatures, are they hot or are they cold?

S: Hot?

ST: Yeah. So we write this out. Write it on the paper. You can put the title, climate in Brazil. OK? (B5)

57
EAL teacher working with bilingual/EAL student

EAL: What you must do now, you need the book, we look at this. Now can you tell me, in summer, let's look at the questions here. The rainforests do or don't have seasons as we know them?

S: Don't.

5 **EAL:** What is a season, seasons?

S: (laughs as she tries to explain) Spring, summer.

EAL: Yeah, brilliant, great. OK. Temperatures are cool or hot all year round?

S: Hot.

	EAL:	We are not talking. Of course we are talking of Brazil now, yes?
10	S:	Yes.
	EAL:	OK. You remember where Brazil is?
	S:	Hmm.
	EAL:	Good. Err, there is rain all month. Now what you have to do is, how much rain is there every year in England, in London?
15	S:	80?
	EAL:	8, 80, this is?
	S:	(laughs) 800.
	EAL:	Thank you. Now what we have got to say is there is 800 millimetres of rain in London, how much rain is there in Brazil, do you know?
20		How do you find out how much there is?
	S:	You have to look at the temperature.
	EAL:	Not temperature.
	S:	At the rain.
	EAL:	And what must you do to the rainfall?
25	S:	You have to look.
	EAL:	What do you think you have to do to see how much there is for the whole year? This is how much rain there is in this month.
	S:	340.
	EAL:	And what month is that?
30	S:	January.
	EAL:	So if you want to find out how much rain there is every month, what do you have to do?
	S:	You have to look at all these number.
	EAL:	Not look at all these numbers, what is the word that we say?
35	S:	XXX (inaudible)
	EAL:	If you were to take 340, 360, what would you be doing?
	S:	Oh, times.
	EAL:	No, not times. What is that number, I mean symbol? It is not times, it is?
	S:	Add.
40	EAL:	So you must add those numbers, OK? (B3)

Perhaps the most striking feature of these extracts (56–7) is how similar they are. Both teachers dominate in terms of amount of talk. A quick tally of the length and number of turns produces the following descriptive statistics:

Total number of words in each extract:

- Subject teacher, Extract 56: 207 (number of turns 6)
- Student, Extract 56: 7 (number of turns 5)
- EAL teacher, Extract 57: 244 (number of turns 16)
- Student, Extract 57: 70 (number of turns 16)

Average number of words per interaction:

- Subject teacher, Extract 56: 34.5 (207 divided by 6)
- Student, Extract 56: 1.4 (7 divided by 5)
- EAL teacher, Extract 57: 15.25 (244 divided by 16)
- Student, Extract 57: 4.37 (70 divided by 16)

However, the extracts also differ, as can be seen by the length of interactions and number of turns between pairings. I will draw on the literature presented earlier to help with this analysis. First, I draw on the analytical tools developed by the input-interactionists to describe modified input. I will then use a functional analysis to show how the ST and the EAL teacher foreground particular functions over others, which in turn index wider discourses in education, some of which come with higher statuses in the secondary school context. Finally, I will comment on the concept of responsiveness developed in both Mercer's and Jarvis and Robinson's work.

The ST asks nine questions:

(1) You done that?
(2) Yes?
(3) It is hot in summer and cold in winter?
(4) In the rainforests, it is?
(5) Is it cold?
(6) It is hot all the time, isn't it?
(7) The temperatures, are they hot or are they cold?
(8) 26 degrees centigrade is hot, isn't it?
(9) OK?

All nine questions are display questions. That is, the teacher's questions require the student to display their understanding of the topic according to the teacher's agenda. The grammatical construction of the questions includes: declarative sentences with rising intonation; tag questions; simple 'be' questions. All questions are formed so that the student need only give a closed one word answer. The total range of possible answers to these questions is: 'yes', 'no', 'hot' or 'cold'.

The EAL teacher asks 18 questions:

(1) The rainforests do or don't have seasons as we know them?
(2) What is a season, seasons?
(3) Temperatures are cool or hot all year round?
(4) Of course we are talking of Brazil now, yes?
(5) You remember where Brazil is?
(6) How much rain is there every year in England, in London?
(7) 8, 80, this is?
(8) How much rain is there in Brazil, do you know?

(9) How do you find out how much there is?
(10) And what must you do to the rainfall?
(11) What do you think you have to do to see how much there is for the whole year?
(12) And what month is that?
(13) So if you want to find out how much rain there is every month, what do you have to do?
(14) What is the word we have to say?
(15) If you were to take 340, 360, what would you be doing?
(16) What is that number, I mean symbol?
(17) It is not times, it is?
(18) OK?

All 18 questions are display questions. However, the grammatical construction of these questions is much more varied than in the ST's extract (56). The range of question types used in this interaction includes: 'yes/no' questions; 'wh-' questions; tag questions; declaratives with rising intonation. Clearly noticeable is how much longer the actual questions are and how they are far more grammatically complex. Also of note is that at least five of the questions are open and require the student to move beyond a one word answer. In addition there is a greater range of topics covered by the closed questions. Possible answers include: 'yes', 'no', 'hot', a number, a month, a mathematical symbol.

A distinction can also be made around the notion of teacher responsiveness (Jarvis & Robinson, 1997; Mercer, 1995) in the two collaborative extracts (56–7). The questions the teachers ask display different levels of teacher responsiveness. In the ST's extract we see the teacher develop opportunities for the student to display the 'right answer'. The teacher restricts the interaction opportunities to one word answers where there is a 50% chance of getting the right answer. In fact, when the student gets the answer wrong, the teacher tells the student the right answer and then checks comprehension by asking the question again later with another 'yes/no' question. There is only one interaction which might be called an 'extension' (Jarvis & Robinson, 1997). This happens at lines 8–9 where the teacher takes the student's definition of the seasons as the weather and goes on to build on the idea of weather as going up and down. There are few opportunities for negotiated modification in the teacher/student interaction or interest in second-language development. There is, however, numerous opportunities for the transmission of subject content and a good deal of the imperative.

Commands/imperatives (directive function):

- Join the dots to give a line graph. Join.
- Join with crosses.

- Look at this and think.
- Write it on the paper.

The teacher is using the directive function here to get students to complete the task. We also see the referential function in full use.

Transmission of subject knowledge (referential function):

- This is a bar.
- A rectangle is a bar.
- These are all what we call a bar graph.
- Seasons are winter and summer.
- Seasons equals winter, spring, summer, autumn.
- Weather, yes it goes up and down. So it is a season. Winter, summer, spring.
- We have our winter holidays, summer holidays. In England. In Turkey, it is hot in summer and cold in winter?
- 26 degrees centigrade is hot, isn't it?
- We don't need sweaters and it is hot in January, February, March, April, May, June, every month.
- Every month it is high.
- So we can say there is no seasons.
- The rainforests don't, do not, do not have seasons.

The subject teacher sees his professional role to deliver the curriculum, to make sure students cover a certain amount of material and that they have the correct answers. The ST is working within a professional and political climate that requires the successful achievement of particular outcomes, especially in year 10, which precedes the students' final year of compulsory school education and their examinations.

The EAL teacher, on the other hand, does not feel the same pressure to transmit subject content. Like the ST, the EAL teacher does foreground the referential function and the focus is very much on subject content. However, the subject knowledge is not transmitted through the imperative or declarative but through the interrogative. The EAL teacher asks numerous questions which strive to develop the student's knowledge. In terms of responsiveness, there are many examples of 'extend and build'. The correct answer to the open display question in line 5 (Extract 57) allows the teacher to compliment the student and move the discussion from a definition of the seasons to the concept of a range of temperature. In fact, the EAL teacher uses his questions to guide the student through the task. His questions are used to check comprehension of the key term 'season', to get the student to define a season, to establish that some places have constant temperatures, to check the student understands the location of Brazil, to check that the student can read a graph/figure, to check knowledge of numbers in English and key mathematical symbols. This is not achieved through the declarative, nor by telling the student, but rather from building the story through questions. Moreover, the EAL teacher creates opportunities to use the metalinguistic function and look at language itself in the interaction. This happens in lines 16–18 and again in lines 34–9 in the talk about numbers and mathematical symbols. There is also more evidence of the expressive function in the EAL teacher's discourse through the wide use of compliments. Of additional grammatical interest is the EAL teacher's use of modal verbs.

Use of modals:

- What you must do now.
- You need the book.
- Now, can you tell me.
- Now, what you have to do is.
- And what must you do to the rainfall?
- What do you think you have to do to see how much there is for the whole year?
- So you must add those numbers.

The use of modal verbs by the EAL teacher detaches him from ownership of the task. What is of interest here is the lack of either the imperative or the use of 'I' or 'you' to direct the student. The EAL teacher constructs the task as if it has its own agency. That is, the agency is presented as if it were in the task itself rather than with the teacher. For example, instead of the teacher saying, 'what I want you to do is X', a modal is used, 'what you need to do is', 'what you have to do/must do', etc. This is contrasted with the ST's talk, where there is evidence of ownership of the task and a clear direction from the teacher of what is expected of the student (Creese, 2000).

Chapter Summary

In this chapter I have argued that research on classroom interaction needs to view school classrooms as more complex than one teacher working with a class of students. One teacher classrooms are simply not the reality for many teachers and students in schools. There are often a number of teachers' discourses in the classroom and this impacts on the nature of interaction. We need a greater understanding of the similarities and differences in teacher talk in the classroom. We need to understand the overlap and underlap in the ways teachers talk to students so that we can be better informed of how teachers with different roles might complement one another in the classroom.

Teachers with different professional roles are under different professional pressures. While it might be easy to look negatively on the ST for not asking more questions or on the EAL teacher for not doing more whole-class subject teaching, we need to view this in a particular political climate. STs are under heavy pressure to transmit an outcomes-orientated curriculum in classes of 30 or more students. Certain aspects need to be covered, information needs to be exchanged, the children need to pass exams. Talking to the many appears potentially more satisfying and successful than working with the few. Similarly, EAL teachers are under a different set of pressures. EAL teacher work, described in Chapter 3 as facilitating, accessing, scaffolding and often working with the few, is positioned as support, helping and generic. In many cases, it is described as work without skill or a particular knowledge base.

I have suggested that the two kinds of teachers' different professional pressures lead them to interact differently in the classroom. Spending time with students and guiding them through a series of questions allows the EAL teacher to respond to the students' learning needs in nuanced ways. Speaking to the whole class about subject curriculum, owning the tasks and moving students through a syllabus allows STs to deliver on core secondary school aims.

Teacher responsiveness and teacher negotiation are important skills. The knowledge of accessing and facilitating, of the role of language in learning and of second-language learning processes are important in any classroom. Such knowledge and skills are particularly important to bilingual/EAL students as they learn a new curriculum in a new language. For these students, negotiation opportunities, which allow for input to be modified to form meaning, are of great importance. Support work or, perhaps better, 'support talk' is a pedagogic skill of great importance in multilingual classrooms. It needs to sit equally alongside other dominant classroom discourses, such as the transmission of subject knowledge.

In the next chapter we go on to look at other ways in which EAL teachers and STs discursively distinguish themselves in the classroom through playing out different institutional roles.

Note

1. A version of this paper is to appear in the *International Journal of Bilingual Education and Bilingualism* (see Creese, in press).

Chapter 5

The Discursive Positionings of Teachers in Collaboration

Introduction

This chapter builds on the analysis of Chapter 4. It again takes the classroom as the site to look at teacher interaction patterns. However, whereas the previous chapter undertook a predominantly functional analysis of teaching and learning exchanges, this chapter takes a wider look at how STs' and EAL teachers' classroom interactions index school and societal discourses on education and diversity.

In order to do this, the chapter is organized along the following lines. First, a working definition of discourse is given which is used to explore the idea that discourses work at different levels seemingly at one and the same time endorsing and contradicting one another. In this section, two other key phrases for the chapter, 'teacher professional discourse' and 'institutional discourse' are explored. Following this discussion, I present transcripts to consider the professional discourses associated with EAL teachers and STs, and how these are linked to institutional and societal level discourses around education.

Definitions and Levels of Discourse

> Discourse is a means of talking and writing about and acting upon worlds, a means which both constructs and is constructed by a set of social practices within these worlds, and in doing so both reproduces and constructs afresh particular social-discursive practices, constrained or encouraged by more macro movements in the overarching social formation. (Candlin, 1997: viii, in Sarangi & Coulthard, 2000: xv)

This quote is helpful as it makes several points that I wish to explore in this chapter. First, the idea that discourse both reflects and constitutes a social context. Because discourse is language-in-use it not only reflects the social and political context but also plays its part in shaping that context. As teachers, the way we speak in the classroom is constrained by the classroom context. However, as teachers we also play our part in reshaping and transforming contexts. This is not to say that we have access to any kind of discourse at any time. The context itself imposes its own patterns of interaction on the way we can speak, as do our own personal histories. Our life experiences affect which discourses we feel able, or want, to take up or use, and therefore the way we construct ourselves through discourse (Cameron, 1997). Moreover, we do not all arrive in a social context on the same level ground. That is, different institutions and their social contexts value our individual, personal and professional discourses in different ways (Bourdieu, 1977).

A second issue which the quote above alludes to is that of power within language use. The point being made is the importance of looking at how discourses in micro and macro contexts interact to inform one another. In looking at this interaction between local and societal discourses we come to see not only how meanings are produced and transmitted but also how institutional roles are established and power relations developed and maintained (Wodak, 2000). As others have argued, power and dominance are usually organized and institutionalized (Fairclough, 1997; van Dijk, 1993). Language plays a key role in maintaining institutionally dominant discourses and the ideologies which underpin them. These discourses and ideologies are often far from transparent to the individuals within the institution. In fact they become 'naturalized' and, therefore, are no longer seen. The work of critical discourse analysis is to 'unnaturalize' these discourses and make transparent who the winners and losers are when particular ways of speaking come to dominate. As educators, we rarely stop to consider how our own and others' language use positions us, and those with whom we work, within the institution. A focus on discourse can help us to do that.

Discourse analysis may help to capture the complexity of classroom and school life by looking at a whole host of competing and seemingly contradictory factors at once. A discourse analysis approach provides a means of understanding how discourses become ordered in ever-increasing hierarchies of authority (Fairclough, 1989, 1995; Wodak, 2000), and how these become linked together through linguistic symbols and structures (Blackledge, in press). Texts are therefore always multi-authored (Geertz, 1988) and heteroglossial (Bakhtin, 1973), that is, occupied by the voices of others. These theories allow us to understand how particular educational hierarchies become established and are shifted. It also allows us to understand how teachers feel able to take up some discourses and not others (Cameron, 1997; Fairclough, 2000; Gee, 1999; Heller & Martin-Jones, 2001).

The critical discourse analysis (CDA) has sought to increase consciousness of how language contributes to the domination of some people by others (Fairclough, 1989: 1). Fairclough describes orders of discourse as socially conventionalised practices which are available to text producers in particular circumstances. Examples would include discourse practices associated with social domains, for instance: the school classroom, parents evening, the political debate, the literary review, and so on. Fairclough argues that the methodologies of CDA provide the tools to better understand the permeability of social boundaries in contemporary societies (Fairclough, 2003, in Blackledge, in press).

Another example of levels or orders of discourse comes from the research of Roberts and Sarangi (1999) and Sarangi and Roberts (2002) working from a more interactional sociolinguistic perspective. They have investigated how different modes of talk are not equally transparent to people within institutions. They have looked at interactions in the oral examination of the Royal College of General Practitioners (RCGP), a prestigious institution which controls entry into the medical profession for doctors. Sarangi and Roberts describe three kinds of experience which student doctors are asked to call upon in their oral examination: professional, institutional and personal experience. These are each linked to modes of talk or discourses. Sarangi and Roberts show how international students taking the examination fail to recognize that 'personal' values are expected to be demonstrated in the distanced and analytic language of the institutional mode. These students failed more often than home students, and Sarangi and Roberts argue that international students were experiencing a discursive difficultly in recognizing the distinction between professional, personal and institutional modes. They go on to argue that interactional management of hybrid discourse is partly what constitutes success in RCGP's oral examination and that international students need additional support in being socialized into these discourses and learning how to mediate them.

EAL Teachers and Discourses of Institutional Power

EAL teachers may unwittingly take up institutional discourses which help position them in particular ways. We have already explored some of these in terms of the discourses of facilitative and transmission pedagogies. In what follows in this chapter we will look at other patterns of interaction that help to position EAL teachers in their classroom contexts. This analysis groups these classroom interactions around three sub-headings: the giving of answers; the use of institutional structures to endorse status hierarchies; and teacher-to-teacher talk.

Giving answers

We have seen in Chapter 4 how one EAL teacher asked many more questions than the ST he was working with. In Extract 58, we look at a related point. This shows a different EAL teacher again engaged in asking many questions, while the collaborating ST is more willing to give out answers. In the following two extracts (58 and 59), the EAL and subject teachers are working with two different students on the same task. The first extract is a non-bilingual EAL teacher working with a bilingual student.

58
EAL language specialist working with bilingual student – Technology, year 10
EAL: Right, what is the first thing you are going to do? Where is your design brief? Get your design brief. Good. Right, that is the first thing. Did you fulfil this? Did you do this? So the first things is (writes) did I fulfil ... Do you know that word? '**The design brief**'.
S: That means to complete it.
EAL: That's right. Did I actually fulfil it? Did I actually achieve it? Did I do it? That was your brief. Do you think you actually completed it?
S: Erm. No, because I haven't put the batteries in.
EAL: No, I mean the idea.
S: Yeah.
EAL: So, you can write a paragraph here, of what the design brief was, my design brief was to der der der der. (writes) What's the past tense of that?
S: 'ed' is it?
EAL: Funnily enough! So you can ask yourself a series of questions, like on the board look. So what went well out of this? Designing, the planning, the making and the evaluating.

The language specialist here is attempting to get the student to complete the task by guiding them through what is expected of them. The pedagogic style is very much that of facilitator rather than transmitter. That is, she asks questions and encourages the student to arrive at an answer herself. However, the subject teacher in the same class adopts a rather different style of teaching.

59
Subject teacher and student (non-bilingual) – Technology, year 10
ST: You can also say how you got around this line here. You know, instead of colouring it in with black felt, you actually put metal around it, didn't you? That's an important point.
S: Yeah.
ST: You want to say how you did that. That is important. And you want to say about how you changed the size.
S: I didn't change the size.
ST: Yeah, you wanted to do it this big to start with and then you decided on this big.
S: Oh yeah. Do I have to do that as well?
ST: Yeah, put that down. Also put down about colour. You wanted it grey, but we didn't have any grey so you had to have it black.
S: Right.
ST: Get all those things down. (A5)

In this extract above the subject teacher gives more explicit instructions on what should be included in the finished piece of work. There are fewer questions and more direct guidance on what the student should write down. Perhaps one reason for this is that subject teachers are under pressure to make sure students have the answers as external examinations and nationally published results will place their school in a league which compares them with other schools. Giving the answer is one strategy for keeping students grouped more closely together. Whatever the pedagogic merits of such action, the two approaches outlined in Extracts 58 and 59 mark the teachers' discourses as different. There are many examples of STs giving students the answer before they move away from them and on to the next student.

60
Subject teacher and student (non-bilingual) – Technology, year 10

ST:　Do it outside please because it will be . . . Bring your stuff over here. You can't work there, well I can't at least.

S:　Sir everything has gone wrong today. Look if I stick that there it is going to be obvious that it has been cut.

ST:　Yeah

S:　I've got to file it down to make it look flat.

ST:　Look, what you need to do is actually put a flat edge on this and, I'll be there in a couple of minutes all right? Erm, what you need to do, put it on that machine over there and just take the flat edge off this or get a file, give this a flat edge and then it will stick on it because it is flat.

S:　All right then.

ST:　Because at the moment you have got one bit that is a curved bit so only one bit is touching. So what you need to do here is=

S:　Should I get that bit flat as well?

ST:　Yeah get that bit even flatter. If I were you, what I would have done I would have done is have just a wooden bit down, so the wooden bit was here.

S:　So I should stick it up to the metal?=

ST:　Was it sticking here? Was it sticking here?

S:　No, it is sticking here. It is just like the, erm, the pencil overlapping it.

ST:　All right, no problem. (A5)

61
ST:　(in groups) Do you know what that word there is? That's average. Do you know what average means? It means like if you take over a long time and say what the most common thing is over that long time, that's what average is OK. So in July, the temperature goes up and down, up and down, up and down doesn't it, but the average is what is generally tended to be. The most common temperature. Do you understand that right? (student reads) Right, so we want to look for the July map and we are looking at the south east. Point at the south east for me, right what temperature does that say? Yeah, and what's the number at the end of that line? OK. So is that one true or false. (true) Excellent well done. Can you carry on like that? (C7)

62
ST: How are you getting on Ayşe? Do you understand that? No? We've got 20 identical tomato plants. That means 20 tomato plants that are exactly the same. All right. That is the number for food A. That food A produces those tomatoes, yeah? Then food B produces these tomatoes, yeah? Now calculate the range for these each plant. Right, the range is from the smallest one to the biggest one. So you are taking 1 from 20. What is 20 take away 1?

S: 19.

ST: 19, good. So the range for that is 19, what is the range for that? So we said=

S: XXX

ST: Go on=

S: 9.

ST: No. We say 20 is the biggest number there and the smallest number is 1. Small. Smallest number is 1. Biggest number is 20. So the range is the biggest number take away the smallest number (pause) which is 20 – 1 which is 19, yes? Now what is the range for that?

S: Seven. (pause) Eight.

ST: Go on, write it down for me. Let's have a look.

S: Six.

ST: Six. Well done. It is 12 take away 6, so it is 12 take away 6, and the range for that one is 20 take away 1, so it is 19. And that is 6, yeah? So you calculate and then answer those two questions, all right. Good girl. (B6)

Each of these examples (60–2) has the ST making sure that the student has the problem resolved before leaving them:

- Look, what you need to do is actually put a flat edge on this.
- It means like if you take over a long time and say what the most common thing is over that long time, that's what average is OK.
- Well done. It is 12 take away 6, so it is 12 take away 6, and the range for that one is 20 take away 1, so it is 19. And that is 6, yeah?

There was a pattern in the language use of STs around the confirmation or giving of answers.

In the next example, we can see what happens when a student does not get the answer he expects. This is an EAL teacher from school C working with a bilingual student in a different design class.

63
EAL teacher working with an individual bilingual student in class
S: Write it, Miss. Answer it.
EAL: No, you do the answer. I am giving you enough help, you have to do your own work, otherwise you're not learning.
S: I am learning.

EAL: You have got to learn how to do it.
(and later with the same student)
S: Miss, let's answer the questions now.
EAL: Well, you can do that yourself, I am not going to.
S: I . . . I can't.
EAL: Yes you can.
S: I can't.
EAL: (pause) I am not doing any more for you, I have done a lot for you already.
S: (big sigh)

'Learning' is interpreted by this EAL teacher as the student working out the answer for himself. The student disagrees with her. This EAL teacher's practice differs from the ST's. EAL teachers appear to engage in more question-asking and less answer-giving. Again, my intention is not to say which approach is 'better' but to show how the teachers position themselves differently through such discourse.

Endorsing status hierarchies

There were three ways in which EAL teachers and STs differed in their use of professional discourses. The first was through reference to examination structures; the second was through reference to different colleagues for professional support and back-up; and the third was structures for praise.

Throughout the information gathered, there were many examples of STs referring to the grades students would get for their work. The statements made by the STs were often made as statements of fact in the third person. Some of the most pertinent remarks have been set in bold in the extracts below.

64
ST, Geography class, year 10
ST: This is temperature. These numbers here refer to temperature. These numbers here refer to rainfall. And it has got two axes. OK? And then if you looked at that again. I think you would find that the weather does not change from month to month from day to day.
S: It doesn't?
ST: It does not change. It is very much the same weather throughout. OK? So do that again. Or just go over that.
S: I don't want to do that again.
ST: You must do it. It is absolutely essential. **This is where you'll get the A as opposed to the B, or the C as opposed to the D.**
S: Sir, I'm not that clever.
ST: Yes, you are that clever. And you should be working, you should be aiming for a top grade.
S: Sir, I don't understand that question.
ST: I gave you a lot of help.

65

ST, Technology, year 10

ST: You don't have to get everything done on it, obviously if you do, you are going to get a better mark. And you are very capable of getting a top grade in this aren't you? The only trouble is you muck about in the lessons too much, don't you? Yeah?

S: It's not my fault though, it is my surroundings, my atmosphere.

ST: Perhaps it's not your fault, but you have also got to take responsibility for actually getting the work done, haven't you?

S: But I will get the work done sir.

ST: **Try, because this will give you quite a good mark, I know you are very capable, I know you can get good marks, you know you can, but the examiners are going to look at your folder now and say a big fail, isn't he? He doesn't know who you are, he doesn't know you are very capable. That's what happens. You go for a job. Somebody else goes for a job, who is not as capable, you know, you are streets above this other bloke who goes for a job, and he has got his piece of paper saying GCSE grade, Technology, grade A, and you could have got a C or a D or any other grade, but you fail, and they turn around and give him the job. How are you going to feel?**

S: XXX

ST: He's got the job! He's a doughnut. Aren't you? But he's got the piece of paper, so it is up to you. If you can get this done, you can get a good mark for it, but you have actually got to get it done, all right? (aside to me) Classic comments! (A5)

66   I don't want to show them all to you because you will get bored. I'll just take out the ones that are relevant. This is a piece of research about what children like and what they can do in bed and what they can't because they are stuck in bed, the things that they need, very small children. Things to play with on the side of the cot. Not complicated just beautifully set out. **This is definitely going to get an A**, because there is a lot of work and all the work is, looks excellent. That is an exam project that she did. Let me see if I can find something else that you can see. That is research. That is all about different material, that is about safety. Everybody in this class can produce sheets of A3 like that. Everybody can. It is not complicated. It is a matter of self-confidence and what you know you can do. (C10)

The subject teachers in these extracts (64–6) show themselves to be representatives of the examination system and interpreters of that system (. . . this is where you'll get the A; you are that clever; I know you can get good marks . . .). There are no examples of the EAL teachers in support mode interpreting student work in this way to assign potential grades with such confidence. EAL teachers do speak of general study skills in relation to examinations but not to actual grades. Instead, EAL teachers refer to STs when they wish to have their message endorsed and backed-up.

67

EAL: You've been to Mr Roberts? Mr Roberts gets you all to make borders doesn't he? Yeah? Mr Porter makes people to make borders.

S: No.

EAL: Mr Sullivan gets people to make borders. You put a border around that and it makes it look a hundred times better. A border. All right? So if you put a coloured border, all you need to do is take a ruler and draw a coloured line around it and you have got a border.

S: Yes, Miss. (A2)

68

EAL: So do what you can? **Because Mr Porter is very worried about your technology.** - - - and you must cover the work, because you can't catch up. If you let it go now you cannot catch up, this is the time to work hard try to get into it and even get ahead if you can. Yeah? To give yourself a chance. Right, I hope that was useful to sort things out.

S: Thanks Miss.

EAL: Right. (C1)

69

EAL: How many homeworks do you owe **Mr Fitch**? (C1)

70

S: But I haven't got the orange juice or the egg because they both smashed.

EAL: Oh no! These are not going to come out as they should are they? **I might ask Mr Holly to see if he can go and butter up the staff, get you an orange juice.** You know you might have to give us 30p or something from the canteen. Is that all right? And then ask them if they have got a spare egg. I need to see your recipe. **Mr Holly, can you help as out of a corner here**?

ST: What sort? (A1)

71

EAL: It is going to look good that.

S: Miss can I finish it off at lunch time?

EAL: If Mr Holly is around, yeah. Most lunch times I am actually in the other building, that is the problem. Or if I am here I am doing homework club.

S: Will you be in the upper building today?

EAL: Yes, I will.

S: Will I be able to do this in the upper building?

EAL: If you take it all over, but you won't be able to do it now because it isn't dry, is it?

S: I know, but can't I take it over?

EAL: Not like that.

S: I'll hold it and let it get dry, and put it in my desk like that in English.

EAL: **Well, Mr Holly needs that stuff next and he is over here, so you can't take that.**

S: Haven't we got that in the other building?

EAL: Well, we might have.

S: Well, can I not put a little bit in a bottle or something and take it with me?

EAL: (with regret) No, no. That needs to dry off anyway before you put any more on.

S: No, I am not. I just want to get this all done here basically and then um you know.

EAL: Leave it as it is and do a second coat now. Because that looks really nice now.

S: A second coat?

EAL: Yeah, after that's dried. After that's dried. That is really beautiful. I love the way the lines are coming through on the wood, that looks really nice. OK. Leave it on the side to dry. **Er, Mr Holly, should she leave it on the back to dry it?**

ST: Er, leave it in that room here.

EAL: Oh all right. (A1)

72

EAL: **You do what Mr Timothy said.** You find the lowest number, the highest number, so the mode is between 125 and 142. OK, so they range from this to this.

S: Yeah, that means that one there is wrong.

EAL: (long pause) **Let me ask Mr Timothy.** (to ST) She is doing the mode of the height here and they range from 125 to 142, right?

ST: What she needs to do is check out which numbers occur most often. For example, count=

EAL: yeah=

ST: How many times 125 occurs.

EAL: Yeah, and then?

ST: And then the one which appears most and check out how many times 128 occurs, how many, the number which occurs most, that will be the mode.

LST: OK.

ST: 125.

LST: (to student) OK. Right, **so Mr Timothy said what you have to do**, are you listening, you have to go through each number 125 to 142, and then 126, 127, 128, etc. Go through this number and see how many times each one occurs and tally it up and the one that occurs the most is the mode he said. (B1)

Summary of data from Extracts 67–72

- Mr Roberts gets you all to make borders doesn't he? Yeah? Mr Porter makes people make borders. Mr Sullivan gets people to make borders. You put a border around that and it makes it look a hundred times better.
- Because Mr Porter is very worried about your technology . . . and you must cover the work, because you can't catch up.
- How many homeworks do you owe Mr Fitch?
- 'Mr Holly, can you help us out of a corner here?'
- 'Er, Mr Holly, should she leave it on the back to dry it?'
- 'You do what Mr Timothy said . . . Let me ask Mr Timothy . . . Right, so Mr Timothy said what you have to do, are you listening, you have to go through each number 125 to 142, and then 126, 127, 128, etc.'

In Extracts 67–72 we see many examples of the EAL teacher endorsing the status of the ST. The EAL teacher's reference to the ST by name helps lend respect to that teacher's work/knowledge/skills. There is a kind of deference towards subject teachers that helps to reinforce knowledge hierarchies in the subject classroom. In many of the extracts, the EAL teacher could have chosen to use 'I' instead of the name of the ST. For example, the EAL could have said, '*I would put a border around that*' or '*How many homeworks do you owe us*'? Moreover, there were many examples of the language specialist positioning the subject specialist as the problem solver, there were few instances in the transcripts of subject specialists positioning language specialists in this way. STs drews on higher structures for endorsement of their message. They did this either through reference to examination structures, already mentioned, or directly through recourse to senior management.

73
ST: Perhaps a visit to **Mr White** (Head of English) would help you to see sense. (C6)

74
ST: Now I am sorry you are finding this a little difficult to concentrate on but believe it or not when you get into the exam next summer you are going to have to read this in silence to yourself. The same amount of work before you answer the questions. You have got to get use to this. I know it is hard. Right. (A9)

75
ST: Right. Now the GCSE examiners love tables so you better get used to looking at them. The writing is minute, so I hope you have got good eye sight. I haven't. (C5)

76
ST: And in the exam you won't have me to explain each source or help you with the questions. So we have got to build up your independence, working on your own. (B7)

As well as using the ST as a problem solver, expert and threat, EAL teachers also use the subject teacher as the bestower of praise. This is related to their position as being expert enough to judge good work (Wolfson, 1981). From interview data we have an ST commenting:

77   Normally what happens with Deirdre (EAL teacher) would be if somebody has done something really good she'll show it to me for additional praise, which I think is quite nice in a way. (C7)

And from the classroom transcripts:

78
(*Context: the EAL teacher is working with three students in the corner of the room. She is doing different work from the rest of the class. The ST visits her group.*)
ST: How are you getting on? That looks good.
EAL: They are drawing the developed world in pencil,=
ST: Hmm=
EAL: =you see and the developing world they've got in pen.
ST: Hmm, and you will do a key won't you to show the difference between developed and developing? Very good.
EAL: It is coming up nicely isn't it, Mrs Smith, Hmm? (B4)

79
EAL: (to Mrs Rubins – the ST) A very good homework record this week. A couple of people blew it but mostly it is much much better than last week. (C4)

Teacher-to-teacher talk

This section presents data of teachers talking to one another in the classroom. The recordings are not of joint teaching sessions but rather other interactions throughout the lesson. Many of them happened at the beginning of the lesson. I present this data as further examples of how the teachers' language use indexes their institutional roles. That is, we see the EAL teachers in support mode relying on the ST for information about the students and the lesson content. There are differences in the ways teachers talk to one another when they work in partnership mode (see Chapters 6 and 7). The teachers A1 and A5 are working in partnership with one another. Teachers A2 and A8 are also working closely. Both A5 and A8 are newly qualified teachers. In total there are 20 occurrences of teachers talking to one another in class from the audio recordings. These can be classified in the following way: suggestions (one instance); materials (five instances); talk about students (four instances); lesson planning (three instances); personal talk (two instances); requesting permission (one instance); problem-solving on behalf of teachers (two instances); and subject clarification (two instances). Examples are provided below:

Suggestions

In this extract we see the EAL teacher make a suggestion to the ST about the presentation of work:

80
ST:　(to EAL) I think most of them have finished. I just thought I could do these.
EAL:　Have you got a title for the map?
ST:　Oh good idea. Right, I had better draw their attention to that. (A2 and A8)

Materials

In these extracts we see the EAL teacher ask the ST about materials. It is the ST who knows where materials are stored, whether particular materials exist and how many sheets of paper students should have for each task:

81
EAL:　Are these their folders? Aren't they big and bulky, aren't they? Where are you going to put these?
ST:　Put them in there.
EAL:　Why don't we put them in the office for the time being?
ST:　Yeah.
EAL:　They take up too much space, don't they these folders? (A1 and A5)

82
EAL:　How many bits of paper are we having? Two bits each?
ST:　Yeah, that'll do.
EAL:　Have you got any rough paper? No? (A2 and A8)

83
EAL:　Oh no, we haven't got any A3.
ST:　Yeah, A3 is in there.
EAL:　Oh yeah. (A1 and A5)

84
EAL: John, do you know where the word sheets went to?
ST: They're in there.
EAL: The top one. (B3 and B5)

85
ST: I don't know what I am doing.
EAL: That's all right!
S: Miss, is it only one?
ST: Yes, one between the group.
EAL: (to ST) We didn't get on to the questions did we?
ST: Ummm?
EAL: We didn't get on to the questions did we?
ST: What, those questions, do you want to do them?
EAL: No, I was just saying.
S: XXX
EAL: Shall I go around and check?
ST: Yeah, there should be one each of each.
EAL: What one per group or one per person?
ST: Yeah, one per group.
EAL: (to ST) Have you got this one? One per group, not one per pair. So, one per group.
S: XXX (inaudible)
EAL: Well, if we have got any to spare we will come back. Can you just sit down. (to ST) Is this one per person or one per group?
ST: XXX (inaudible)
EAL: Per person. Right, one per person. Right. (A2 and A8)

Talk about students

In these four extracts we see EAL teachers and STs talking about their students. As I mentioned at the beginning of this section on teacher-to-teacher talk, this pairing of teachers were working in partnership mode and there was continuity in their teaching. In Extract 88 it appears that the teachers are in disagreement with one another about Anthony, but in fact their collaborative relationship meant they could debate Anthony's moods in a spirit of solidarity. Sharing knowledge of students in this informal way seemed to consolidate the relationship between these partner teachers:

86
ST: It is so much better when half the class is away, isn't it?
EAL: Yeah, there are a lot of them away. Where are Adam and Ricky going?
ST: Ricky wants to move school, apparently. He is not coming in now. He is moving. His mum has been creating all sorts of problems. About it is the school's fault that Ricky hasn't done any work in any subject.

EAL: Well, he isn't going to get any GCSEs at that rate, is he? I mean, he is a truant basically.

ST: Yeah. He is very capable but I keep telling Craig.

EAL: Well, Ricky is his big mate isn't he?

ST: Yeah. (A1 and A5)

87

EAL: Are a lot of people away today?

ST: Anthony could join them couldn't he? Seem to be. We can't have Anthony on his own.

EAL: No, shall we put those three with Anthony and that will be a group then.

ST: Unless we move Anthony onto there rather than have everybody moving.

EAL: Yeah, we'll do that. (goes to Anthony) (A2 and A8)

88

ST: Anthony is in a foul mood.

EAL: Who?

ST: Anthony.

EAL: No, he is not. I thought he was in a really good mood.

ST: He just pushed the table. Germane accidentally jogged the table and he pushed it back and said 'don't you push the table like that'.

EAL: Oh! I thought he seemed really happy.

ST: He just turns doesn't he? (A2 and A8)

89

ST: Oh you can leave your stuff Fatima, because you'll probably come back, won't you? You can leave your bag. You'll probably only be gone 10 minutes or so. It's a career interview. (to EAL teacher) Has she got enough English to?

EAL: I doubt it very much.

ST: Who will she need there then? Where is she from? She is Bangladeshi, isn't she?

EAL: Maybe they have.

ST: I doubt it. I wouldn't have thought that far ahead. (A2 and A9)

Lesson planning

These three extracts are examples of partnership teaching. We see the EAL teacher taking the lead, making suggestions and we see STs seeking the endorsement of EAL teachers. In the first extract in particular, we can see the joint construction of an idea to change the following week's lesson plan. All the extracts are full of good nature and the endorsement of one another's ideas:

90
EAL: If we don't cook next week because I don't think all of them have got their folder sorted do you? We do the test next week and then we have one special before Christmas.
ST: That will be nice.
EAL: And we can ask them to do something Christmasy if they want to.
ST: That would be excellent, that would be brilliant that would.
    The last week=
EAL: So mince pies=
ST: Is next week the last week or the week after next?
EAL: Well, I think next week is supposed to be the last week. But I don't think it matters if we do one more.
ST: No, but we haven't got time because the week after that is year trips. Next week is the last one.
EAL: Next week is the last week for cooking? Right. Shall we do that then? They can do anything special for Christmas.
ST: A special Christmas one, yeah. As long as they can=
EAL: As long as they can get their own recipes together=
ST: And organize time plans and stuff. I wouldn't want them coming in with just a recipe and saying 'I want to make this' without them actually having prepared it as well.
EAL: Yeah. + + + What do you think? Would it work?
ST: I think so.
EAL: Are they going on a year trip?
ST: (to class) Are you going on a year trip? (A1 and A5)

91
ST: Miss Harrington, what do you think about keeping them doing this rather than the practical at the moment? This is just as many marks. This is just as many marks. That's the problem. In fact their folder work is 75% of their marks.
EAL: Well, let's get them to the stage where they think they will finish their folder and then they can start the practical if they want to. They'll have to come back and do the practical at another time.
ST: That's why I said on Monday. (A1 and A5)

92
ST: I was going to do that afterwards, do you think?
EAL: OK.
ST: =to remind them.
EAL: And then is that it?
ST: And then I can set them on their homework.
EAL: Yeah.
ST: Explain their homework. (A2 and A8)

Personal talk

Teachers in partnership are more likely to engage in informal talk which creates a positive rapport between them (Nias, 1989):

93
ST: (at break time the teachers stay in the workshop to help those students who wish to continue with their work) Miss Harrington, do you want a cup of coffee? (A5)

94
EAL: Oh I don't want to be here.
ST: I went home early last night I felt so rough.
EAL: I went home at half past nine.
ST: I fell asleep and when I got in I felt so ill, I didn't have time to cut these up. Because I just felt so rough last night.
EAL: They look good. Let's have a look. You do the register. Can we get them to do something?
ST: Right, everybody should be ready now. (to one student) Anthony, sit down please. Why did you come late? (A2 and A8)

Requesting permission

This is an example of an EAL teacher in support mode. She is not able to get the ST's attention neither is she clear about what the students have been working on. The decision for her to have the bilingual students work on a different task appears arbitrary. The ST has not had time to look through the new task. We also see evidence of the ST and EAL teacher constructing the bilingual students as under the remit of different teachers ('**go through it with my group**'), rather than being shared by both teachers:

95
(*The EAL is talking to the ST just before they go into the lesson*)
EAL: Have we finished the population pyramids in that class? 8 something, 8 B?
ST: XXX (the ST is half talking to herself about the need to find some work she is looking for)
EAL: Well, what is it in the end, can you remember?
ST: Well yes, I know what I am teaching.
EAL: Yeah, but what is it?
ST: Interpretation of graphs.
EAL: Ah, right. Thanks. So we are still on that, right. I've found some slightly easier work that John . . .
        (ST is doing other things)
EAL: Right. I've found some easier work on population on pyramids that John prepared. Can I **go through it with my group**? . . .
ST: Yes.
EAL: Because if it is interpretation then they will find it hard, yeah? (B4 and B8)

Problem-solving on behalf of teachers

These two extracts come from teachers working in a support mode relationship. The EAL teacher is focused on improving the bilingual students' homework submissions throughout the school. She therefore needs to hear from the ST about which students are submitting homework and which are not:

96
EAL: Hello. Is it mainly drawing?
ST: Yeah, it is today.
EAL: If it is just drawing then there is no point . . .
ST: Yes, it is the drawing.
EAL: And are you happy with their having done their homework?
ST: Well, Adnan hasn't done anything. I don't know if you can give him a hand. XXX I mean he is coming up with excuses every week.
EAL: Sorry, which table?
ST: Over there at the end, that table, the one in the middle.
EAL: With the blue shirt? Right, yes, he always makes excuses. Right, I'll have a word with him then. (C1)

97
EAL: Hello. Homework?
ST: Right.
EAL: Did they . . .
ST: Very disappointing, really. I am going to have a word with a number of those children today.
EAL: I'll go and have a go with my target people. (C1)

Subject clarification

EAL teachers would ask STs for clarification about subject matters. However, there were no examples of STs asking EAL teachers for clarification on language-learning, linguistic diversity or study skills:

98
EAL: What is freezing point in centigrade?
ST: Sorry?
EAL: Freezing point?
ST: Zero degrees
EAL: (referring to text) So it would have to be . . . Right! (ST laughs) (C2 and C7)

99
EAL: It says two lots of people were responsible for punishing them.
ST: Yeah, there is an overlooker and a parent in that one.
EAL: Oh right.
ST: Yeah? Because that is the father.
EAL: But did he actually do the punishing?

ST: Yeah, because he pushed her and she broke her arm, didn't she? And the reason he pushed her was because she didn't do, she was tired, so

...

S: Miss! (A2 and A9)

I captured relatively few instances of teacher-to-teacher talk. However, those that I did record show how teachers working in different collaborative modes talked to one another differently. Those working in partnership modes appeared to have more informal and collegial interactions in class (and, from observation, also outside of the class in the staffroom). Partnership teachers also shared knowledge of materials, lesson plans and individual children. Those EAL teachers in a support mode appeared to position the ST much more as a problem-solver concerning information such as materials to be covered and progression through the syllabus. These occurrences are summarized below:

- John, do you know where the word sheets went to?
- Can I go through it with my group? ...
- And are you happy with their having done their homework?
- What is freezing point in centigrade?
- But did he actually do the punishing?

The lack of continuity for EAL teachers in support mode meant they relied on the ST to bring them up-to-date with work. This helped position the EAL teachers as helpers, as they were not setting a shared learning and teaching agenda but rather a separate one.

Chapter Summary

This chapter has looked at how teachers' discourses uphold and challenge school systems and structures, which discursively mark out the two kinds of teachers as having different roles. The chapter has attempted to move beyond the teachers' classrooms interactions to institutional and societal discourses of power. Whereas STs use the school's hierarchy and examination structure to encourage and discipline students, EAL teachers tend to refer directly to STs to achieve the same ends. This has the effect of supporting already established hierarchies. In the teacher-to-teacher interactions we can see evidence of how the different kinds of relationships the teachers form with one another impact on their language use. These relationships are linked to modes of collaboration. Teachers in partnership mode form closer relationships, and there is evidence of shared agendas and overlapping knowledge about students and their learning. Teachers working in support mode do not have such continuity of experience, and their interactions are more about catching up. EAL teachers working in support mode ask more questions of the ST regarding materials and subject content. We take up these themes in the following two chapters.

Chapter 6

Teacher Collaboration in Support and Withdrawal Modes

Introduction

This chapter looks at various configurations of teacher collaboration between EAL and subject teachers when working in support and withdrawal modes. It describes how these relationships impact on teacher and student views of diversity within the school. This chapter, and Chapter 7 on partnership teaching, suggest that our understanding of teaching relationships is important in creating effective teaching and learning opportunities in mainstream classrooms. The chapter is organized along the following lines. First, literature on teacher collaboration is reviewed. This is embedded in a discussion of institutional cultures and teacher change and development. It is argued that teacher collaboration can only take place within institutional cultures which are open to change and learning themselves. Second, models of the different kinds of teaching relationships I observed across the three schools are described. These are grouped as different modes of collaboration: in this chapter, as support and withdrawal; and in Chapter 7, as partnership. A short vignette describing a classroom event is given to capture each mode. In this chapter and in Chapter 7, I will argue that partnership teaching relationships present the best opportunities for the transformation of the mainstream classroom. This is because partnerships work within already established institutional structures. However, these partnerships are rare, and even when they are established are not without their problems in terms of lack of overall institutional support. Support and withdrawal modes also provide good instances of teaching and learning, however these modes of collaboration tended to reinforce pedagogic divides. This is not the fault of the support mode itself, but rather the prestige attributed to transmission pedagogies and their discourses in the current climate of market-driven approaches to education.

Cultures of Individualism and Collaboration

Nias (1993b) points out that historically teaching as a profession has emphasized the importance of the teacher's autonomy and personality. Teachers are encouraged to be self-reliant and autonomous in making their decisions about curriculum and teaching methods. Their relationship with their students within the closed walls of the classroom keeps interference out and allows teachers a certain amount of ideological freedom to articulate their own views. Teachers bring their own ways of perceiving the world into their classroom.

Yet of course, the reasons for this professional individualism, as Nias points out, 'are also profoundly cultural' (1993a: 141). The training that teachers receive and the organizational structure of schools seem to discourage cultures which develop professional interaction and shared knowledge with other fellow teachers. For example, teachers are generally trained to work with children in classrooms, not with adults in schools: 'They are given little understanding of schools as institutions or preparation for negotiation or conflict resolution among their colleagues' (Nias, 1993a: 145).

Moreover, not only are teachers given little training in dealing with their fellow staff, there are often negative consequences for seeking such interactions. For example, teachers are unlikely to seek help in situations that could be embarrassing or stigmatizing, and which may prove threatening to the teachers' views of themselves (Rosenholtz, 1989). Rosenholtz (1989: 44) has shown how the organizational set up of the school is important in encouraging collaborative atmospheres:

> Norms of collaboration don't simply just happen. They do not spring spontaneously out of teachers' mutual respect and concern for each other. Rather, principals seem to structure them in the workplace by offering ongoing invitations for substantive decision-making and faculty interaction. . . . In other words, faculty members' involvement in decision-making about the technical matters of teaching appears to be one organizational vehicle that lends substance to their performance-based interaction.

As Rosenholtz points out it has become axiomatic in sociological literature that organizations must change and renew themselves by keeping abreast of situations which present problems and uncertainties. Schools must remain 'viable, and productive . . . adapting to ever changing needs. In short, successful organizations must have the capacity for regulation and self-renewal' (Rosenholtz, 1989: 71).

The work of Fullan and Hargreaves (1992) also emphasizes the importance of a school's organizational structure in bringing about classroom effectiveness. Like Nias and Rosenholtz, they also argue that it is cultures of individualism that restrict teachers from sharing their expertise, and thereby limit teachers' potential and competency. They also argue the need for schools to keep up with the fast pace of social life. Hargreaves (1994: 158) argues that many secondary schools struggle to keep pace:

> Secondary schools are prime symbols and symptoms of modernity. Their immense scale, their patterns of specialization, their balkanized structure and bureaucratic complexity, their persistent failure to engage the emotions and motivations of many of their students and considerable numbers of their staff are just some of the ways in which the principles of modernity are expressed in the practice of secondary education.

This literature makes a distinction between schools which have developed collaborative cultures and those which have developed isolationist cultures. Rosenholtz (1989) prefers the terms 'moving schools' in contrast to 'stuck schools'. His research argues that collaborative cultures lead to diversity, the identification of common problems, joint problem-solving, security and openness. However, there are also warnings against false realizations of collaboration which Hargreaves describes as superficial, comfortable, complacent, conformist and contrived (1994: 155). Most in education would support the notion of 'moving' and collaborative school cultures. And yet the reality of schools, particularly large secondary schools, is very far from this ideal:

> Open collaboration, extensive collegial conversation, mutual observation, and interactive professionalism are not yet an integral part of most teachers' working lives. In the main it is privacy, individualism and isolation that remain the persistent and pervasive conditions of teaching ... It is, therefore, not at all surprising that teachers often associate help with evaluation, or collaboration with control. Isolation and individualism are their armour here, their protection against scrutiny and intrusion. (Fullan & Hargreaves, 1992: 55–6)

> ... the organization of schools, especially large secondary ones, frequently impedes the development in schools of discussion groups representing varied perspectives. In schools which are tightly organized into departments or faculties, it may be difficult to bring teachers together across curriculum boundaries. (Nias, 1989: 32)

And in terms of EAL and subject teacher collaboration, Arkoudis (2003: 165) makes a similar point concerning balkanization into subject-specific departments:

> ESL, unlike other subjects in the secondary school curriculum, has attempted to arch over all curriculum areas and assist mainstream teachers in catering for the needs of their ESL and LOTE (language other than English) background students. This has been difficult because ESL teachers have entered specific discourse communities where pedagogy and subject knowledge were viewed differently (Siskin & Little, 1995, in Arkoudis, 2003: 165)

For the most part then, the sphere of decision-making in schools is narrow and promises of teacher empowerment and self-determination remain at the level of rhetoric:

> Empowerment is, in its own right, a compelling force in its potential to achieve organizational excellence (but) above all it is imperative that we recognize what empowerment is *not* ... Empowerment is *not* kidding teachers into thinking preplanned initiatives were their ideas. (That is entrapment.) Empowerment is *not* holding out rewards emanating from positive power. (That is enticement.) Empowerment is *not* insisting that participation is mandated from above. (That is enforcement.) Empowerment is *not* increasing the responsibility and scope

of the job in trivial areas. (That is enlargement.) Empowerment is *not* merely concluding that enlarged job expectations just go with the territory. (That is enslavement.) Empowerment is, rather, giving teachers and students a share in important organizational decisions, giving them opportunities to shape organizational goals, purposely providing forums for staff input, acting on staff input, and giving real leadership opportunities in school-specific situations that really matter. (Renihan & Renihan, 1992, in Hargreaves, 1994: 69)

As the above quote alludes to, teacher collaboration requires commitment at management level (see also Creese *et al.*, 2000). It requires an understanding that particular discourses are more powerful than others and that the school needs to play an active role in mediating these.

In this section I have reviewed a variety of literature which argues that teachers have received little training on how to work with other teachers. Moreover, teachers often work in institutional cultures that, through their very structures and practices, do not encourage easy collaboration.

How Teachers Deal with Change

I have argued throughout this book so far that the inclusive policy of mainstreaming is predicated on changing the classroom to make it more inclusive of the learning and language acquisition needs of bilingual students. Policy documents indicate that supporting teaching collaborations is one important means of bringing about this change. I have also argued that placing two teachers in the classroom requires teachers to adapt and adjust to this new teaching and learning context. It is fitting, therefore, to consider how teachers deal with change.

Teaching has been described as an open-ended activity (Fullan & Hargreaves, 1992: 58) in the sense that when the school day finishes and you go home, you always have work to think about. It has also been described as an inclusive activity in the sense that it draws on interests which would otherwise be used outside the classroom (Nias, 1993a: 141). What this amounts to is that teaching requires a heavy investment of the self in such work. Nias (1993a: 141) puts this as follows, 'Teachers appear to construe the purpose and meaning of their work in terms of its impact upon the self'. The very act of teaching, then, is about projecting one's identity:

> And you cannot change the teacher in fundamental ways, without changing the person the teacher is, either. This means that meaningful or lasting change will almost inevitably be slow. . . . Teachers become the teachers they are not just out of habit. Teaching is bound up with their lives, their biographies, with the kinds of people they have become. (Fullan & Hargreaves, 1992: 36)

Change, therefore, that threatens teachers is likely also to threaten teachers' perceptions of themselves and perhaps to damage their confidence and self-esteem (Nias, 1993a: 147). Or as Fullan and Hargreaves say, 'Ignoring or riding roughshod over teachers' purposes can produce resistance and resentment' (1992: 30). The task then becomes how to allow for change which is viewed by teachers as opening up possibilities for them rather than increasing their anger or silencing them completely. In the next section we look at the possibilities of teacher collaboration as a means of bringing about individual teacher and institutional change.

Teacher Collaboration

Cohen (1981) found that team teaching provided the means for greater professional and personal interaction, as teachers discussed and challenged each other's ideas about students, grouping arrangements, the curriculum and classroom management. Nias (1989) found in collaborative teacher groups there were no boundaries drawn between personal and professional concerns, and that this in turn led to a more enriching work environment. Hargreaves (1994) found that team-teaching situations could be either: *development partnerships*, which were voluntary, informal and spontaneous, sustained and evolving, organic and responsive, and with low prediction; or *implementation partnerships*, which were imposed, brief, mechanistic, discharging of specified duties and with high prediction.

Within the ESL field, the descriptive taxonomy offered by Bourne and McPake (1991) is the best known. Bourne and McPake (1991: 12) make a distinction between support teaching and partnership teaching, and the intermediary position of co-operative teaching. Support teaching involves the language-support teacher working with a targeted child or children in a lesson in which the curriculum is planned and delivered by the subject teacher. The intermediary position of co-operative teaching, in contrast, involves the two teachers planning the curriculum and teaching strategies together, taking account of the needs of all children in the class. The teachers have equal status and shared responsibilities, taking it in turns to lead the class. The last type of teaching relationship is that of partnership teaching. According to Bourne and McPake, this last kind of relationship adds to the co-operative model in the sense that it also allows for the teachers to develop the curriculum while also developing themselves. Here, the emphasis is on reviewing practice, setting short-term goals, 'experimenting' (teacher-action research), evaluating joint work and disseminating the results to the rest of the school (1991: 13). Bourne and McPake express a clear preference for partnership teaching. In a sense, the three categories are presented as a hierarchy of collaboration, with support teaching as the less favoured form of support and partnership as the preferred model.

In fact, the literature of support and advisory teaching has recognized the great diversity of relationships that teachers form with one another and the problems that this entails for role definition (Biott, 1991). There have been various attempts to classify types of support/advice. Dyer (1988, in Biott, 1991: 8–9) determines support as in three broad categories:

(1) support for pupils;
(2) support for teacher/pupils; and
(3) support for curriculum and materials development.

This classification maps onto the distinctions that Bourne and McPake made (see above). Biott (1991), however, breaks these categories down further. These are given in full here so as to show the great diversity in the kinds of support possible:

(1)   Direct pupil support (or one-to-one support)
    (a)   In-class support: obviating problems as they arise in a lesson.
    (b)   Preparational support: to prepare the pupil for an ongoing lesson (e.g. teaching sight vocabulary of key words).
    (c)   Remedial support: pupils are withdrawn into a separate group for extra tuition (may have little impact on the whole-school approach).

(2)   Teacher/pupil support
    (a)   General class support: team teaching in which the teachers' roles are ideally not distinguished.
    (b)   Consultative support: to respond to immediate problems or to 'get ahead' of potential problems.
    (c)   Analytical support: to detect what might be going wrong in organization, preparation or in the learning process.
    (d)   Observational support: to observe a specific point in classroom organization, lesson preparation or the pupil's learning strategy (likely to follow (c) above).
    (e)   Substitutional support: the support teacher takes over the teaching of a lesson.
    (f)   Specific support: the follow-up to the analysis of a difficulty (recommended only as a specific focus where direct pupil in-class support is practiced).
    (g)   Specific withdrawal: for a short time span, as part of the general support strategy.

(3)   Support in curriculum delivery
    (a)   Planning support: support in planning to identify potential pitfalls for pupils.
    (b)   Material (preparation): help to make materials or make commonly used support materials accessible to certain pupils.
    (c)   Curriculum support: support to maintain the integrity of the curriculum for low attainers. (Dyer, 1988: 7–10, in Biott, 1991: 8–9)

It is not clear whether Dyer intended this classification to be a continuum or a hierarchy. In my own work, I have found that teacher collaborations often contain elements of all three classifications within one teaching relationship, and often within one teaching session.

Within teacher collaboration literature, terms such as 'support', 'team teaching', 'collaborative teaching' and 'partnership' continue to be popular in distinguishing different kinds of teaching relationships. Indeed, I have continued to use them in this book. In many ways though, they do little to get at the complexities of the professional relationships that teachers form with one another. These relationship modes are overlapping. That is, it is common to find language specialists in multiple relationships each with differing levels of commitment. In any one classroom an EAL teacher might be engaged in giving individual learning support for part of the lesson while noting how to adapt the curriculum and analysing how teaching and learning aims might be improved (see Vignette 1). In any one school a language specialist may work in partnership with one teacher, in a support mode with another, and choose to withdraw students while working with yet another teacher. Here it is important to recognize that withdrawal is also a mode of collaboration if it is done successfully. Teachers need to keep one another well-informed if a child is taken out to work on supplementary aims.

EAL literature has generally favoured partnership teaching over support and withdrawal teaching. Generally, I would support such a position. In all three schools involved in this study, support and withdrawal modes tended to marginalize the EAL teachers. In support mode EAL teachers were not seen to be at the centre of institutional teaching practices. However, I also argue in this book that support work often provided very important learning opportunities for individual children. In some cases this individual work was evidence of the most concentrated learning going on in the classroom. I would be wary of arguing that working in support mode is always second rate, and that withdrawal is always third rate. In both modes of collaboration, teachers worked on important teaching and learning outcomes. Indeed, I would argue that, rather than one mode of collaboration being intrinsically better or worse than another, it is the discourses of government policy at the highest level that underpins what counts as teaching and learning in secondary school classrooms and impacts on how these different modes are viewed in schools. If individual support work and withdrawal were properly planned into policy, implemented and evaluated carefully, then these modes could also have a higher status within schools along with the discourses and pedagogies which support them.

In the rest of this chapter and in Chapter 7, we look at 10 examples of different kinds of teaching relationship grouped broadly under the headings outlined earlier from Bourne and McPake (1991) of support and partnership, and one that I have added, withdrawal. Although the last would ostensibly appear not to be a collaborative relationship at all, it is included here because withdrawal in two of the schools in which information was collected occurred regularly and always required some kind of teacher collaboration.

The ten collaborative relationships can be shown graphically (see Figure 3). They are used to capture general trends in the data. The graphs are not intended to be exclusive. They illustrate both bilingual and non-bilingual EAL teachers at work. Readers will quickly be able to add to these from their own experiences in multilingual schools. Moreover, the graphs are not being used to make a comment on the pedagogic quality of interactions. So, for example, the lack of lines between students is not intended to indicate that students are isolated in class, nor is the vertical line between teachers and students intended to suggest the relationship is one way only.

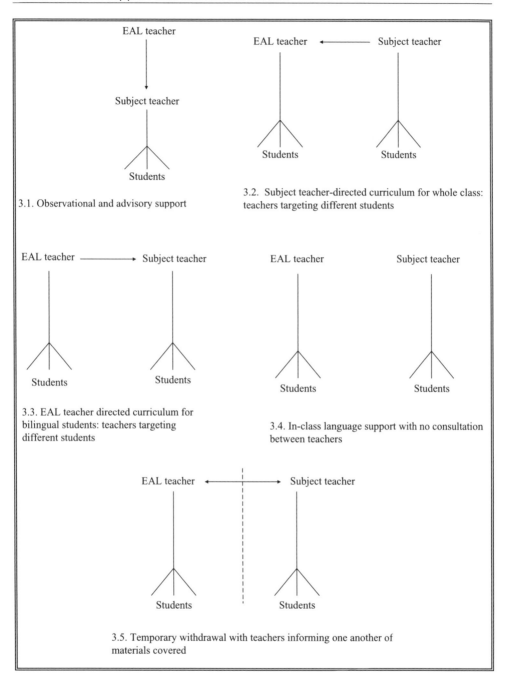

Figure 3 Ten modes of collaboration

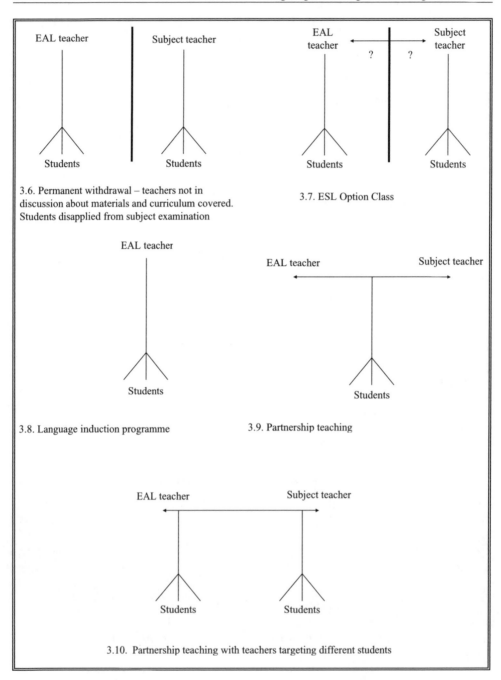

3.6. Permanent withdrawal – teachers not in discussion about materials and curriculum covered. Students disapplied from subject examination

3.7. ESL Option Class

3.8. Language induction programme

3.9. Partnership teaching

3.10. Partnership teaching with teachers targeting different students

Figure 3 (continued)

The graphs are to give a quick thumbnail sketch of the relationship mode in which collaborating teachers organized themselves. They capture general trends in data across the three schools studied in this book. The arrows between the teachers show their interactions concerning the aims of the lesson. The diagram trees show whether teachers are working with particular groups of students or the whole class. Where there is a vertical line between the two teachers (and the students they are working with), this shows a withdrawal situation. The dotted line shows temporary withdrawal. Of the ten modes of collaboration, four are given as support, two as partnership, and four as withdrawal.

In order to illustrate these various collaborations, a number of vignettes are given (see p. 000–0). The two partnership modes are illustrated with vignettes in Chapter 7.

Support Modes of Collaboration

A distinguishing feature of the support mode of collaboration is the EAL teacher's lack of control of time and place in the classroom. EAL teachers involved in support do not have the kind of continuity of time found in partnership teaching. Because EAL teachers working in support mode are attempting to cover and target as many students as possible rather than, for example, a single subject area and one teacher, they are not present in all of the classes of any particular subject area. Thus, they cannot be part of the setting and marking of homework because they will have missed some lessons in-between. This lack of continuity is recognized as a problem for the all teachers involved. Because of the lack of planning or consultation time in schools it can mean that these EAL teachers do not know what they will be doing in class until they get there. Moreover, it also means that the ST cannot be completely sure that they will have support for a particular lesson, and cannot plan their lessons with this provision in mind. The upside of this lack of continuity is that support teachers can be more flexible in responding to teachers' and students' needs. They can take themselves off the timetable to work on a materials task, or to work with a child who needs attention. The downside is that the support teaching can be ad hoc.

When an EAL teacher was working in support mode they tended to stand either at the side or the back of the class, working with individual students or waiting for the ST to finish any class-fronted teaching. STs tended to interact with more students in the class for shorter amounts of time, whereas EAL teachers often worked with a smaller group of students for longer periods of time. Moreover, STs were involved in a broader range of classroom activities, so the teaching interactions were interspersed with sorting out materials, etc. EAL teachers in support mode, on the other hand, did not have this variety. They were engaged in working with smaller groups of students on a learning task without the same level of interruption. STs managed the class with more students approaching the ST for help. These students, however, tended to be monolingual rather than bilingual. The following are some written accounts illustrating the support mode of collaboration.

Observational and advisory support

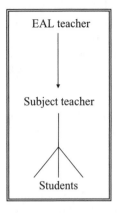

Figure 3.1
Observational and
advisory support

In this support mode of collaboration the EAL teacher attends the ST's classroom in order to offer specific advice on how the ST might improve an aspect of his or her teaching to make it more inclusive of bilingual students. The giving of such advice through observation is agreed upon by the two teachers beforehand. It is placed under the support mode of collaboration because the EAL teacher often attends only some of the classes of the ST, who then hopes to apply these suggestions in the remaining lessons. The EAL teacher does not have joint responsibility for the outcomes of the class. The following is an example of the EAL teacher visiting the class in order to make comments to the ST. These comments are included as an example of this kind of support.

Vignette 1
Year 8, religious education

The ST is going over parables with this year 8 class. The theme is Christianity, and Jesus' miracles. Before he starts on the theme, he spends about ten minutes recapping on the previous lesson. The EAL teacher is sitting at the side of the class taking notes. The ST then writes the word 'miracle' on the board. He asks the class what the word means, and they volunteer magic, skill, luck. All the boys are answering. The ST then uses two London football teams as an example of what a miracle is not. After the teacher-fronted examples he tells the students to open their books at page 34. As a way of disciplining a child the EAL teacher asks him which page he should be opening. He replies cheekily, 'Page 34 Miss, why don't you know?'. The students read aloud and answer the ST's questions. After this has finished the ST sets up the new activity, which requires the students to work in groups of three. They are to imagine they are groups in the crowd that saw Jesus doing his miracles. One student reads the worksheet to the whole class. Once the children are in groups, the EAL teacher goes to work with the Turkish bilingual students who have formed a group of three. Only one of these is a stage 1 bilingual, the others are around stage 3 or 4 (upper intermediate). She prompts this group by first asking them what they should be doing for the task. Both teachers then move around the whole class working with different children. At the end of the activity, the ST goes around the class calling on students to tell what they saw. The Turkish-speaking group do not want to answer. As the lesson ends, the ST writes the homework on the board. The EAL teacher is looking through some textbooks.

After the lesson the EAL teacher tells me that with this ST she spends one lesson observing and then prepares the material for the next lesson. She explains that she rarely has the time to coordinate work with teachers. She covers so many different lessons. She likes working with this particular ST because he at least follows up her ideas. She then writes down her comments for the ST:

Toby

Some thoughts on the miracles lesson, year 8. Good to elicit meaning of 'miracle' and to get examples. Of the two stories, the feeding of the 5000 was the most straightforward, but the healing of the Centurion's servant was quite difficult to follow. Quite a few students were confused as to the actual sequence of events. Therefore, either a different more straightforward story should be used or some work needs to be done by the students to clarify exactly what happened, e.g. giving them five or six sentences about the story to put into the correct order. Good to elicit exactly what was miraculous about the two stories.

The role play (empathy activity) was an <u>excellent</u> way of supporting stage 3/4 bilingual students who need opportunities to discuss things before writing them down. Many other students benefit from this as well. It gives them ideas, etc. of what to write.

Hope this is of some use.

Lucy

Vignette 1 shows the EAL teacher engaged in both advisory and support teaching. In this relationship the advice role in particular was negotiated with the ST before the observations started. The EAL teacher's role is centred on making the teaching process as creative as possible. One of the factors influencing the relationship these teachers chose to develop was the best use of the EAL teacher's and ST's time. Realizing that she could not possibly work as widely as she would have liked, she chose to work with a teacher who she knew would be open to her ideas.

Subject teacher-directed curriculum for whole class: Teachers targeting different students

Figure 3.2 captures a situation in which the ST directs the whole class with the EAL teacher using the same material but with targeted students.

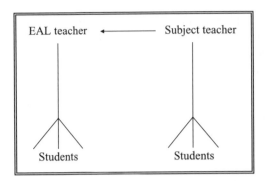

Figure 3.2 Subject teacher-directed curriculum for whole class: teachers targeting different students

Vignette 2
Year 10, geography

All the students are using the same geography text simplified by one of the EAL teachers. The fact that the whole class can use the same material is seen as a sign by the ST of the booklet's success.

As the lesson starts the ST assigns a page number. This is translated to the relevant Turkish girls in class. The Turkish-speaking girls immediately start calling for the Turkish-speaking bilingual EAL teacher's help. The class seems to be divided into two. The 'able' girls sit in the front two rows and are assisted by the ST teacher (these children also come from a variety of different ethnic backgrounds). The early-stage bilingual children and less-able children sit in the back two rows. In the third row three bilingual children sit together – one from Vietnam, one Turkish-speaking and one French-speaking from Africa. Next to them are two Turkish girls (stage 1). In the back row is a louder group of white English (one of whom has special educational needs) and Turkish-speaking students (around stages 2–3). At the very end, next to an English-speaking girl, is a Turkish-speaking Cypriot – a stage 1 – who is considered to be very bright and has been pointed out as such. The bilingual EAL teacher wanders around explaining most terms in Turkish and using Turkish for explanations. He goes from one group of targeted individuals to another. Rarely does he help the other students in the class. Rarely, also, does the ST help the bilingual students. Moreover, the students usually only call on 'their teacher'.

It takes a while for the girls to settle down (in the third row the girls are introducing themselves to one another). The bilingual students cover one or maybe two exercises. They have bilingual vocabulary sheets to help them. The ST tells me that presently the students are almost all working on the same material. This is also seen as a success.

Three minutes before the class finishes the ST brings the class focus back to the front and does a written summary on the board. This looks at the changes in the Norfolk Broads.

After the class the bilingual EAL teacher makes a brief note of what is covered in the lesson (this record-keeping is required of all the EAL teachers in this school).

Later in the break the ST tells me that he knows that sometimes he cannot do what is right for the students – because there are so many demands on his time. Thus, he was only able to give the answers to the text without explanation to one student who didn't understand due to language difficulties.

This vignette shows how the ST is primarily concerned with teaching subject content and he sees the main function of the bilingual EAL teacher as helping him to achieve these aims. Although this ST does direct the objectives of the class, he has asked an EAL staff member to make changes to the teaching material so that it is more task-based and all students can do the same work. The two teachers target different children throughout the lesson. The ST sees the need to push the 'able' students, while the bilingual EAL teacher sees his responsibility as keeping the bilingual students up with the curriculum content.

EAL teacher-directed curriculum for bilingual students: Teachers targeting different students

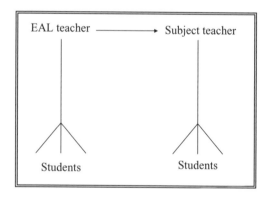

Figure 3.3 EAL teacher-directed curriculum for bilingual students: teachers targeting different students

As can be seen from Figure 3.3, in this mode of collaboration the teachers are working with different students and on different or additional material. Moreover, it is often the EAL teacher who requests that the targeted group work on different/additional activities. This support mode of collaboration is interesting because it does not fit the description of support in the Bourne and McPake typology (see p. 000), in which they suggest that the support mode requires the ST to plan and deliver the curriculum. I wish to argue here that although EAL teachers are fitting into the general scheme of things, they are able to play out aims which may be different from those of the ST. This continues to be in a support mode however, because the teachers target different groups in class, with the ST retaining overall class control.

Vignette 3(a)
Year 10, construction technology

When we (the EAL teacher and myself) come into the class the technology teacher is at the front showing previous good work done by students. She is explaining that she wants similar work to be produced by the children. The children are listening quietly and attentively. The teacher now moves the children on to getting started with the practical work, which they set about doing eagerly. Their aim is to make a container. Now the EAL teacher starts to move around to the bilingual children. While one of the boys is sawing a piece of wood, she asks him what the name of the tool is in English. He does not know and is not interested. She turns to the other bilingual children around her and asks the same question. None of them want to get involved and are anxious to continue with their work. She goes back to the individual boy and asks him whether he has done his homework. He has not, nor does he remember what it was. She collects several of the children around her. She reviews with the boys what was expected from them in the homework, 'I gave you these questions and I wanted you to write in Turkish, you haven't done it. Read to me what it says'. He reads about storage spaces. The EAL teacher summarizes 'to put things away when they are not being used. So if you store something, that is what it means. Storage space. You are making a storage space. My purse is a container. My wallet is a container. A bag is a container. So a container can be anything.' None of the children are paying much attention. They are looking around and are keen to get back to their practical work. The EAL teacher tells them that what she is saying is also learning, 'if you can't write it you won't do well'. The boys are now dying to get away. They make faces, and don't listen. They look at their watches and tap their fingers. Finally the EAL teacher finishes telling them about their homework and they rush off to do their practical work.

This is an example of the EAL teacher having aims beyond those of the subject teacher, focused on language-learning. The overall difficulty of pursuing language aims within the secondary school classroom is fully taken up in Chapter 8. In Vignette 3(a) the EAL teacher has confirmed with the ST beforehand that she will be checking the bilingual students' homework completion. This often involves taking the bilingual students to one side. The EAL teacher sits with the bilingual children grouped around him/her and works on this task while the rest of the class are engaged on something else.

The following is an example of a bilingual EAL teacher working on a different task with one individual student. A discussion of bilingual pedagogies can be found in Chapter 9.

Vignette 3(b)

Today I meet Neşe, a bilingual Turkish-speaking teacher who has been in Britain since 1988. She has been taking a Qualified Teacher's Status (QTS) certificate this term so she has been doing less teaching than usual. She has instructor status at the school.

Neşe is not a mathematics teacher by profession. She trained in English, but says that she doesn't feel too bad with the subject at this level, and that anyway she is helping them with the language, not necessarily with the maths. 'The Turkish bilingual children are often not bad at maths.'

The mainstream teacher has great difficulty with this class because they have been 'messed around' so much. Neşe sits at the back of the class with Metihan. Metihan has been in England for five years. He and his sister have just been statemented as children with SENs. He had no schooling in Turkey. Since then his education has been unsettled as he has been a pupil in many different schools in Germany and England. He is not really literate in Turkish, although more so than in English. Neşe feels that he has made some progress over the last year. He now recognizes mathematic symbols, can say the Turkish word for them and is starting to search for the English word.

The class is working on tasks at their own speed. Neşe feels these tasks are too language-based and so gets some other work for him, checking with the teacher first. She consults the mainstream teacher on several occasions and at one time asks for another book, which the subject teacher leaves the room to go and fetch. While she is out of the class the noise level goes up but Neşe does not get involved. Another student asks a question to Neşe. However, she says she is sorry but she does not know the answer (after trying) and that he needs to ask the other teacher.

The discipline in the class is very bad. The students are making all kinds of noises and hardly stop when the ST asks them to do so. When they do, it is for a very short time. A boy who comes into the class and who is looking for the teacher to deliver a message approaches Neşe and myself. 'Miss, can I get something from my brother please.' At first we don't think he can be talking to us and we don't hear him. He is confused (as are we!). Another child rescues us: 'They are not teachers. She's the teacher.'

The children are all getting on with their project work. Neşe starts working with Metihan. First she looks at the text and goes through the English. She asks Metihan to read a worksheet in English. Now she translates into Turkish. She tells him not to worry about the maths but are there any words he doesn't understand. He asks the meaning of the following words: 'what', 'hen', 'each', 'the mean'. Neşe translates for him. She draws a picture of 3 hens and 12 eggs. She now asks how many eggs each hen has. He says four. Now she asks which sign they are using (all in Turkish). He chooses the correct sign and writes the sum in his book. Now Neşe writes in English. 'Each hen has four eggs'. He now repeats the exercise using 16 eggs and 4 hens. Again when he has done the calculation, Neşe writes the answer out in English. Neşe tells me that she is going to use a booklet that they used in year 7 so that there is some consistency between her and Metihan, working together. She says she will check with the ST first.

While Metihan is working, Neşe is translating the books. When he has finished she goes over it with him. She asks comprehension questions in English. 'What is the mean in number three? How many eggs are there in number five?' He answers in Turkish but when she persists, he answers in English. Turkish is used to work out the calculation, English to record the result.

Another sum. Neşe tells him to work it out on his calculator (in Turkish). He says 'aklımda yapmak istiyorum' ('I want to do it in my head'). We both laugh and encourage him. He smiles at himself. She now shows the relationship between multiplication and division in Turkish. When referring directly to the worksheet she uses English, but explanation and instruction are in Turkish.

'Can you write marbles?' He pauses. 'Can you find marbles here?' He points.

There are five minutes to go. Neşe and Metihan have stopped work. However, they have worked harder than the rest of the class, which has been making lots of noise and most of the children do not seem to be on the task. Neşe tells me that she would like to give him a gold star. In the remaining minutes she chats with him about his football team and family, etc.

This lesson is an example of how an EAL teacher is able to still do focused individual work with a child despite not being recognized as a 'teacher' by other children in the class. She is clear about who she is there to help and stays focused on that child.

In this last example, the bilingual EAL teacher is working on material which is different from the rest of the class and she has cleared this with the ST. Although the EAL teacher says that she is not teaching maths but English, she is indeed focused more on the content, with English being used mostly to record results. Here is an example of some very good one-to-one interactional teaching in which the individual needs of the student are the starting point. Such one-to-one teaching in the context of the mainstream is often disparaged, with the support teacher being referred to as a 'whispering radiator'. However, this student was able to be a part of the atmosphere of the mainstream classroom (however troubled this might be) while receiving help that was perceived by the teacher and student to be valuable. The EAL teacher did not become involved in disciplining the class. She directed her attention to the needs of the individual rather than the whole class. Of course, not all instances of such one-to-one teaching can be claimed to be as valuable. The point I wish to make overall here is that EAL teachers are able, within the support mode of collaboration, to direct their own aims to a certain extent – with positive and negative results.

In-class language support with no consultation between teachers

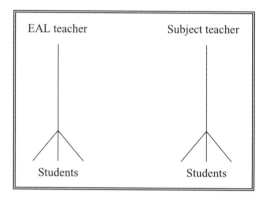

Figure 3.4 In-class language support with no consultation between teachers

As can be seen from Figure 3.4, in this mode the two teachers do not consult one another about the curriculum or the students with whom they are working. This usually means that the EAL teacher follows the curriculum set by the ST but with little or no consultation. Thus, this mode of collaboration is similar to the subject teacher-directed curriculum for the whole class mode, in which the ST directs the EAL teacher in terms of the lesson aims. However, here the ST does not tell the EAL teacher either before or during the lesson what will be covered in the lesson. The EAL teacher is often expected to pick this up as the lesson goes on. Moreover, this lack of consultation also points out a pattern in that the ST tends to see the EAL teacher as having specific students to work with, who rarely come under her own domain and tutorage.

Vignette 4
Year 10, Information Technology

In this class there are two groups working on different activities. For example, none of the Turkish students are doing the homework because it is considered appropriate only for the higher-achieving children. However, the Turkish-speaking bilingual EAL teacher is not aware of this and neither are the bilingual children. The ST mentions this particular instruction only once and they do not hear it. However, the ST does spend ten minutes speaking about the homework to the whole class. When she has finished this, she stays at the front of the class working on her own materials at the computer terminal.

The bilingual EAL teacher walks around the class working with bilingual students at the computers. She corrects spelling mistakes on their computer questionnaire. The bilingual EAL teacher and bilingual students are code-switching.

Two girls from outside come in and look for the ST, who has temporarily left the class. They only approach the bilingual EAL teacher when they cannot find her. She does not really know how to help them. When the ST comes in she directs them immediately.

The ST spends the whole lesson working on her own at the front doing paper-work. The bilingual EAL teacher goes around to various students. She disciplines the Turkish students both close-up and across the room, first in Turkish and then in English. She jokes with them and calms them down: 'sakın ol, saçmalama' ('calm down, don't be so silly!').

At the end of the lesson one of the Turkish boys picks up the homework that the others have to do. He says to the ST, 'What's that, Miss?' She says, 'homework, but not for you'. He only hears homework and takes it away.

This example shows the ST as distinguishing clearly between what she perceives her role to be and that of the bilingual EAL teacher. Although she could involve herself in the language needs of the bilingual students she chooses not to. She is unable to impart the curriculum herself and so she passes the responsibility over to the EAL teacher. The support role of the EAL teacher, thus, becomes very large indeed, and in fact she takes over many of the roles of the ST. One possibility would be for a role reversal to be implemented in which the ST played an EAL support role. However, the ST here chooses to withdraw completely.

Withdrawal Modes of Collaboration

Withdrawal was used in all three schools involved in the research for this book. I have included withdrawal as a mode of collaboration as in all instances it required STs and EAL teachers to collaborate although this was done in differing degrees.

Temporary withdrawal

As shown in Figure 3.5, this withdrawal occurs for only part of the lesson and is agreed upon by both teachers. Either one may suggest that the students are taken out temporarily to work on a particular skill.

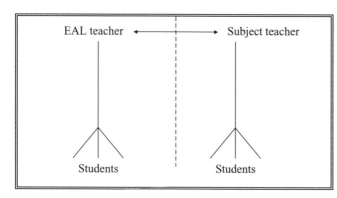

Figure 3.5 Temporary withdrawal with teachers informing one another of materials covered

Vignette 5
Year 8, English

The EAL teacher and myself go into 8P to withdraw four students from their English class. They are very reluctant to leave. Two are Vietnamese, and the other two girls are Turkish. In particular, the two Turkish girls are resentful about leaving. This is especially evident when they hear their form singing 'happy birthday' to their tutor.

We push two tables together. They group themselves as far away from the EAL teacher as possible. Before the reading starts she talks about the using the library – if there is one near them, do they use it? Do they listen to tapes? She talks about study skills, getting help from others, their teachers, watching English TV, etc. The EAL teacher then gets them to talk about their books and read a little passage from each. When they struggle she asks one of the students who is sitting next to them to help. This gives them conflicting tasks because they have also been told to read their own book silently. She praises them for their reading strategies – continuing to the end of the sentence even when they don't know a word and then going back to it. She praises all of them for their reading. She tells them it has improved. They respond well to this praise – smiling openly. There is a discussion about reading aloud, initiated by one of the Turkish-speaking girls who says she finds it much more difficult to read aloud than to read by herself. The EAL teacher agrees with her, but says sometimes it is good to hear how the word should be said. The EAL teacher says that everyone has problems reading aloud and uses herself and me as examples of people who can't pronounce or understand everything we read.

Both teachers agreed that it was a good idea to take the students out of the class so that they could get more individual help from a teacher. Back inside the mainstream class the other students were doing the same activity, that is reading, although they were doing this silently.

Permanent withdrawal: Disapplication from national curriculum subject, with EAL instruction

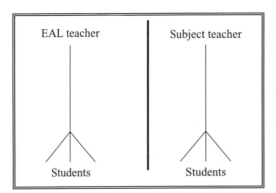

Figure 3.6 Permanent withdrawal – teachers not in discussion about materials and curriculum covered. Students disapplied from subject examination

This kind of withdrawal occurred in only one of the schools. In this school, bilingual children were withdrawn from the subject area of English because it was felt to be too difficult for them. Although the children were withdrawn, there was no other curriculum in place for them, and this led the EAL teachers to feel resentful towards the STs, who they felt should be providing this additional material. In such withdrawal classes, the EAL teachers either introduced their own material, which tended to come from EFL textbooks for teenagers, or they developed work around what they knew of the national curriculum for English. In Vignettes 6(a) and 6(b), I present an example of both. Each is an example of the same bilingual EAL teacher working with the same group of students. Vignette 6(a) shows the bilingual EAL teacher working within the English subject curriculum. He is working on an activity that they would be expected to do had they stayed in the mainstream class.

The students in this class responded well to being able to use their first language to express themselves. If this was the aim of the lesson, the class was a success. However, the bilingual EAL teacher seemed to have mixed aims. The first aim was focused on encouraging students to use their first language to express themselves. The second was on the teaching of specific English vocabulary to allow them to complete a key stage 4 English-speaking task. The bilingual EAL teacher felt uncomfortable about using the first language for teaching the curriculum.

Vignette 6(a)
Year 10, English

All the pupils in this group are Turkish-speaking and the class is conducted almost totally in Turkish with vocabulary in English being taught through translation. They have written a childhood experience in Turkish and later they will have to translate it with the bilingual EAL teacher's help. One girl starts off by reading her work out to the class. The others listen. At the end, the EAL teacher says how much he liked it. The EAL teacher now comments on the form of the writing (need to make the distinction between village and city, needs paragraphs). Fatoş seems really pleased that it has been well received.

Now the bilingual EAL teacher goes around the class asking if they have done the writing and how much they have written. He tells them if this is enough. Now he tells them about the need to write in English. All of this is done in Turkish. The theme now becomes: what they did this morning. He gives examples in Turkish, but writes key English words on the board. Students have to use these words. They start. Some obviously find it easier than others. One girl who I helped could not get started at all. The atmosphere is very quiet and hard-working.

The teacher now sets homework. They must do the same, but write what they do in the evenings. Again key words are written on the board.

In this lesson, Turkish was really valued, and the students clearly felt this also.

Instead, it only seemed acceptable if supporting the learning of English. This issue is developed further in Chapters 9 and 10.

The second example of permanent withdrawal shows a situation in which the bilingual EAL teacher was responsible for the curriculum. We see the bilingual EAL teacher following an EFL textbook.

Vignette 6(b)
Year 10, English

This week a Somali girl has been moved out of this withdrawal English class, leaving only the bilingual Turkish students present again. She has been moved into another withdrawal class which is more mixed, but a younger year.

Before class starts the bilingual EAL teacher complains that it is difficult to teach a double period when the mainstream teacher has not provided any material.

The class unfolds in the following way. There are lots of comings and goings. The bilingual EAL teacher waits for things to settle down. He has chosen to use the EFL text *Hotline*. The students have to copy the text into books because it is too expensive to write on the photocopies. They listen to a conversation on the tape. This is very very simple. They listen two or three times. The bilingual EAL teacher writes missing words on the board. The girls read one sentence each. This is too easy for them.

There is then a similar exercise. Instructions are in English and Turkish. The students are working hard. The bilingual EAL teacher comments, 'Look how hard you are working'. One of the students finds it surprising too!

The EAL teacher now moves on to setting up the next exercise, which he does incorrectly. He says he has not had time to prepare and apologizes a lot. Towards the end of this part of the lesson, he writes homework on the board. Students now change activity and start reading a story. They have been working on this story for several weeks. One student summarizes the story so far in English. The teacher translates in Turkish. Another student reads, and says afterwards to herself that she didn't understand anything. Teacher questions are in English, then translated into Turkish. The girls answer in Turkish.

In an after-class discussion the teacher said he felt this was a bad lesson. I agreed with him! The problem was that it did not seem to be focused on either appropriate second-language instruction – in terms of the students' level – or on developing literacy in relation to the English curriculum. Students were already competent at making requests, etc. in situations that required formulaic daily English.

Some very focused work was done in withdrawal situations, but as the EAL teachers themselves warn, unless there is a curriculum already in place, withdrawal can offer a non-stimulating atmosphere.

ESL option class

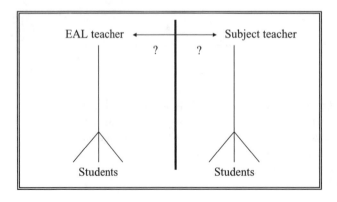

Figure 3.7
EAL option class

This option had a slot on the timetable for students in years 10 and 11. The rationale behind it was to allow students to bring the work they were doing in other curriculum exam subjects to the option where they could get help from the EAL teachers. They have dropped one examination subject to take the option.

Vignette 7
Year 10, EAL option

There were approximately eight students in the class and all had brought their own work to do, although some were much more inclined to do it than others. They sat in friendship groups. A group of five Turkish students worked together at the end table. Two other Turkish students sat on another table and did not interact with the others. A stage 1 Vietnamese boy sat on his own. The EAL teacher asked me to help him, which I did for the hour. We worked on the alphabet and using dictionaries. We worked well together and both of us were very happy to see each other around the school later on. The EAL teacher thanked me and pointed out how hard it was when there was only her in the room. It was obvious how much attention a stage 1 student needs in order to feel helped. It was very rewarding to be able to do this.

The ESL option like the withdrawal situation found in Vignette 7, does not have its own curriculum and was set up as a support service to students in their exam years. The option, therefore, works when students bring their own work and does not when they are not prepared. There appeared to be little liason between EAL and ST teachers.

Language induction programme

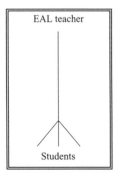

Two of the schools ran an induction programme for newly arrived bilingual children. This induction ranged in duration from half a term to one term, and children missed their afternoon curriculum classes for three days a week while they attended an intensive language course in 'survival school English'. As well as English instruction, the aim was to help orientate children into how British schools operate.

One of the aims of the induction class is to provide a transition into the mainstream when they first arrive.

Figure 3.8 Language induction programme

Vignette 8
Mixed years, EAL induction

There are six students in this class, four are Turkish-speaking and the other two are half-brothers from Bangladesh. The EAL teacher starts by returning the students' homework. Now she goes through her regular routine of, 'Take your jacket off and put it over your chair, and put your bag under your chair. Take your equipment out of your bag – pen, pencil, rubber, ruler, folder, diary, dictionary.'

Now the EAL teacher encourages them, 'All of you are managing quite nicely and should be able to do well with a bit of help in your classes. Ayşe, you are finding it hard. You must read and write words. Find out what they mean.' From this she starts to talk about study skills. 'Who watches English TV? If you watch Turkish TV, what do you watch? Are you watching the news? It is very important that you know what is going on in the world when the teacher asks the class.' One of the students interrupts,

S: Miss, they are showing Kurdish and Turkish dead people.
EAL: Is that what they are showing on the news? Can anyone tell me what is happening?
S: In Turkey, Miss?
EAL: No, not in Turkey, in a lot of Europe?
S: Hitler, Miss.
EAL: No, that was a long time ago . . .

Again she switches back to study skills:

EAL: You need to talk to people in English. You need to read and listen to tapes at the same time. You should also read books in Turkish and Bengali to make sure that your own language gets better. You should read more difficult things than you can read in English . . . What should you do in class if you don't understand? You can write things in Turkish, it helps you to keep things in your head.

After this reminder about study skills, she moves on to a more interactive lesson on the family.

Chapter Summary

This chapter has presented literature on teacher collaboration and change. It has looked at how EAL teachers work in support and withdrawal modes. I have argued that although a lot of good work is done in these modes, these kinds of relationships tend to place the work EAL teachers do on the periphery within the school. Other much more powerful discourses dominate the secondary school classroom, and the work done in support mode through facilitation appears to count for little at the school and wider societal discursive levels. In chapters 7 and 9 we turn to look at two kinds of provision that appear to address bilingual students needs by more clearly fitting into or challenging school participant structures. These are partnership teaching and bilingual pedagogies. In Chapter 7 we look at teaching partnerships as a mode of collaboration. We will see that despite some problems, this mode continues to offer hope in bringing about the kind of institutional change necessary to make the mainstream secondary school classroom inclusive.

Chapter 7
Teaching Partnerships

Introduction

This chapter extends from Chapter 6 in its aim to describe different forms of collaboration between teachers. The focus here is on teacher partnerships which are defined as:

> Pairs or groups of teachers working together inside and outside the classroom to develop a curriculum responsive to **all** pupils' language needs and abilities. (bold in the original) (Bourne & McPake, 1991: 1)

> Partnership teaching is a term which implies attempts to construct specific conditions for more than one teacher to support pupils' learning. (Levine, 1990: 30)

The literature discussed in Chapter 6 is also relevant to issues raised here. As in Chapter 6, I use vignettes to illustrate different examples of the partnership mode. I also draw on interview data and some classroom transcripts. Towards the end of the chapter, we look at the difficulties which partnering teachers face from within their institutions.

Partnership Modes of Collaboration

EAL teachers in the partnership mode of collaboration target a specific subject area. This results in greater timetable continuity than for those EAL teachers working in support modes. In the vignettes presented, we will see that some of the advantages of partnership teaching include: the possibility of a more democratic classroom as teachers and students negotiate; a greater variety of aims incorporating some language-learning as well as subject-learning; materials developed by teaching partners tend to be recycled and become part of the department's bank of materials, whereas material developed by EAL teachers outside of partnerships may be lost or never used again; teachers feel they are learning from one another.

Only two pairings of STs and EAL teachers in the three schools described themselves as being in a partnership teaching situation. The remaining eight EAL teachers described themselves as being in support mode. The two EAL teachers who were

132

in a partnership were working with newly qualified STs. This is a common arrangement and has been noted elsewhere (Gardner, in press; Lee, 1997). As Alison Lee's work on language specialists in universities shows (1997: 76), it is not uncommon to find 'experienced and highly institutionally literate literacy specialists' working intensively with more junior staff'.

However, although the EAL teachers were more experienced than their ST partners, there was always an atmosphere of both teachers learning from one another. They shared educational beliefs and principles. EAL teachers in partnerships see themselves in a balancing act of finding a person they can work with, developing good teaching practice for all children in the class and making sure that this good practice is disseminated to a wider audience in the school.

Primarily, the success of partnership teaching is in the building of shared repertoires and the extension of new knowledge. Teachers working in partnerships liaised with one another about students' needs and between them were able to build up a more sophisticated portrait of the students they taught. They were also the ones likely to be engaged in personal conversations with each other and to consult before, during and after class on how the lessons went, on what could be done to improve them and what to do next. In this way, these partnerships can be said to extend beyond the classroom to further afield in the school. They often resulted in the EAL teacher temporarily 'joining' the department with which they were working (however, the reverse did not seem to be true, that is, STs did not join EAL departments for their meeting). This meant that EAL teachers could belong to two reference groups in the school: the EAL group and subject department. Teachers in partnership sat with their teaching partner and his or her department colleagues in staff meetings or in staff briefings at the beginning of the day. Moreover, they often ate lunch together and sat together during break-time. Thus, partnership teaching encouraged the breaking down of compartments which make up secondary schools.

Partnership teaching

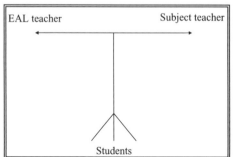

Figure 3.9 Partnership teaching

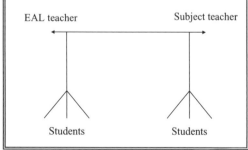

Figure 3.10 Partnership teaching with teachers targeting different students

In Vignette 9 the two teachers worked together in two areas of technology: food and construction. In the food area the EAL teacher was as familiar with the subject as the ST, whose particular area of expertise was in construction.

Vignette 9
Year 10, food technology

The EAL teacher started off the lesson by taking the register, sorting out materials, and introducing the theme. She told the students what the two teachers wanted to cover in the course of the lesson. Both teachers say either 'we want you to' or 'Mr X and I want you to'. During the class-fronted instruction, the teachers come in and out of each other's instruction time, adding information or assisting and joking with one another. They also ask one another directly for help. This was an equal lesson in terms of teacher-fronted instruction. Perhaps this was because both teachers felt relatively comfortable with the subject area. This was a double lesson which spanned the break. During the break, one of the teachers, this time the ST, went off to get coffee for the EAL teacher, while the latter stayed and chatted to the children who wanted to stay in the class.

This short vignette highlights several issues of partnership teaching. First, the teachers refer to one another as joint experts, as opposed to the ST being the only expert in the class. Second, the teachers managed to blur their roles. Both were engaged in subject teaching and concerned with linguistic sensitivity. And finally, as an outcome of their teaching, they became friends and chose to spend their break-time in one another's company, where they continued to discuss their collaboration.

In the second mode of partnership collaboration the teachers have the same features of collaboration, but tend to work more with targeted groups of students. Importantly, in this form of partnership it is not necessarily the EAL teacher who works with the targeted bilingual children and the ST with the others. The teachers may allow the students to be self-selecting about the teacher with whom they wish to work.

Vignette 10
Year 8, geography

The ST teacher starts the class with 'Now what Miss Smith and I will do is help you. . . . We'll spilt you up into two and I will take one group and Miss Smith will take the other. . . .' Again, the two teachers are using 'we'.
The teachers are doing the same activities. Both teachers are sorting out material for students. They make eye contact a lot.

The ST has more students approaching her. The EAL teacher works with a white girl at the beginning of the class. The ST does administration work such as writing a slip when a student wishes to leave the class and dealing with visitors to the class. When the ST leaves there is no difference in the class noise level and the class do not seem to have noticed.

When she returns the two teachers spend time at the front answering students' questions.

When the bell goes the two teachers are at the front. The ST is doing class-fronted discipline. She is the one that dismisses students individually.

Both teachers move around the class and approach all groups easily. However, they also have groups with whom they stay longer. These are either self-selecting groups (the teachers tell me at interview that some students get on with them more easily than others) or the EAL teacher works longer with the targeted bilingual students.

The teachers enjoy one another's company, both in and out of the classroom, and can often be found together in the staffroom.

Teachers working in partnership appear more aware of the need to position themselves equally in class and actively seek to share their responsibilities. They think through their various roles and how these might be perceived. There are possibilities of learning from one another. One ST describes his work with his partner EAL teacher in the following way:

> 100 I tend to be up front at the beginning of lessons. I tend to like to have a couple of minutes to actually say what I want them to do in that lesson. Noreen does it as well. I think she's doing it more now which is good. Now it's more joint but at the beginning it tended to be more me. I think it was because Noreen wasn't sure where she stood on that. I think she's more confident now. She can say what she wants now. . . . I think it is important at the beginning that they know what is expected of them and what the goals are for this lesson. I tend to have more responsibility in the instruction, but now Noreen has been through the year and she's got more confidence, she takes over and does some things. Perhaps in the food area Noreen takes more control . . . probably because she feels more confident with the content and I feel less confident, and the work is more hers than mine in the food. We've worked it out together but because she has more capability within the area of food, more of the ideas have come from her. (A5)

His partner EAL teacher shares similar views.

> 101 This year I feel a bit more confident with the content material. I mean, like last year half of the stuff was so new that it meant my learning the skills as well on the trot and I was literally at times just keeping ahead of

the students. . . . I think that's a good learning experience for me. I can actually empathize with what the students are going through when I'm trying to learn it new as well, I'm trying to learn new skills from that teacher in the same situation and I'm trying to sort of elicit from the teacher what it is he wants us to do and I've actually been in a position to say to the teacher that I didn't understand what we're actually meant to do. You know, I've got no experience of this subject, could you just run through or could you explain so and so. Afterwards, that teacher has said to me that was really useful to him to have that feedback because you get to a certain stage with every subject, particularly the visual ones where you just take for granted so much of the vocabulary and so much of the explanation, that you don't realize, so it has been useful for them (the STs) having someone in my position in the classroom, it's taught them a lot about how to visualise things. (A1)

Teaching partnerships can provide opportunities for professional development for both teachers. In many ways, we see partner teachers merging their different knowledge to produce a new, extended and cohesive knowledge. Through such sharing, partner teachers produce new communities of practice and extend their networks throughout the school. Through their teacher collaboration the boundaries of subject knowledge are pervaded and the networks which form around subject expertise become less exclusive. The sharing of knowledge becomes easier and more fluid. One example of this is the willingness to teach new subject curriculum knowledge as described by both ST and EAL teacher in Quotes 100–1. Another example is the ST's openness to taking on language issues in the classroom. In the following extract, an EAL teacher is describing her partner teacher's attitude to language.

102 Adrian is very much interested in the linguistic side of what he is doing and accepts that there is a linguistic side to what he's doing and the cliché 'everyone's an English language teacher', and he takes that seriously, as I do, and in fact I think sometimes he's quite glad for his own benefit to have my second opinion on stuff, because his own use of English at times lets him down, and he knows that. He often gets kids to spell things for him so I think, you know, it's the atmosphere that everyone is learning at the same time and I like that. (A1)

The ST himself had something similar to say:

103 I think it (language instruction) should be joint. I think I should get involved in language instruction as well. Perhaps because I taught English as a foreign language and am bilingual I do know some of the pitfalls. I have lived in countries where I can't speak the language and I know the situation, what it's like to be in a room when someone is giving a lecture and you don't understand much of what they're saying. (A5)

This ST is aware of the necessity of a focus on language not only because of his relationship in the partnership mode of collaboration, but also because of his prior experience as a language teacher and as an English/Spanish bilingual himself. He is looking for overlaps in the two teachers' knowledge. Teachers in partnership actively work to present an agreed and common agenda to the class. In the following interview transcript we see how one ST described this process.

> 104
>
> **AC:** Do you, do you really think that the children see you as equal?
>
> **ST:** No, no, they do know, but there is not a stigma of Susan talking to somebody.
>
> **AC:** How do they know?
>
> **ST:** Because they know I am a humanities teacher and they know that Susan is a language-support teacher so that is how they know. But at the beginning we actually put an awful lot of effort in with things like they were coming up to me to get their toilet notes signed and I would say go to Miss Smith. And we made an awful lot of effort in the beginning to make sure that in the lesson, that at the end of the lesson we both said you have done very well. We would both dismiss, so you know we made a huge effort at the beginning so that they knew, and there was one incident at the beginning where I was on an inset and most of the year group were out and there were four kids in so she sat with them and they were playing cards and one of them got a bit naughty and Susan sort of corrected him, tried to control him and he said to her 'you are not my bloody teacher, you know, Miss Potter is my teacher, you're not', and she told me about it and we both went to him and we said to him: 'And you are not coming back into our lesson you know until you have apologized and XYZ.' And um he actually did try to come in when Susan was away once and I said no, you are not coming in until you do and so we were quite fastidious about doing that sort of thing which I think helped, but they do still, because I am a humanities teacher. (C7)

In this extract we see how partnership teachers are consciously aware of the need to break down the structures which get built up around support and subject teaching. These teachers worked at presenting themselves in particular ways in the classroom and attempted to stand up against the inequalities that have developed around support work.

Despite the role and relationship differences in partnership teaching that teachers worked to establish with one another, and which marked partnership modes as distinct from support and withdrawal modes, children could still distinguish between the status of the two teachers. The following extract is a longer version of the classroom transcript with which this book began. The ST here is the same person as in Extract 104, where the ST discussed how she and her partner EAL teacher work to present a common and united front to troublesome students.

In Extract 105 the ST is working with three students who debate with her what constitutes a 'real teacher':

105
S1: Miss, what have you got that for (referring to the tape recorder)?
ST: Because she wants to erm record what I am saying and what Miss Smith is saying and then she can play it back and she can see if there is a difference between the two of us.
S1: There is.
S2: Yeah, I think there should be a difference.
ST: Why?
S3: Miss, you're the better teacher aren't you?
S2: So we can see it in different ways.
ST: Say what you mean?
S2: XXX (inaudible)
ST: So you mean it gives you a bit of variety.
S2: But Miss, teachers might have different ideas about work and like.
ST: Hold on a second. (to the whole class) Er, it's getting far too noisy in here.
S2: I said like if I don't understand and Miss Smith explains to me and I still don't understand and I call you over and you tell me a different thing, like two different things.
ST: So we see it from two different ways you mean?
S3: But you're the proper teacher aren't you?
ST: Well no. We are both proper teachers.
S3: She's like a help.
ST: No, that's not true.
S3: That's what it's like because when you are both in, you are like the proper one.
S1: Yeah.
ST: Yeah, but sometimes Miss Smith takes the lesson doesn't she?
S1: Yeah, but that's because ...
ST: When I am not ...
S2: Yeah that's because she is still a proper teacher because Miss Smith takes class as well. She still qualifies as a teacher. (C7)

In this extract we see the importance that both the ST and the students give to whole class subject-based teaching: **'Yeah, but sometimes Miss Smith takes the lesson doesn't she?'**; **'Yeah that's because she is still a proper teacher because Miss Smith takes class as well. She still qualifies as a teacher.'** 'Taking the class' is what makes a real teacher according to the interactants in the extract.

In another example, we see an EAL teacher criticized for making decisions in a subject area which was not her own. In the incident reported below, we see Noreen and Adrian, the two partner teachers in school A, come up against institutional structures that block Noreen from making joint decisions with Adrian about curriculum content in the area of food technology. Adrian is the ST assigned to this subject, but by his own admission he describes Noreen as more of an expert in this area than himself. His own expertise is in construction technology. The following is drawn from my field notes:

Vignette 11

When I first arrive at the school today, Noreen (the EAL teacher) is upset. She tells me about two incidents which are the cause for this. The first one concerns Helen, the head of technology, the department in which she is supporting and does partnership teaching. Helen challenged her yesterday about what she and Adrian (her ST partner in construction and food technology) had been doing in the food lessons. Helen told them that they should be following her syllabus (sausage rolls instead of vegetarian samosas; fruit loaf instead of barbecue). This discussion escalated into Helen saying to Noreen, 'That is what happens when non-subject specialists get involved'. This obviously hurt Noreen a lot and she, along with two technology teachers, decided to take the matter further and discuss it with Helen's line manager, by going first through the deputy head. Later that morning, Noreen heard from Adrian that their line manager had asked to see the two technology teachers but not herself. She asked him to ask the line manager why this was so. Later, Noreen explained to me that she does not enjoy working with Helen, she does not have any opportunity for input into the lesson.

The second incident involved one of her partnership teaching classes – year 11 construction – which erupted the day before and got out of control. Noreen felt that one of the male students had threatened her with intimidating behaviour. She had disciplined him for his involvement in pushing over one of the bilingual children – Zyneb – while she was doing up her shoelace. Ciğdem – a Turkish-speaking child who is bilingually fluent in English – got involved when Noreen was trying to sort it out. She challenged Noreen's authority by saying: 'Who do you think you are? You can't tell us what to do. You are only here to teach <u>them</u>.' (A1)

This incident greatly upset the teacher involved. Both the head of department and student who questioned her authority did so by challenging the very heart of her role as an equal classroom teacher. Not only was she challenged individually, but the school's structures enforced this by not including her in discussions around the incident.

Partnership Talk

In this chapter I have argued that teachers in partnership are more centrally involved in classroom and school work than those working in support and withdrawal in terms of the roles the teachers assume. In this section I look more particularly at partner teachers' talk in class.

Partnership teachers often referred to one another in class. In doing so, they endorsed one another's work and rightful place in the classroom. The following extracts come from the classroom transcripts of one partnership pair in school A:

> 106
> **ST:**   (to the whole class) Now, I'd like to do practical work and I know Miss Harrington wanted you to do practical work. She was more forceful than me and she won out. (A5)

> 107
> **EAL:**   (to individual students) Oh no! These are not going to come out as they should are they? I might ask Mr Holly to see if he can go and butter up the staff. Get you an orange juice. (A1)

> 108
> **S:**   All right, then. Where is the machine?
> **ST:**   Just behind Miss Harrington? (A5)

> 109
> **EAL:**   (explaining to an individual student) If Mr Holly is around, yeah, you can work in the class. Most lunch times I am actually in the other building, that is the problem. Or if I am here I am doing homework club. (A1)

In the above examples, each teacher presents the other as problem solver/decision maker or as an equal presence in the class. Other instances can be found in Chapter 5, where examples are given of teachers talking to one another informally in class. The evidence from these transcripts shows that teachers working in partnership mode know their students better and, together, are more able to accommodate students' needs.

However, even in partnership pairings we have seen that the way subject curriculum is taught by the two teachers positions the two teachers differently within the class. EAL teachers in partnership do attempt to engage in whole-class teaching in subject content, but they still do it less than STs. As the ST in Quote 100 pointed out, his partner EAL teacher did more teacher-fronted work as she became more comfortable with the subject area. In the same quote, the ST also mentions how he likes to do some whole-class teaching at the beginning of the lesson. I have shown the importance of the whole-class lesson introduction and lesson summary for a number of subject teachers. The point being made here is that the IYS interaction pattern, described in Chapter 4, is often not used by the EAL teacher and, therefore, marks them out as discursively different from the STs, who make this a routine formula in their classrooms.

Interestingly, EAL teachers in both partnership and support mode follow similar interaction patterns when working with individual and small groups of students. They are more willing to ask questions and do not move so quickly to provide answers as STs.

In Extracts 110 and 111 I contrast the EAL teacher's and the ST's interactions with two students. The students are different but the topic of the conversation is the same (using strong glue for doing practical work), and both teachers are working with the same class in the same lesson. In the following extract the EAL teacher is working with a bilingual student learning English:

110
EAL: Let's go outside. (they go outside) We have got to go outside because this is . . . (pauses to let student fill in gap)?
S: Smelly.
EAL: Smelly, and it might make you go phew! Like that, right. I don't know which end you want to use, but probably that end there. And you need a little bit at a time to put on the back, OK? Which side, are you going to do that side, yeah?
S: Yeah.
EAL: Put a tiny little bit on as you go along the edge. Is it working? The other side, yeah, that's it, like that. The thing is that you have to leave this, you have to leave it for a couple of minutes and it goes tacky, you know like? (shows with her hands)
S: Yeah.
EAL: You know tacky, and when it has gone tacky you can stick it down. I don't think it has to cover it but just do the corners. That corner. There is some more. It is actually quite dangerous this stuff. Right you have to leave it there now for a few minutes, possibly about five minutes. Just leave it like that, and then you stick it on later, all right?
S: Yeah.
EAL: Let's put that back in the cupboard. Come back inside, I don't think anyone is going to touch it. (they go back inside) (A1)

In this extract the EAL teacher weaves vocabulary learning with a task. Moreover, this EAL teacher asks lots of questions – comprehension and confirmation checks – to make sure that they are understanding one another. There are commands too, and these are focused on completing the task. However, a language/vocabulary focus is never far behind:

- 'The thing is that you have to leave this, you have to leave it for a couple of minutes and it goes tacky, you know like?'
- 'We have to go outside because this is smelly, and it might make you go phew!'

The aim of completing the task is mitigated by making sure that the student is comprehending the task. However, unlike her colleagues working in support mode, the EAL teacher takes full responsibility for the task. That is, she uses 'I' to 'own' the task. I have argued in Chapters 4 and 5 that in support mode the EAL teachers tend to use passive and modal verbs to distance themselves from task ownership. The EAL teacher in Extract 110, in contrast, uses 'I' to direct the student:

- 'I don't know which end you want to use, but probably that end there.'
- 'I don't think it has to cover it but just do the corners.'
- 'Come back inside, I don't think anyone is going to touch it.'

However, these 'I's are embedded and are also expressed in the negative.

Now let us look at what the ST does when working with a non-targeted child:

111
ST: This is evo-stick. Take it outside to use it, yeah?
S: XXX
ST: You need to draw that? I'd leave it as it is actually.
S: No. There's a line.
ST: Yeah, I know, but people can see it is as line. No problem. Leave it as it is, that's fine.
S: It would be better to cover it.
ST: No, it would be better to leave it. I'm sure.
S: All right.
ST: Yeah? I've got some stuff to put on it actually as well. So get yourself an apron and take it outside because the fumes are really dangerous, come and get, (to other students) mind your backs. Remember to spread it both sides, get an apron on please, remember to spread it both sides with this, yeah? Put it on both sides, yeah?
S: Yeah.
ST: Do it outside please because it will be ... (to another student) Bring your stuff over here. You can't work there, well I can't at least. (A5)

This example of an ST's speech captures many of the points I have been making in this book. First, 'I' is used to stamp the ST's authority on the task. That is, s/he owns the subject and the tasks which s/he sets for its learning:

- 'I'd leave it as it is actually.'
- 'No, it would be better to leave it. I'm sure.'
- 'I've got some stuff to put on it actually as well.'

I would argue that there are qualitative and quantitative differences in the teacher talk displayed in Extracts 110 and 111. The ST uses the imperative voice more and far fewer embedded 'I's. His discourse is confident around his subject knowledge and directing the students through the task. The EAL teacher also 'owns' the task, distinguishing her from the work done in support mode, however she is less assertive around ownership of the task than the ST. The EAL teacher displays a more facilitative pedagogy. She provides building blocks for the student to develop her vocabulary and her subject knowledge through the asking of questions and embedding. Partnership teaching allows EAL teachers to become more fully engaged with the curriculum agenda while honing their skills as scaffolders of learning.

Across the three schools involved in this study, partnerships were rare and difficult to maintain. They received little institutional support to sustain them. Teacher collaboration, and the skills that went with doing it successfully, were not supported by any of three schools. This, I would argue, indirectly reflects a lack of commitment on the government's part to finance policy change in the form of teaching partnerships to make the mainstream classroom more amenable to diversity. It also reflects a wider societal discourse on education which promotes the transmission of subject-learning in secondary schools. Clearly, transmission of subject knowledge is key in secondary school education. However, our classrooms are very diverse and other pedagogic skills and knowledge are also important if we are to respond to this diversity of need. The skills and knowledge which go with teaching and learning in small group interactions and with meeting individuals could be better supported in key policy documents.

Chapter Summary

The 10 modes of collaboration described in this chapter and Chapter 6 cannot be described as discrete. However, they do reflect data patterns. Moreover, all of the collaboration modes encouraged both good and bad examples of lessons, as the teachers involved would themselves point out. However, it was only in the partnership teaching mode of collaboration that the EAL teachers were likely to be viewed as having a similar status to that of the STs. This was primarily because the ST in this collaborative mode valued the aims of the EAL teacher as equal to their own, and similarly the EAL teacher valued those of the ST. In fact, they shared both classroom objectives and responsibility for the children. These differences between support and partnership modes of collaboration are summarized in Table 2.

This chapter and Chapter 6 have outlined the various teaching relationships between EAL teachers and subject teachers in secondary school classes. It has been argued that partnership modes of collaboration allow teachers to go some way towards transforming the mainstream classroom into a place where children have access to equal educational opportunities through a recognition of their individual needs. However, Chapter 6 has shown that support and withdrawal modes of collaboration also have their place within schools. The argument I have made is that, generally, partnerships allow for language concerns to gain a more central place on school agendas, whereas support modes tend to limit EAL teachers' abilities to influence school policies and practices around the needs of linguistic minority pupils. However, support and withdrawal work allows for intensive scaffolding interactions in mainstream contexts. It is not that there is anything fundamentally

Table 2 Partnership and support modes of collaboration

Partnership mode	Support mode
• Same aims as ST.	• Different/additional aims from ST.
• Exchange of ideas.	• Advice is one way.
• Teachers play a greater number of roles and these are more fluid.	• Teachers' roles are fixed.
• EAL teacher targets subject area.	• EAL teacher targets students.
• Teachers refer to one another as joint experts in the classroom.	• Both teachers refer to ST as expert.
• Teachers are friends.	
• Materials developed are reused.	• Materials developed by EAL teachers are lost.
• Teachers interact with whole class.	• Teachers target individual students.
• Continuity in timetabling.	• Lack of continuity in timetabling.
• EAL teacher share a sense of achievement for students' success.	• EAL teachers feel less responsibility for subject achievement.
• EAL works directly to the exam system.	• EAL teacher works through the ST within the exam system.

wrong with support work; it is that only particular teachers do it and the pedagogies they use do not have equal status with the whole class transmission
pedagogies and discourses which subject teaching draws upon. If STs were able
to get more involved in facilitative and individual teaching and learning interactions, and to see this kind of work endorsed by government policy, then the
importance of facilitative pedagogies would be more convincing for all classroom
participants.

Chapter 8

Content-based Language-learning and Language-based Content-learning: Learning a Second Language in the Mainstream Classroom

Introduction

This chapter considers the possibilities of the mainstream secondary school classroom in terms of the opportunities it provides for the acquisition of English and the learning of subject content. In doing so, it looks at how subject and EAL teachers use various resources to deliver on the dual and overlapping aims of language-learning and cognitive development. Specifically, it looks at the possibilities of a focus on language, form and meaning within the mainstream subject classroom. A discussion is developed that considers what we mean by a focus on language within curriculum-focused classrooms. An argument is made that 'language work' must extend beyond a focus on form (grammar) and the teaching of key symbols (vocabulary). Instead, a language focus must capture the ability to understand the role language plays (along with other signs and symbols) in the creation of meanings and knowledge in school life.

In keeping with the theme of this book, these ideas are embedded in a discussion of the collaboration between EAL and subject teachers. The chapter is divided into the following sections: the rationale for language-learning in the mainstream classroom is reviewed by visiting the literatures of content-based language teaching and input/interactionist second-language acquisition; we then move to focus on research data through which the possibilities of learning English in mainstream secondary school classrooms are discussed; and a specific example of text adaptation is given at the end of the chapter. This example demonstrates how an EAL teacher adapts a text previously produced by an ST. It considers how changes in language impact directly on the construction of subject knowledge and explores the possibilities of how such adaptation allows a focus on language.

Content-based Language Instruction

There is a growing literature which argues the benefits of content-based language instruction (Adamson, 1993; Brinton *et al.*, 1989; Freeman & Freeman, 1992; Kessler, 1992; Mohan, 1986; Mohan *et al.*, 2001; Richard-Amato & Snow, 1992). However, as Davison and Williams point out, 'Definitions of language and content integration in the ESL literature are complicated by the diverse theoretical origins and orientations of the field.' (2001: 54; see also Valdés, 2004). The various models of content-based instruction such as theme-based language instruction, sheltered content instruction and adjunct language instruction (see Brinton *et al.*, 1989 for a full summary), all describe the benefits to be gained by integrating content with language-teaching aims: '. . . content-based instruction aims at eliminating the artificial separation between language instruction and subject matter classes which exist in most educational settings' (Brinton *et al.*, 1989: 2). Similarly, Mohan (1986: 18) argues that the dual aims of language- and content-learning can be met in the content-based classroom:

> Language learning in the communicative environment of the *content* classroom furthers the goals of language teaching by offering a context for language. It provides language use in a context of communication about important subject matter. Language learning in the *language* classroom can further the goals of content teaching by offering learners help with the language of the thinking processes and the structure or shape of content. (italic in the original)

Content-based language instruction is considered to be beneficial to second-language learners because it provides students with meaningful content that is input rich because of its relevance to students' lives. However, even proponents of content-based language instruction are aware that factors, other than rich input, are also important in the second-language learning process. For example, Adamson (1993) points out that background knowledge (such as previous knowledge of a subject area, knowledge of how the school system works, etc.), pragmatic knowledge (such as communication skills) and language proficiency are all factors which affect learning language through content and vice versa. Adamson (1993: 114) argues that students need to develop academic competence which he describes as amounting to,

> (1) the ability to use a combination of linguistic, pragmatic, and background knowledge to reach a basic understanding of content material; (2) the ability to use appropriate strategies (which vary according to the degree of basic understanding) to enhance knowledge of content material; and (3) the ability to use appropriate strategies to complete academic assignments with less than a full understanding of the content material.

Of course, all children need academic competence to do well at secondary school. Indeed, others have argued that the very basis of secondary level education is to teach students to achieve such a competence. That is, formal schooling is about building concepts through language to allow children to make increasingly sophisticated generalizations (Scribner & Cole, 1973). Scribner and Cole (1973: 555) define formal education as:

> any process of cultural transmission that is (i) organized deliberately to fulfill the specific purpose of transmission, (ii) extracted from the manifold of daily life, placed in a special setting and carried out according to specific routines, and (iii) made the responsibility of the larger social group.

Bilingual children find themselves in a context where they must use a language that they are learning to learn a subject that is new to them. That is, they must simultaneously learn a new language and the academic competence that other children are also there to learn.

The work of Jim Cummins has considered this process in detail (1988, 1991, 2000; see Baker, 2001 for further examples and clarification). Cummins has made a distinction between basic interpersonal communicative skills (BICS) and cognitive/academic language proficiency (CALP). BICS is said to occur in context-embedded contexts, which allow the learner to make meaning from clues in the context. An example of this is body language and the use of non-verbal visuals. CALP, on the other hand, is said to occur in context-reduced academic situations. The language of secondary school classrooms and the teaching of, say, analysis or hypothesis testing, would be an example of language that has been 'disembedded' and abstracted. For

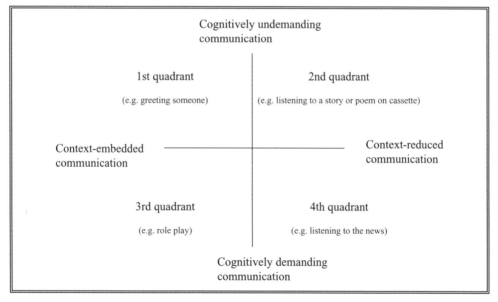

Figure 4 Cummins' quadrants

Source: Baker, 2001: 172

Cummins, it often takes one or two years for a child to acquire context-embedded second language fluency, but five to seven years or more to acquire context-reduced fluency (in Baker, 2001). Cummins' theory is often represented diagrammatically (see Figure 4). Cummins' quadrants intersect learning in context-embedded and context-reduced communicative contexts with cognitively undemanding and cognitively demanding tasks (1988, 1991, 2000) and offers the teacher a pedagogic framework considering instructional implications. Cummins (1991, 2000) has also helpfully listed how other scholars have made these distinctions:

> Vygotsky (1986) – spontaneous and scientific concepts
> Bruner (1975) – communicative and analytic competence
> Olson (1977) – utterance and text
> Donaldson (1978) – embedded and disembedded thought and language
> Bereiter and Scardamalia (1981) – conversation and composition
> Snow *et al.* (1991) – contextualized and decontextualized language
> Mohan (1986) – practical and theoretical
> Snow (1991) – contextualized and decontextualized.
>
> (1991: 71; 2000: Ch. 3)

It is an awareness of the importance of this distinction that Cummins makes between context embedded and context reduced which is at the cornerstone of EAL and bilingual EAL teachers' work in the mainstream classroom. Either through use of the first language, or from scaffolding language and thought through the second language, EAL teachers assist in creating learning opportunities for bilingual students. A large part of an EAL teacher's expertise is in teaching academic skills and advising STs on how this can be achieved in the context-reduced environment of the school. Already an excellent literature exists giving suggestions to practitioners on how best to achieve this (see Gibbons, 1993, 2002; Gravelle, 1996). Indeed much of this practice-oriented literature speaks of the importance of scaffolding pedagogies and combining language and curriculum aims.

However, Cummins' original conceptualization of CALP has been criticized for presenting a view of academic language as 'abstract'. This is problematic not only theoretically, as it could be argued that no discourse exists without a context (Gee, 1999), but also pedagogically, because CALP presents academic literacy predominantly as a matter of cognition with the attainment of higher order reasoning skills as the goal. This view is in opposition to one of academic literacy as socially constructed and linked to the standards of the elites (Clark & Ivanič, 1997; Ivanič, 1998, 2004; Street, 1999). According to Valdés (2004: 121):

> Cummins himself (2000) . . . has to some degree moved away from describing academic language abstractly and now describes academic proficiency as 'the extent to which an individual has access to and command of the oral and written academic registers of schooling'.

Another point of importance to Valdés (2004: 123) is:

What I am questioning is whether academic language can, in fact, be taught or learned effectively in the self-contained, hermetic universes of ELL classrooms. I am arguing that in order for students to eventually engage as writers in what Guerra (1997: 252) has called 'the arduous act of struggling with a clash of voices' the classroom must be opened to multiple texts and multiple voices. Students must be encouraged to see themselves as having something to say, as taking part in a dialogue with teachers, with students in their classroom, with students in their school, with members of their communities, and with other writers who have written about issues and questions that intrigue them.

This quote is helpful here as it focuses us on our context. Unlike the 'hermetic universes' of ELL (English language learner) classrooms which Valdés describes in the US context, the bilingual students in the three London schools were not isolated for the most part in withdrawal contexts. Indeed, they were expected to learn academic literacy in their mainstream contexts. EAL teachers, bilingual and non-bilingual, were crucial in this endeavour as they were the ones who were predominantly given the responsibility of helping students move towards academic literacy. We will see in this chapter, and in those that follow, that some STs made few concessions to specifically developing the academic literacies of bilingual students.

My specific intent in this chapter is to describe how the content/language interface is played out by collaborating teachers in the particular context of three London secondary schools. Before we turn to the information gathered it might be helpful to briefly consider another literature which has concerned itself with language teaching in content-focused classrooms.

Language-learning in Content-focused Classrooms

Wong-Fillmore (1991: 52) summarized the major components needed for second-language learning:

(1) *Learners* who realize that they need to learn the target language and are motivated to do so; (2) *speakers of the target language* who know it well enough to provide the learners with access to the language and the help they need for learning it; and (3) a *social setting* which brings learners and target language speakers into frequent enough contact to make the language learning possible. (italic in original)

The mainstream classroom has all of these criteria. However, despite such a rich environment, second language acquisition (SLA) seems to suggest this is not enough. One particular approach to SLA (the input/interactionist research) suggests a focus solely on meaning, such as in the building of concepts, may not leave enough space for second-language learners to focus on the language itself (Harley, 1993; Long, 1983; Musumeci, 1996; Pica, 1995). Increasingly, researchers point out the necessity of the conscious, cognitive side of language-learning, and in doing so, give implicit support to the argument that the process of learning a second language (at least after early adolescence) is different from that of learning the first. That is, the first language may be a 'natural developmental process', which the vast majority of children are able to achieve with relatively little difficulty, but the learning of the second does not show the same fluidity in later adolescence and after. Such a view promotes the argument that language learners should be considered as hypothesis testers and problem-solvers rather than *acquirers* who, being naturally endowed with a language-acquisition device, do little but take in the language data undiluted while filtering it through their language faculties until it takes the target form (White, 1987).

It is clear that all learners need some kind of input to learn a language, whether it be their first or second. Learners need access to the sounds, words and combinations of words that constitute a particular language. When Corder (1967) first introduced the term 'input' as a theoretical construct, however, he meant more than a source of the language itself. Corder's original definition of input spoke more generally of *what is available for learners to select to go in*. Corder's definition points toward what the learner *does* with positive data that s/he receives about the language, not simply what that positive data is made up of. Corder's definition is such, however, that it can be interpreted in many ways. Where each approach to the study of input seems to differ primarily is in how input is taken up by the learner. Increasingly, attention is being paid to the importance of pointing out to learners what is not apparent from language data itself.

Recently scholars have suggested that more direct forms of feedback need to be provided to the learner. That is, learners need to be guided or shown how their language is non-target like. Research literature suggests that learners need to actually *notice* what led to the communication breakdown before they can act on it (Schmidt, 1990; Schmidt & Frota, 1986). Schmidt and Frota argue that the gap between the learners' interlanguage and the target language must be consciously noticed by learners in order for them to acquire target-like forms. Moreover, they also argue that a sole focus on communication and meaning may mean that learners and their interactants do not have the opportunity, time or even inclination to notice this gap. These areas are now being investigated with new attention given to the importance of consciousness in noticing modifications (Long, 1991) and what the negotiation process can and cannot provide (Pica, 1991).

Pica has argued that asking learners to participate in communication and attend to content-learning may result in a lack of opportunity to focus on the grammatical aspects of communicative competence (Pica, 1995: 384). Harley (1993: 251–5) has argued that students and teachers may fail to attend to the language code in analytic activities in content-based communicative classrooms. She argues that the focus on language becomes implicit rather than explicit. Musumeci (1996) found that teachers in content-based language classrooms behaved in the same way as in any subject-focused classrooms. That is, when teachers perceived that students did not understand them, they modified their input but rarely did they get the students to modify theirs. Teachers did not give linguistic feedback, nor were incomplete messages renegotiated. Instead, the teachers took pride in the fact that they were able to understand students' language however inaccurate or opaque. That is, teachers made extraordinary efforts to create meaning from students' output. In this way, Musumeci argues that the teachers carry the linguistic burden of the class. Such is the emphasis on understanding the content in the subject-based classroom that both teachers and students find it difficult to admit to not understanding one another. Musumeci concludes by arguing that creating negotiation opportunities, in which the student and teacher can directly focus on form, is crucial in content-focused classrooms:

> In order for teachers to indicate that they have not understood and students to modify, negotiation cannot be interpreted as repair or imperfect or failed communication, rather, it must be regarded as an important component of the learning experience. (1996: 321)

Data from my research supports such findings. In the subject-focused mainstream classroom, bilingual students are rightly focused on the content and meaning of new concepts. There appear to be few opportunities for a focus on the relationship between form and meaning in language; that is, the role language plays in structuring meaning. A focus on form is most likely to occur in one-to-one EAL teacher and student interactions. However, within these one-to-one interactions there are also some examples in the research findings of students rejecting an EAL teacher-initiated shift of focus from content to form. We will look at such data in this chapter.

English as an Additional Language in the Mainstream: Whose Responsibility?

Subject teachers showed little interest or awareness in the importance of 'input' in creating language-learning possibilities across the three schools. The exception was the ST working in partnership mode. Whereas EAL teachers generally felt the need to manage input, subject specialists passed this responsibility back to the students themselves. In this section, I will look at the interview data to analyse how subject teachers and EAL teachers view English language-learning possibilities in the mainstream.

Subject teachers

112 I guess what I am trying to say is that there has to be a motivation there and if the motivation is getting girlfriends or keeping them or whatever then that is fine, if it is making friends then that is fine, if it is doing well at school then that is fine, but I don't think a lot of the kids in our school

are motivated by GCSE results because they see it as beyond them anyway which is something I suppose we should be addressing. But so they need the motivation to do it and then I suppose they pick up, at the start they do it by hearing other people talking and trying to make sense of what they are saying and become familiar with the alphabet if that is different with the alphabet they are familiar with. (C7)

113 I find learning my own language difficult enough! How do they learn it. Ah, I haven't . . . tricky one isn't it. It seems as if kids all learn it at a different rates and in different ways. Some kids can pick up another language very very quickly. You get some children who come to the class and have got very little language and within two weeks they are as fluent as anybody else umm . . . I think a lot of it is to do with their personality and their ability to learn . . . umm but as a general rule . . . I think they learn by being part of something and having a need to. I think the ones who don't learn tend to be the quiet ones who are really very introspective anyway. I think the ones who are outgoing who want to communicate who want to find out who have got energy are the ones who tend to pick it up quickly. So I think you just put them in a stimulating environment and they will learn it in no time (laughs). There is the answer (laughs). (C5)

114 I would say it is the same way you learn a first language. Being involved, being surrounded by a language through experience. Observation, listening, coping, practising. Exactly as you would do a baby who learns to walk by practising and falling over and making mistakes and learns to speak by listening and trying a second language also. (A6)

115 Well from my own experience of going to countries on holiday, it is by going there and talking to people, and basically, it seems to come, doesn't it. I've been to Spain and I've been to Russia, you have to do some basics things to get by. I would learn words, and look them up in a dictionary as I went. I don't think it would be sitting down and writing great tracks of things you would learn the language first and then you would change it into written. (A7)

116 Well, I learned a second language being completely immersed in that language – learning through doing and generally . . . It wasn't very specific or grammatically based. It was the case of some grammar but a lot of experience as well with the grammar being in context. You need to have it in context and learn as you go on. I think if you kept at and just learned the specific language, specific grammar points, you don't see any relevance to them. Often you need to actually have situation to learn and learn through doing activity, seeing it. (A5)

117 I don't know, it is quite a difficult one. Sometimes I am quite convinced in my mind that the only way the majority of bilingual children are going to

learn English is by integrating all the time with English-speaking students and also with an English-speaking setting and atmosphere and therefore I would support bringing children into the same class. (B6)

It is perhaps not surprising that many of these STs cannot articulate how a second language is learned. They do not receive any input on SLA during their initial teacher training. Indeed, in many ways the study of second language acquisition is still in its infancy. However, there is much that we do know about the importance of input, output, interaction and language-processing. Quotes 112–115 emphasized the learners' role in terms of what motivates them: interaction with people, doing well in the exam system, being involved. The teachers therefore put the onus on the learners themselves, rather than on their role as teachers in managing input and output opportunities for language-learning in their classrooms. The subject teachers highlight the individual and idiosyncratic nature of language-learning and relieve themselves from managing the input to make it comprehensible or responding with feedback in helpful ways. The majority of the subject specialists saw this as the responsibility of the bilingual student. I would argue that this data reflects the prevailing monolingual culture of inclusive and multicultural schools. Many teachers themselves have little personal experience of language-learning or any professional development in the subject of language-learning, or indeed any training in the role language plays in teaching. The ideologies of inclusion and multiculturalism as practiced by these teachers shows a monolingualizing tendency (Heller, 1999).

Responding to the needs of bilingual students is the responsibility of both kinds of teachers and meeting the second-language learning needs of bilingual students is supposed to be a shared responsibility. STs in this data showed almost no awareness of how language might be learned in their classrooms. They also showed no evidence of how they might combine a language focus with a content focus. This was left to the EAL teacher. However, as I have argued throughout this book, this could only happen when STs and EAL teachers were working in partnership mode. This arrangement across all three schools was the exception rather than the rule. Quote 116 comes from one of the partnership teachers in this study. He speaks of the importance of the environment, i.e. action that the school can take rather than the individual child. This includes providing the right context, providing opportunities for learning by doing and integrating the child. This is also true of Quote 117 where the ST is bilingual himself.

EAL teachers

EAL teachers also emphasize the role of the environment and the individual as important elements in the language-learning process. However, for them the reverse is true: rather than focusing first on the individual, they tend to highlight the role of the environment:

118 You know they have to understand the context of why they are learning this language in the first place, it is fair enough if it is just to get you to the shops and around, which is a very important part but also if you are going to have to be in the exam system then you are going to have to learn that this [is] how it is written down as well. I mean it is just access to it, you know, it is like how do you teach somebody how to read, I don't know how to do that either, and yet people learn, I don't know if there is [a] true and trusted formula for teaching someone to read but I think . . . once the germ is there [there are] certainly things you can do to improve the vocabulary to enlarge it, I think it has just got to come through familiarity, with the look of words, with the sound of them, the repetition, hearing things. Yeah, I don't know. You must tell me! (C2)

119 I think some of them [students], well I am sure that some of them think that it is not the way they should be learning English. I am sure that some of them have a very sort of traditional view of how they should be taught English, based on a more sort of TEFL [Teaching English as a Foreign Language] type thing. And I suppose that depends on where they come from and what experience they have had with learning English before. I mean I have had students who have said to me can you recommend a grammar book that I can get because I want to study grammar. And I think one or two cases it has been sort of can you help me when I get this book. Will you help me, will you teach me it? And when I have tried to explain that I don't think that this is a useful thing for them to be doing and that it is much better for them to be concentrating on their class work and that I can help them with that and that through that you know certain grammar points might come up that we can look at, but I don't think that they appreciate that argument at all. I think they have got set traditional views on it. . . . I mean when I am presenting things in class I think I do look at words and forms and things, or maybe I am more aware of it than content teachers. (A2)

120 I think the characteristic of learning another language is to feel frustrated and I usually say to parents when they're bringing their kids in, you know this is going to be a frustrating time. There will be some days when nothing seems to have gelled, nothing has gone right and other days when you feel great, because you've finally understood something, some days you feel tired – some days you just don't want to participate, and I think that only when other people have learned other languages or have remembered their experience of learning other languages can they possibly understand where the children are at. I mean, they've [subject teachers] got to stop seeing the children as being the source of frustration and start to see their own lack of ability to communicate with them as the source of frustration. (A1)

121 I like to get them [students] to the stage where they can see basic patterns, so that they can begin to see that because there is a pattern you can change

the elements of that pattern and make new sentences, new patterns, because eventually you actually begin to see how it works. That also helps their reading and writing. (C1)

122 No, I suppose I'm a traditionalist. I would like them to take away an idea, embedded in a sentence. + + + Because I find it difficult to think except in sentences, so if I get the time I like to describe everything in sentences but then I was trained in the sixties. I mean it sounds defensive but it's not meant to sound defensive. Yes, I was trained in English as a foreign language where it was all form and no content. (B4)

123 They hear a word and they hear a word and they hear a word. And they read it and they read it and they read it and it is in a vague concept. Therefore they have an English concept of what a tree is or a Turkish concept of what a tree is. And the different types of trees stick in their head as the subject expands. And the fact that it is repeated from subject to subject and you get to see the word from different angles because it is repeated. That is the theory, I think. I think that is the practice for some of them. I think some of them should not be taught like that. I think some of them won't learn like that. I think some of them should be taken out and made to go home and learn a list of words and I think then they might achieve something. I think that fundamentally, grammar is the icing on the cake. It is a secondary, rather than a primary. . . . I would always go down the simple grammatical forms that we use for a basic description and I would also follow that down. But I don't do it when I have gone past a certain point and we are into content. (B3)

124 Well I know the problem. You see what I am trying to do in accessing the content is that I am always trying to emphasize certain keys words within the context and say these are the key words within this passage and these are the key English words that you have to learn. So that I am not simply trying to communicate in Turkish so that they know the content, I am trying to point out what the important words and phrases are so that they can learn the important key expressions. So it isn't a case of one cancelling the other. I think bilingualism can assist in the acquisition of language, so I do both in fact, I don't do just one to the exclusion of the other. I think I am doing them both at the same time. (B1)

125 They should try and use their language, I mean try and speak in English more but at the same time I don't think we should deprive them of their own language if they are good at it. If they have a high vocabulary in Turkish and they can communicate better in Turkish I think they will probably be better in English. (B2)

We see a wide range of attitudes to second-language learning expressed in this extracts. The comments range from the importance of language in context, the need for repetition of language across the curriculum, the role of grammar instruction in content classrooms, the role of grammar in the language-learning process, to the non-linear nature of language-learning, and the patterned nature of syntax. Like the STs, there is evidence that some of the EAL teachers do not feel comfortable with their knowledge of the second-language learning process. However, rather than place the responsibility on the language learner they are more likely to emphasize the importance of context in the language-learning process. Quotes 124 and 125 come from bilingual EAL teachers. Understandably, they highlight the use of the first language in learning the second, and in also learning the content. This topic is taken up again in Chapters 9 and 10.

Is this Content-based Language-learning?

Let us now look at some actual language-focused work captured in the classroom recordings. We will see the bulk of this is done by EAL teachers, but there is one instance of an ST engaging in a focus on form. In the following extract the ST is reading through a student's work with the student. When the ST is reading, I have indicated this by an underline in the transcript:

> 126
> **ST:** Which one, all three, or just the bottom one?
> **S:** Just that one.
> **ST:** (reads) <u>I enjoyed doing the practical work. It's</u>. There is no comma in <u>it's</u>. Yes, there is, yes there is, it is difficult. But write *it is*, yeah, because you should only put 'it's' when it is spoken. Or when you are writing what someone is speaking, yeah? If you are writing an evaluation *it is*, yeah? Use a full one. (reads her work) <u>It is difficult to draw the space.</u>
> **S:** Shape.
> **ST:** <u>The shape.</u>
> **S:** Did I put space?
> **ST:** Yeah. Let's get that changed then. <u>The shape,</u> 'comma' <u>but when I look at the</u>
> **S:** (laughs)
> **ST:** <u>When I looked at the shape,</u> when I *first*, when I *first* looked at the shape, yeah?
> First, yeah? Because that is the first thing you do, right? <u>When I first looked at the shape, it looks</u>=
> **S:** It was=
> **ST:** No, not was, because was is the present isn't it? It looked. Sorry, was is the past. <u>It looked easy to draw and make but when I started</u>, is that started?
> **S:** Yeah.
> **ST:** <u>But when I started to draw it took me</u>
> **S:** Long time.

ST: A long time, yeah? Because *a* long time. Not long time. It took me *a* long time to draw. Yeah? Don't forget to put that in, yeah? Fine. I never did. <u>I never *done*</u>. Don't use done in that context. I never did something like that. Sorry. I have never done. It is a different tense. You are in the past here, you have got to keep in the past in the same sentence <u>and I found it interesting to make</u>, yeah? OK. That is fine. No problem.

ST: Miss Harrington, do you fancy a cup of coffee? (A5)

This is the only example of a subject teacher specifically focusing on language form in my classroom transcript data. This ST was working in a partnership and was aware of the importance of a focus on language around subject-learning and also of creating opportunities for second-language learning. In the extract above, we see the ST foreground the metalingual function and its focus on language form. Both the ST and the EAL teacher in their partnership were keen to promote language awareness in their co-taught classes. Despite the problems the ST faces in his lack of linguistic knowledge regarding the past tense, his profiling of language work in the subject-based classroom shows an attempt to share his EAL partner teacher's agendas. However, the transcript also shows the importance of linguistic knowledge if this kind of work is undertaken.

The bulk of language work done in mainstream classrooms was initiated by EAL teachers. There are several examples of this on the following pages. These are drawn from various data sources and include classroom transcripts and observational field notes. We turn first to look at how EAL teachers attempt to combine a subject and language focus. One common strategy was for EAL teachers to concentrate on explaining key subject vocabulary. For instance, Extract 127 shows a blending of language and content focus:

127
EAL: What is the total, what do they equal? What do they equal, add them up, add them up. What do they equal, what do they all equal? All right, if you come here, come here a minute. Bring your chair around here. What are you on? Which part are you on? Are you doing this? Have you done this? You will have to wait, you will have to wait. (He has four students grouped around him now)

S: Very hard sir.

EAL: It is not very hard, it isn't very hard. You are pretending it is very hard.

S: What does pretending mean?

EAL: All right. What does pretending mean? It means you think it is very hard, but it is not very hard. OK. Like when you are an actor, you know you are an actor, that is pretending. When you act you pretend. It is not quite true, you think it is true but it isn't true. All right, you add all these numbers together.

S: You can't do that sir because there is 1, 2, 3 number.

EAL: Yes, you can.=

S: No you can't do that, no.

EAL: Yes you can. Look, what is 340 + 360? is?

S2:   700.

EAL: Yeah, if you add another 70, that's all right, that will be 770. You can add three figures. You can add any numbers! (girls laugh) (moves onto another group of students)

EAL: Now what does, what happens when it is raining. Sorry. What is the temperature, the climate in a rainforest?

S: Very hot.

EAL: OK. The temperatures are very high, very hot everyday. Because it is so hot a lot of water evaporates from the rivers and forests. Now what does evaporate mean? (no pause) Evaporate is when, evaporate means when water changes from liquid to vapour. So you know when you have a kettle and you turn on a kettle, what comes out of the kettle?

S: XXX

EAL: Yes! So what is the right answer? (student points) Yes! Good. So here you have a kettle.

S: (said in aside to her friend) *Unlamiyorum* (I don't understand)

EAL: Here is a very badly drawn kettle, OK. When the water boils, what comes out of here. This is called steam.

S: What?

EAL: Steam. Yeah. Water evaporates to become steam. Yes. Now. So evaporate is when water changes. Do you understand? Do you understand? All right. Now. In the equator the sun rises at 6 o'clock it evaporates the mists. So the water goes into the sky, yes, it becomes hotter, hotter. The evaporated water condenses into clouds, it changes into clouds, now what are clouds. Do you know what clouds are?

S: Yeah. (student from Vietnam) (Turkish girls don't answer)

EAL: Do you know what clouds are? In the sky, there is the sun, there is the sun, and here is?

S: Clouds.

EAL: A cloud.

S: Yeah.

EAL: Yeah, This is like this, from a kettle. Do you understand. Yes?

S: Yes.

EAL: Do you understand? The condensed water. (B3)

An interesting feature of the discourse is the number of questions that the EAL teacher asks the students. Moreoever, the EAL teacher's focus on the language as a code is of further interest. The first instance of this comes from the students themselves when they ask for the meaning of the word *pretend*. However, for the most part it is the EAL teacher who chooses for the students the key words on which they should focus their attention. EAL teachers are very much concerned with making sure students know the meaning of key words. In the following example, the microphone was on the EAL teacher who was working with one student. The ST is talking to the whole class while the EAL is whispering to the student and pointing to text and pictures:

128
ST: That even when they are pregnant.
EAL: (whispering throughout) She is pregnant.
ST: They still have to pull this strap around her waist to work.
EAL: She still has to work.
ST: And pull the coal out. So it is hardly surprising that four out of her eight children were born stillborn.
EAL: This means dead [stillborn]. It means four of her children were born dead.
ST: And she was doing this even on the day that she gave birth. (A2 and A9)

In this example the EAL teacher is mirroring the key words that the ST is using to the whole class. She does this by either simply repeating the word again (as in the word pregnant) or by explaining a concept further (stillborn means dead). Both these extracts (127 and 128) attempt to balance content- and language-learning aims. They are examples of EAL teachers working in an ad hoc manner with subject material to make it more accessible to bilingual students. Their aim is for bilingual students to learn subject knowledge and new English vocabulary simultaneously. We see in these transcripts the EAL teachers focused particularly on conveying the meaning of key vocabulary by attempting to introduce greater context around the text.

In the next example we look at an EAL teacher who has chosen to do a different task with her students within the content-based classroom. This task has a language focus that aims to teach quantifiers: few, a few, many, high, low. In negotiating with the ST to use different material from the rest of the class, the EAL teacher has the following conversation (reported earlier in Chapter 5):

129
(*the EAL teacher is talking to the ST just before they go into the lesson*)
EAL: Have we finished the population pyramids in that class? 8 something, 8 B?
ST: XXX (the ST is half talking to herself about the need to find some work she is looking for)
EAL: Well, what is it in the end, can you remember?
ST: Well yes, I know what I am teaching.
EAL: Yeah, but what is it?
ST: Interpretation of graphs.
EAL: Ah, right. Thanks. So we are still on that, right. I've found some slightly easier work that John . . .
(ST is doing other things)

EAL: Right. I've found some easier work on population on pyramids that John prepared. Can I go through it with my group? ...

ST: Yes.

EAL: Because if it is interpretation then they will find it hard, yeah? (B4 and B8)

This interaction gets off to a bad start and is illustrative of what happens when the two teachers have not been able to exchange information before a lesson.

After this discussion, the EAL teacher goes on to work with a small group of bilingual students within the mainstream class. The bilingual students and teacher are grouped together around one table and each have a separate worksheet. Throughout the transcript that follows the teacher and students are referring to the worksheet. The EAL teacher undertakes the following activity with the bilingual students that she has described as easier:

130

EAL: Number two. Right.
(student reads)

EAL: Mexico birth rate, high or low?

S: High.

EAL: High, good girl. Mexico has a high birth rate. So cross out low. Cross out low. Good. Now, Mexico old people. Many or not many? Many, not many?

S: Many.

EAL: Many or not many?

S: Not many.

EAL: Not many. Number three. A few. Not many, a few. So cross off lots of. Few is not many. Few, not many. So cross out this one, Hatice. Lot of. Cross. Yeah? That is the birth rate. Death rate. Dying. Yeah? These people are born here, they're dead. High death rate. High death rate. Ahmm right. OK. Can you try Sweden? You do number five, number six, number seven, number eight, Sweden. You do it yourselves please. Sweden. Can you do this now yourselves. Sweden. This is Sweden. A lot of babies. No, not many. Few, that one. No, a lot of babies. No look, not many. Lot, few, lot, few. Good. Yes, good. Few birth rate, few babies. Low birth rate. Yeah good, look see. See here, they are dying. Here not dying. Good girl. OK. Right so you can copy this here in pen this writing. Emis you can copy in pen. Copy in pen. Have you finished, yeah? No, Sweden, not many. Few. Look not many. See not many. OK give it to me and I'll check. (B4)

I would argue that the aims of this activity were not clear to the students or perhaps to the teacher herself. This did not make the activity 'easy' at all. The EAL teacher seems to have two aims: language and content. There is a conflation of these aims. The EAL teacher has not made clear to the students her intention to teach quantifiers, or the interpretation of graphs. Bilingual students do not often receive language-focused instruction in their mainstream classrooms and they may well have been confused about what was required of them in this task. The EAL teacher uses many directives, simplified noun phrases with rising intonation as questions, and display questions. There are few opportunities to negotiate throughout the task and the majority of talk is done by the EAL teacher herself. Without a well-planned syllabus of how language and content can interact, there is a danger that the rationale for a language focus will be unclear to the bilingual students. Moreover, a language focus, like a subject focus, must be thought through and provide opportunities for negotiation and the optimal context for second-language learning.

Another example of the EAL teacher doing different work from the rest of the class is shown in Extract 131. Here the EAL teacher is working with a bilingual student who has speech and language difficulties. She started the interaction by talking to him about his reading but switched to getting him to concentrate on specific sounds:

131
EAL: /d/
S: /td/
EAL: /d/
S: /td/
EAL: drop the /t/, /d/, /d/. Can you put XXX together and then try /d/
S: /d/
EAL: That's better, much better. Say day.
S: Day.
EAL: Day.
S: Day.
EAL: Good. If you put your two teeth together and say day.
S: Day.
EAL: It works. Good.
S: /d/
EAL: Have you seen your speech therapist?
S: No.
EAL: Since your operation? No? Did the speech therapist, last time you saw her, give you any exercises to practice, any sounds?
S: No.
EAL: No? Are you going to see her soon?
S: Miss. I think so.
EAL: You think so? Well, if you don't see her before the end of this term, let me know because we must do something, because you need little exercises to practice, but that could be one of the sounds, if you get your /d/, /d/, /d/, if you say that to yourself . . .
S: /d/
EAL: Every morning and every night /d/, and then you can try words like daddy, day, dog. Just getting that sound and making it harder because then people can hear it. The way you say it we can't hear it.

S: Yeah.

EAL: And then we don't know what you are saying and so we have got to practise getting that sound right. (C1)

In this extract the EAL teacher is in the class to help the student with his reading. However, she first focuses on his pronunciation. She sees this as one of her duties, which is related to the EAL teacher's role of advocator/facilitator/language teacher in the school. In the extract, she refers to the student seeing his speech and language therapist and feels a responsibility to make sure that happens. She is responding to the student's wider personal, physical and educational needs.

The final example below is taken from a withdrawal situation. Here we can also see a shift from a content to language focus. The following excerpt is taken from my field notes.

Vignette 12

Ozcan and Hidir have been withdrawn with the EAL teacher and they are working on their science reading skills. When Ozcan reads the EAL teacher praises him saying: 'Good, you read until the end of the sentence and when you come to a difficult word leave it and then go back to it.' The difficult work is 'environment'. Hidir is now trying to find the word 'flame' by saying, 'yellow thing comes out', which the EAL teacher does not understand. Hidir is frustrated because he cannot find the word in Turkish either. His friend Ozcan cannot guess either. Hidir draws a picture of a tripod to illustrate flame. This leads the EAL teacher to an explanation of 'mono' – one, 'di' – two, and 'tri' – three. This frustrates the boys tremendously because they just want the words 'bunsen burner' and 'flame'. The EAL teacher adds: 'Blue flame good and yellow flame bad.' The boys react and now the EAL teacher understands which word they want and gives it to them asking them why blue is good and yellow is bad. She goes on to remind them to use their word lists in science which have been prepared for them.

Hidir now shows some of his answers already done in his science class. He says 'I got this from Miss [ST]'. The EAL teacher replies, 'Yes, this is probably the answer, it could be that they want the word "soot" here'. Hidir has now understood. Along with the EAL teacher, he tries to explain the word to Ozcan, who only really listens to Hidir who is speaking Turkish. When Ozcan has got it he tries to stop the EAL teacher from going on with her explanation, which is not only a definition of the word, but has expanded to the work of chimney sweeps. He says impatiently, 'Miss, I've got it, I've got it'. Once they have got the word in Turkish they don't listen any more to the English.

Although this is a withdrawal situation, the task remained subject-based and the children were anxious to keep it so. However, as language became an issue in the completion of the task the EAL teacher became more focused on it. The children, on the other hand, wanted to move away from an English-language-learning focus. Instead, their objective was to get the answer. In order to maintain a subject focus, the students drew on their Turkish and English. That is, both languages were being used to stay focused on the subject content. When the language teacher insisted on a focus on language and the metalingual function of language, as in the EAL teacher's remarks on 'mono', 'di' and 'tri' (as in 'tripod'), the students lost interest. The EAL teacher's insistence on using the message to focus on the code was at odds with the students' aim to use the code to make a comment on the message. In making the subject content their focus the students were in line with the STs, who also have as their focus the content knowledge of the curriculum. This over-riding domination of a focus on meaning is in keeping with the SLA classroom-based studies discussed earlier in this chapter. In classrooms where the focus is on subject content, it is very difficult to shift to a focus on form (and its role in creating meaning).

Adapting Texts for Learning English

Below are two excerpts from two different texts used in the same year 10 geography lesson. Text A is the original from a worksheet written by a subject specialist. Text B is the adapted material written by the EAL teacher. Both texts were available for students' use. In fact, students, with some teacher guidance, were expected to choose which text to use. In the end, the ST decided that all students should use Text B adapted and produced by the EAL teacher. The class in which Text B was used consisted of 50% early learners of English.

Text A (by ST)

In Britain, people use the land for many different reasons. The land is a RESOURCE (something that people could use) for producing food, for building homes, offices and factories, or for RECREATION (spare-time activities). All these things change the ENVIRONMENT (surroundings) including the ECOSYSTEM (plant and animal-life). But there are also natural changes going-on that can affect them as well.

(Capitals and punctuation as in the original.)

Text B (by EAL teacher)

<u>Read</u>
Land is a RESOURCE. It is used for lots of different things.
Land is used for growing food, for homes, for factories, and for offices.
Land is also used for RECREATION. People use the land when they are not working.

People change the land. When people change the land they change the ENVIRONMENT. The ENVIRONMENT is the things that are around us.
Part of the ENVIRONMENT that people change is the ECOSYSTEM. The ECOSYSTEM is Animals and Plants living together. People change the lives of plants and animals.

(Capitals and punctuation as in the original.)

A first glance shows that text B is longer than text A. However, although text B has more sentences than text A (11 sentences compared to 3), these sentences are shorter (average words per sentence for text B = 8, whereas for text A = 20). The EAL teacher who made these adaptations is attempting to strip all unnecessary language away so that students can reach the core meaning of the text. In doing so, fundamental changes in the linguistic code are made (there is less embedding, and less use of deictic markers). However, because of the fundamental relationship between form and function in language, what also changes is the meaning of text itself. In text A each key word is bracketed with a simplified gloss, whereas in text B the definition of the key word becomes the proposition of the sentence. This means that the cause and effect processes in the two texts are different. In text A, *All these things change the ENVIRONMENT*. That is, resources (and all examples given of resources) and recreation (and all examples given of recreation) are what change the environment. It is that *people* change the environment through their *use* of resources and recreation for a purpose, i.e. they do things. Text B, on the other hand, does not point to the rationale for people changing the environment. People simply do things to change the environment seemingly without purpose. Text B does not make the link between people using the land as a resource and for recreation, which brings about change to the environment (*When people change the land they change the ENVIRONMENT*). In text B people are behaving in an unexplained way, whereas in text A they are making changes because of the benefits these changes bring. The main purpose of text B appears to be a set of definitions of key concepts. The main purpose of text A appears to show causality and effect.

I would suggest that the two texts have different aims and functions. Perhaps at first glance the adaptation of one text to another appears to be a good example of content-based language teaching, but I would suggest that this is a much more complex matter. The structure of an academic text is important in orga-nizing ideas coherently and logically. The way a sentence is linked backwards and for-wards in the text is important in building up cohesive arguments. When these building blocks are changed, meaning is also changed. When grammar is simplified and vocabulary made 'easier', the relationship between form and meaning is changed. The linguistic changes from text A to text B make causality less apparent. I would suggest that deducing the argument is actually more diffi-cult in text B, rather than easier, because structurally it does not 'build up' and connect propositions.

Interestingly, in adapting text A the two teachers (subject and EAL) appear to share a common agenda. That is, in the adaptation process the focus remains on teaching subject knowledge rather than on the underlying process of meaning-making for example. 'Knowledge' here is the learning of the geography curriculum. Both teachers are committed to teaching key geographical terms. This view of know-ledge as the 'what' rather than the 'how' very much mirrors earlier discussions of transmission and facilitative pedagogies. This approach has been criticized by Jay Lemke. He argues:

> A lot of education today is still oriented to teaching students to read, write and use various kinds of specialised written materials, their accompanying diagrams, and sometimes mathematics. But we teach the content, not the medium. We teach students scientific and technical vocabulary, but we never point out how science systematically turns verbs into nouns and why it does so. We rarely if ever explicitly teach students how to talk science (Lemke, 1990) or how to write science (Halliday and Martin, 1993) and show them how it's different from (and like) telling a story or writing one. (Lemke, 2002: 42)

I would argue that a similar criticism could be made in the way the two collab-orating teachers handled the adaptation process from text A to text B. They were so focused on the subject content that they missed an opportunity to consider the role language plays in the construction of meaning. Moreover, this could have been a valuable learning experience for all the children in the class. Again Lemke argues:

> No attention at all is paid in the curriculum to explaining how complex mean-ings are expressed by combining words and graphic images. Students desperately need to know how to critically interpret combinations of words, pictures, maps, diagrams and specialised symbolic expressions. (2002: 42)

Across the three schools, I saw very few examples of teachers integrating an under-standing of 'how' meanings create the 'what' of the curriculum. There were very few opportunities for teachers to plan together and work out shared subject- and language-learning aims. The order was always the exploitation of the subject curriculum for language work rather than a focus on how language constructs knowledge.

As language specialists we are in a position to understand the role of language in knowledge creation and in social life. We can make it our business to deconstruct subject-based texts for an understanding of how language, graphics and other signs function. This obviously moves beyond the teaching of core vocabulary. The example given in texts A and B (see p. 000) is helpful in illustrating this. Adapting a text should be predicated on shared language- and subject-focused aims. One of the subject aims in the year 10 geography lesson was 'causality'. This theme could have been developed into overlapping language- and content-based aims and outcomes.

Chapter Summary

The argument made throughout this chapter has been that content-based language teaching requires both kinds of teachers to take a greater interest in the role language (and other media) plays in the construction of meanings. Teachers need to pay as much attention to the 'how' as to the 'what' of the curriculum. Subject and 'language work' require an understanding of meaning-making, knowledge construction, academic and other literacies. For EAL teachers, one area of their subject specialism should be an understanding of discourse, and how language functions in the construction of knowledge. An EAL teacher may teach grammar and key vocabulary, but their expertise needs to extended beyond this by helping students make connections across discourses and subject genres so that learning links up.

Throughout this book, I have argued that providing opportunities for language-learning is one of the fundamental tenants of the inclusive policy of mainstreaming. For the most part, this policy has projected language-learning as occurring 'naturally' and in ways similar to first language-learning. This has allowed subject teachers to develop a distanced approach towards language teaching and learning and assists a monolingual ideology.

EAL teachers are more likely to be engage in some language teaching. However, such is the dominance of meaning-making in subject-focused classrooms that a switch to a focus on linguistic structure is often met with student opposition. Students understand that the most important aim in the secondary school classroom is not language-learning but curriculum-learning. Subject teachers appear to feel little responsibility in making language-learning an important aim in their classrooms. Indeed, teachers receive very little information in their initial teacher training to help them achieve this. They are not taught the processes of language-learning nor are they given any training in how to make their subject teaching dovetail with a language syllabus.

In England, we have been very slow in looking at the possibilities of combining subject and language syllabuses within one classroom. Indeed, at policy level we have not really begun to discuss what we might mean by 'language work' in the mainstream. For the most part, there are few opportunities for language-focused negotiation, attention to form or corrective feedback, all factors claimed to be useful in the second-language learning process. Second-language learning is seen very much as a problem rather than a resource in secondary school classrooms. This is because second languages are often viewed as deficient in the sense that they are insufficient for the building-up of scientific concepts which continues to be the primary aim of secondary school education. In the following chapter we look further at the possibilities of using the first language to learn subject content across the three schools.

Chapter 9

Bilingual Teachers and Students in Secondary School Classrooms: Using Turkish for Curriculum-learning[1]

As English-only policies and monolingual language ideologies continue to exert their sway both nationally and internationally, we need bilingual educators to be conscious advocates for the language rights and resources of language minority students and speakers of endangered, indigenous, immigrant, and ethnic languages wherever they may be. (Hornberger, 2004: 169)

Introduction

The focus of this chapter is twofold. The first aim is to focus specifically on the six Turkish/English bilingual EAL teachers from the three London secondary schools in this study. As stated earlier in this book, my interest has been at looking at the work both non-bilingual and bilingual EAL teachers do in the mainstream classrooms of English secondary schools. Despite the policy statement conflation of bilingual and non-bilingual teachers into the generic category of EAL teachers (see Chapter 2), I think it worth considering these teachers separately. The importance and distinctiveness of bilingual EAL teachers' work is described in this chapter and Chapter 10. The second aim of this chapter is to look at attitudes towards the use of Turkish across the three schools, by STs, EAL teachers (bilingual and non-bilingual) and by members of the senior management. Chapter 10 also relates to this second theme as it presents a case study illustrating how Turkish and English are used in managing one specific event in a school.

There are two positive arguments made about bilingualism in this chapter. The first concerns bilingual teachers' ability to use their first language to move beyond 'support' to teach subject content. Their practice is therefore embedded within the dominant pedagogic framework of secondary schooling and keeps the bilingual/EAL teacher and children at the centre of classroom life. The second argument shows the usefulness of community languages to STs. Community languages have a higher profile than might otherwise be expected in a secondary school classroom, mostly because of their value to STs in building-up scientific concepts for curriculum teaching.

Using First Languages for Curriculum-learning

A recent General Teaching Council report in the UK (GTC, 2003) suggests that there are around 9000 minority ethnic teachers working in England's schools. This amount to 2.4% of the teacher workforce. We do not have up-to-date information on how many of these are EAL teachers or how many are bilingual. The most recent survey that broke down non-bilingual and bilingual teachers was conducted in 1989 (Bourne, 1989) and found that the vast majority of EAL teachers are white and non-bilingual in a classroom community language. Although in need of updating, this survey found that 86% of the teachers were deployed as non-bilingual EAL teachers; 9% as community language teachers,[2] and 5% as bilingual EAL teachers (Bourne, 1989: 34). It is likely that the low figures for bilingual teachers persists today, especially as there is no professional route into EAL teaching (Leung, 2001; Ofsted, 2001).

Educational policy in England encourages the use of other languages only for transitional purposes; that is, until the student is proficient enough to learn the subject curriculum through English. The current policy has been developed around an argument that the huge diversity in languages that exists in English schools makes bilingual education in mainstream schooling impossible and undesirable. Bilingual EAL teachers work in a climate in which an emphasis is placed on the use of other languages for transitional and pastoral uses only. Other languages are presented as a rich resource in this transition (see Chapter 2). Neither in policy documents nor in practice do bilingual EAL teachers receive any encouragement to expand their role in using other languages for the teaching of the subject curriculum beyond the transition to English.[3]

Research on bilingual teachers and learning assistants in England has been predominantly carried out in primary schools (Bourne, 1989, 1997, 2001; Martin-Jones & Saxena, 1989, 1996, 2003). Very little empirical work has been done on bilingual EAL teachers in English secondary schools. Research on bilingual teachers in secondary schools is much richer in the US (see Bunch et al., 2001; Ruiz, 1992; Valdés, 1997, 1998). However, the provision of schooling is clearly very different between the two national contexts. In the US, bilingual teachers can be employed to work bilingually within bilingual programmes whether their orientation be transitional, maintenance or enrichment (Baker, 2001). In England, there are no statutory bilingual or dual immersion programmes. Instead, bilingual EAL teachers are engaged primarily to play a support role in curriculum-learning and are employed to use their first languages to ease the transition to English in monolingual subject-focused classrooms or for pastoral reasons to assist in home/school links. Bilingual EAL teachers are not employed to teach the curriculum bilingually.

Nevertheless, if the literature on bilingual teachers in the US context is not explicitly transferable to the English context at programme level, there are elements of the debate in the US which are. Valdés' work has been important in looking at the instructional dilemmas that surround the education of immigrant children in US secondary schools. She has described how the school systems can work against migrant children so that some of them never move beyond ESL or sheltered classes to mainstream classes. Her work shows the unwillingness of some mainstream teachers to work with immigrant children in subject-focused classrooms. She shows the dilemmas mainstream subject teachers face in transforming their classrooms into arenas in which language- and content-learning can be integrated. In one particular case study, she finds that 'like many other mainstream teachers forced to take English-language learners, she [the mainstream teacher] simply directed her class at the ability levels of her majority English-speaking mainstream students' (Valdés, 1998: 9). That is, the mainstream teacher made little attempt to integrate the teaching of language and subject content. We have seen throughout this book a similar tendency for some STs to place responsibility for the bilingual student with the EAL teacher. In this chapter we explore the role the bilingual EAL teacher plays in mediating subject curriculum knowledge and show how STs come to rely on these skills in different ways to their dependence on non-bilingual EAL teachers.

Bilingual Teachers in the Mainstream

Recently, Widdowson has argued that 'guiding the development of bilinguals has to be attuned to the bilingualisation process, and not by the imposition of an exclusively monolingual pedagogy' (2003: 162, in Brutt-Griffler & Varghese, 2004). This is an important argument and recognizes the distinctiveness that bilingual teachers can play in teaching and learning. Widdowson appears to be foregrounding the identities of the bilingual child and, indeed, the bilingual teacher in the teaching and learning process. He recognizes that these processes are likely to differ from those the monolingual child and teacher may have experienced.

In a recent special issue of the *International Journal of Bilingual Education and Bilingualism*, Brutt-Griffler and Varghese (2004) bring together some interesting articles which discuss the importance of bilingual teachers' identities and practices. They quote Johnston *et al.*:

> the more researchers have examined the role of teachers in the processes of language teaching and learning, the clearer it has become that a deeper understanding of teachers and their work requires a consideration of who teachers are: the professional, cultural, political and individual identities which they claim or which are assigned to them. (Johnston *et al.*, in preparation, in Brutt-Griffler & Varghese, 2004: 96)

Indeed, in Chapter 6 of this book we considered the importance of teacher identity in bringing about change and much of that discussion is also relevant to the debate surrounding bilingual student and teacher identities. In an interesting article, Morgan (2004) reviews the literature on learner and teacher identities. He draws on Cummins' framework (2000, 2001) which sees cognitive development and academic achievement as inseparable from teacher–student identity negotiation. Morgan argues against a notion of

> 'teacher identity *and* pedagogy', that is juxtaposed yet separable variable – to a notion of 'teacher identity *as* pedagogy', a conflation or synthesis more in keeping with the continuous interweaving of identity negotiation and language learning articulated in Cummins' (2000, 2001) framework. (2004: 178)

These view of *identity as pedagogy* is helpful here as it highlights the 'identity options or interpersonal spaces' (Morgan, 2004: 178) that bilingual teachers and students face in mainstream contexts. These identity options are constituted through interaction and involve: L1/L2 translation and interpretation, code-switching, group work and explanations about grammar, vocabulary practice and subject content. Morgan calls this kind of interaction 'languaging' (2004: 178). From my research data which follows in this chapter we will see that the bilingual teachers' pedagogies very much draw on this kind of 'languaging' work, particularly the use of movement between languages in the teaching of subject content. We will also see that bilingual teachers' identities are constructed particularly around their use of other languages in the mainstream. Equally, other monolingual speakers within the school construct bilingual teachers' identities around these languages in ways useful to themselves and the school generally. That is, bilingualism in the mainstream school is used by monolingual teachers to maintain dominant pedagogies and ideologies.

In the same edited collection mentioned above, Benson (2004) asks the question, 'Do we expect too much of bilingual teachers?' Her context is bilingual teachers in Bolivia and Mozambique, and she is specifically concerned with the challenges facing bilingual teachers in post-colonial contexts. However, her work is also of relevance here as she raises some important concerns about the nature of roles we ask our bilingual teachers to play and the lack of training which accompanies these demands. She describes five key roles: pedagogue, linguist, intercultural communicator, community member and advocate, and argues that if bilingual teachers are to adequately perform these roles effective bilingual teacher training must include the following:

(1) first and second-language learning theory;
(2) modelling of first and second language teaching methods (oral and written);
(3) modelling of methods for intercultural instruction;
(4) L2 verbal and literacy skills;
(5) L1 verbal and literacy skills, including pedagogical vocabulary;
(6) language and programme assessment, including international studies of bilingual schooling, models and evaluation;
(7) study visits and/or practical internships at functioning bilingual schools;
(8) collaboration with parents and community members.

(Benson, 2004: 215–16)

Table 3 Bilingual EAL teachers in three London secondary schools

Sinchester: mixed, 11–16 years	*Skonnington: single-sex girls school, 11–18 years*	*Soldingstoke: mixed, 11–16 years*
• Nese – from Turkey, female, early thirties; lived in UK for approx. five years. Instructor, training for qualified teacher status in England. Original subject area: English.	• Unal – from Cyprus, male, lived in UK for over 20 years. Teacher, Ph.D. from London University. Original subject area: humanities.	• Nur – from Turkey, female, lived in UK for approx. seven years. Teacher. Original subject area: English.
• Birgul – from Turkey, female, early thirties, lived and studied in UK for approx. five years. Teacher, MA from London University. Original subject area: English.	• Dilek – from Cyprus, female, lived in UK for over 20 years. Teacher. Original subject area: science-trained.	• Yilgin – from Turkey, lived in UK for approx. five years. Teacher. Original subject area: modern foreign languages.

Interestingly, the list of roles which Benson describes bilingual teachers playing very much mirrors the list given in Chapter 3 of this book, which describes the different functions bilingual and non-bilingual EAL teachers can assume in mainstream schools. In a final plea, Benson (2004: 217) argues:

> As Hornberger explains, the paradox is to 'transform a standardising education into a diversifying one' (2002: 30). If we recognise that the monolingual, monocultural classroom is a relic of the past (if it ever existed at all), and if we truly wish to create pluralistic societies full of bilingual and biliterate people, why is there any monolingual or monocultural teaching training? . . . All teacher trainees, not just 'bilingual' ones, could be learning strategies for working in students' first and second languages. All teacher trainees could be developing skills in interculturalism, and all teacher trainees could be learning how to promote biliteracy as a desirable outcome of the curriculum for all students.

These are persuasive arguments. In this and the following chapter, I look at the challenges bilingual EAL teachers face in schools and how they use their first languages to diversify mainstream classrooms.

In each school, two EAL language specialists were bilingual Turkish/English speakers and two were not bilingual in a community language of the classroom. This section focuses on the six bilingual teachers in the three schools and the teachers they worked with (see Table 3).

My data is divided into two sections: the first gives voice to the bilingual teachers and their rational for using Turkish in the subject classroom; the second describes the views of subject teachers in the schools.

Bilingual teachers in the mainstream

In the following section, interview information is presented from the bilingual EAL teachers in which they describe their use of Turkish in the mainstream class-room. We will see that the bilingual teachers see themselves primarily as explainers of information rather than as accessors/facilitators of information. They are primarily focused on conveying the subject content and only secondarily on simpli-fying content so that the students could learn English. Learning English is seen as happening over time, whereas subject-learning is seen as happening in the here and now. The bilingual teachers give an account of the best use of their time in the mainstream as keeping students up to speed with content knowledge. In the following extract a bilingual teacher is describing her role to me:

132 Well, I think if they [bilingual students] think they are keeping up with the content they are reassured that they are not being left behind. Especially with the Turkish kids who have been used to the system where you fail and you have to repeat the same class.

133 I mean, I think they ought to know the content. It is easier if you know the language of the student you are helping. It is harder if you don't know the language. . . . If you know the language you can translate and try and explain it to them. But I think they ought to know what is going on in the class, as well as trying to learn some new words. (Dilek, Skonnington)

This bilingual teacher was originally science-trained. In Quotes 132–3 she describes her primary role as keeping students up with the content area. Her skills of trans-lating and interpreting the subject teacher, tasks and texts from one language into another in a subject that she knew meant that she stayed focused on the subject curriculum message and, consequently, the Turkish-speaking bilingual children followed the same agenda as the rest of the class. She is also aware of how the Turkish students are likely to interpret the English education system and the problems this might cause, and she uses this knowledge to shape her teaching.

The following quote comes from another bilingual teacher in the same school who was also head of the language/learning support:

134 I think our main job ought to be facilitating access to the curriculum. This obviously works in different ways. If the support teacher has prior knowledge of what the content of the lesson was going to be and the nature of the work that was going to be, and if the support teacher had the opportunity of providing additional worksheets or maybe having to

provide some kind of simplified version I think that is what the support teacher ought to be doing. I am finding increasingly that I am not really producing worksheets because nearly all the girls that I support, there are exceptions obviously, tend to be Turkish speakers. **And it isn't only a question of simplifying things, it is easier to explain things in Turkish.** (Unal, Skonnington)

In this quote the teacher speaks as the middle manager he is and refers to the policy documents and the support work he is required to do. However, he also refers to the bilingual work he does that is not captured in these documents. He starts by speaking of 'accessing' the curriculum as 'our main job' and of offering 'simplified versions' of materials. However, he ends by speaking in terms of 'I' and contrasting the effectiveness of 'explaining' as opposed to 'simplifying'. He is able to explain because the majority of students he works with are Turkish-speaking and he shares their language as well as knowing the subject material well. This teacher sees the role of the first language as being very important in teaching and learning subject material. In fact, in Quote 135 we see the same teacher construct of 'learning' to mean specifically subject-learning. The learning of English, on the other hand, which is often seen as an important element of EAL support work, is described as naturally acquired and not part of any taught process:

135 Well, language is a continuous thing isn't it? You acquire it little by little. So yes, language does come along . . . but obviously language is an accumulative thing, isn't it? You acquire little by little, it doesn't all come at once. (Unal, Skonnington)

The bilingual teacher goes on to suggest that the students' English is not adequate for what he sees as the main teaching and learning agenda of the mainstream classroom:

136 On the whole this might be a bad admission to make. I think the amount of language that we initially teach them is not really adequate for their learning. It is only when they really become more articulate that it does become a vehicle for learning really. . . . After all, no matter how much I teach girls at stage one or two they're still not independent and they're simply learning lists of words or phrases or whatever and that really by itself is not sufficient or adequate to enable them to learn. (Unal, Skonnington)

From Quotes 135 and 136 from Unal, we see different constructions of teaching and learning taking place. Whereas subject curriculum is learned, language is acquired. In other words, where the subject curriculum needs to be taught, the second language needs to be acquired gradually over time. In this bilingual EAL teacher's discourse there is support for the use of the first/dominant language for subject teaching and learning. The use of Turkish for this role was endorsed by all six of the Turkish-speaking teachers in this study. Using Turkish in the mainstream subject-focused classroom allowed these bilingual teachers and students to follow the same curriculum as the non-bilingual students. The bilingual teachers were able to use their bilingual resource to keep students focused on subject knowledge.

STs were also aware of the different skills which bilingual EAL teachers brought to the classroom. In the following extract, an Information Technology subject teacher contemplates her own role alongside her bilingual colleague, Nur:

> 137 Nur's job, the difference? Well, in this classroom, Nur has a bigger role than she would have in other classes that I have. In this class she has more pupils as such than I have and so she would do a lot of translation work and I'd be explaining things and she would work with most of the children in this room. I think there are only two that don't need Nur, as such. So I do all the main teaching, I do the main demonstrations and the problems and then she would sort of filter them through her to those who need it. So her role is hard to say, is not more important than mine but it is kind of. (Information Technology teacher, female, Soldingstoke)

In the above quote the subject teacher maintains that there are clear role differences between herself and Nur. The 'main teaching' continues to be done by herself. This includes explaining and demonstrating. Nur's role is to translate and interpret this, as the subject teachers says, 'to filter it'. However, because of the large number of Turkish-speaking children in the class Nur's role becomes 'more important'. Why should Nur's role become more important because there are more bilingual children in the class? The answer seems to lie in the job description this subject teacher has constructed for herself. She sees her primary job as teaching concepts, problem-solving and demonstrating. Without being able to follow what the children understand and do not understand, she is unable to do this job. Nur has taken over this role:

> 138 In this class, they [bilingual students] have a difficulty with the concepts and a lot of the problems are that I don't realize how much they know or don't know, how much they are understanding, because when Nur isn't here, and say we are doing a theory lesson or something on the board and I say, do you understand, they don't say anything and I don't really understand what they don't understand. (ibid.)

From Quotes 138 and 139 we can see that in translating and explaining, Nur's 'support' role has grown into *teaching* rather than *supporting* subject content, and in doing so she is no longer supporting the subject but is teaching it. Translation and interpretation of content from one language to another is a great asset to the subject teacher because she can feel assured that the students are learning content and understanding content. However, in this very process, she feels her role as a subject teacher has fundamentally changed. She sees herself as retaining her subject knowledge expertise but also as losing her pedagogic interpretive skills. Nur, on the other hand, is seen as having both knowledge expertise through translation and the pedagogic skills to interpret whether students understand or not:

139 So I think, Nur, her main role is not really supposed to be translation and you can't directly translate in this subject but she's, she does a lot of explaining ... so Nur trains them to say, this word means or this word wants you to, which I wouldn't be able to do, because I don't really know where they are or what level or understanding they have. (ibid.)

Translating has become explaining and teaching. These quotes from the subject teacher (137–9) highlight what she sees and does not see as her classroom role. One area she claims as her own is the explaining of subject content; so much so, in fact, that when this role is adopted by the bilingual teacher, she describes Nur as having a more important job in the classroom than she does.

One role which the subject teacher does not see as her own is the focus on language-learning which in policy documents is also expected of her in classrooms where bilingual EAL students are learning. Her construction of 'hers' and 'Nur's' students shows that the policy of educational inclusion and entitlement, based on the mainstream classroom providing an opportunity for the most efficient route to English-language-learning, is not working fully in this case at least. This subject teacher sees her job as the delivery of the Information Technology curriculum. She is aware that Nur's Turkish provides a valuable way to deliver this aim, even though it fundamentally changes her job as a teacher. We now turn to look in more detail at how other languages are viewed for the teaching and learning of the curriculum in secondary school classrooms.

Attitudes to First Languages

In this section, we will look at different attitudes and values attached to the use of Turkish in the three secondary schools. A variety of views are expressed. We will see that there is a fair amount of ambiguity around the use of first languages and the role they should play in the mainstream classroom. We will deal with the views of three groups of teachers in the schools: management, STs and EAL teachers (non-bilingual). (The views of the bilingual staff have been given in the previous section.)

We will look at the views of one deputy head in detail in the transcript below. The deputy head's comments demonstrate the often contradictory discourses that exist around the use of other languages in English schools. Her role within the school as senior management shows her struggling to both endorse wider educational discourses on multilingualism while also acknowledging the difficulties schools and teachers face in sustaining these discourses under daily realities. I intend to extract from this transcript several themes that emerge from the way the deputy head describes the work of EAL teachers. The question, the deputy head is responding to is: *What is the role of the mother tongue in the mainstream classroom?*

140
Deputy head, school B (from interview transcript)

(a) It is a difficult one. And I think it is easier to see in terms of the kids. I think I can say it is so supportive for girls to have the opportunity to use their mother tongue for security and for understanding that I think it has a large role to play and we should never say, which is what I think we sometimes do say, 'speak in English, speak in English', as if it were better than speaking in Bengali, or Turkish or whatever the girls' mother tongue is and I think we should not discourage girls from continuing to use their mother tongue, I think it is important that they do so.

(b) I think for staff it is more difficult to draw a line. Undoubtedly, the use of the mother tongue for the bilingual teacher is very useful, particularly at early stages and if there happens to be a Turkish teacher and a Turkish girl then it is brilliant that they can use it. But I don't think that our support system for girls should be dependent on that because we are not all bilingual teachers, we are not multilingual anyway and we have girls, yes as it happens at the moment we have two Turkish-speaking teachers and a lot of girls who have just arrived for whom Turkish is their main language so it is convenient. But I think sometimes there is a danger of falling back on that and forgetting the other ways of accessing, of looking at the material of what is being done and making the English better and the English more accessible and relying a little too much on happening to speak the same first language as the girls.

(c) I don't know, it is a bit waffly but I think it can be almost, it is wonderful as part of the support system for those girls and on occasions like the traumas we've had recently in the school around the racism allegations and all the stuff, and thank God we have got staff with whom the girls can feel that bit safer and that bit more confident and who can also act as interpreters, which is a total misuse of their time but it is good that we have got them.

(d) But the philosophy of language development cannot be based on, can't be dependent on happening to have teachers who speak the first language of the girls, you know. Peter (non-bilingual EAL teacher) has got to be able to be just as successful as a support teacher and, therefore, the work-ings and the approach has to be based on the assumption that you won't happen to speak their mother tongue but when you do, yes it can be a great support, it can be a great pastoral support.

(e) I don't know whether sometimes it stays too much part of the classroom, I don't know. I mean this is vague observation, but whether sometimes a lesson is accessed by translation and I don't know whether that is terribly helpful . . . And if the bilingual teacher is turned into a kind of interpreter sitting alongside of the pupil literally translating from one language to another as opposed to simplifying or something within English, but trans-lating from one language to another then that is great because then the archaeology gets learnt but the English doesn't, yeah and that's the risk. So a mixture, I suppose is what's right, but I think there is a bit of a risk in terms of too much use of mother tongue from teacher to pupil within the classroom. Outside the classroom, yes, for different purposes, but within the classroom it can be risky.

Like other participants within school communities, this deputy head is shown handling and making sense of the contradictory and ideological dilemmas she faces as her allegiances to different positions is continuously and temporarily reconciled and renegotiated (Billig *et al.*, 1988). There is much that I could comment on in this transcript: the different views of community languages as a resource, a right and a problem (Ruiz, 1984) all expressed within the same transcript; the construction of racism and the institutional work the bilingual teachers are asked to do around it (see Chapter 10). However, I wish to focus now on one particular theme that emerged: the power of different pedagogies and the discourses associated with them.

The deputy head makes an argument *against* the use of the first language beyond transitional pastoral support for curriculum-learning. She argues that the support system for learning must be based on English. In particular she uses the words and phrases *'accessing* . . . the material' and *'making the English better and . . . more accessible'* and *'simplifying* . . . within English' (see paragraphs (b) and (e)). These phrases can be traced back to earlier government reports as, indeed, can references regarding the use of other languages as a minimal form of transitional bilingual support (DES, 1985). Indeed, as I have already indicated, EAL teachers themselves describe their work in similar terms. Terms such as 'facilitation' and 'accessing' are key words in professional EAL discourses. One might think then, that this is a clear example of professional and institutional discourses endorsing one another. That is, the facilitation of learning, the accessing of materials and the scaffolding of interaction are endorsed in school institutional discourses of the teaching of EAL. However, quite the opposite is true. The endorsement of support work through English is only given such a favourable approval when set against support work in a community language. The deputy head in Quote 140 is arguing that support for learning should be predicated on English rather than bilingual support.

Interestingly, we see this view endorsed also in one of the non-bilingual EAL teachers' transcripts:

141 I think it [community language] should be used as rarely as possible. And I am not sure if that is because I cannot use it and I am jealous. Maybe it is that slight ego thing, that the way I do it is best and because the way I do it is in English, there is that side of you that thinks this is the best way of doing it. I genuinely don't know which is better. If I push pride stuff to one side, I think Unal – by speaking Turkish to the Turkish girls – has much more immediate access to getting the subject material across, but I think probably, logically, the temptation is for me, the amount of English he gets across is less, whereas with me I get less content across, but more English across. So in reality, if I were to be in a class for four lessons a week, that class would speak more English but they wouldn't pass their GCSEs.[4] But they might at the end of two years have the English

to try the GCSE. With Unal . . ., at the end of the two years, they might not have the English to do the GCSE but they would have the content to do the GCSE. Whereas if you have the two of us supporting [a] class, like in geography, that might be the best combination. I'd like to think that all the Turkish girls will be entered for the exam. There are some that won't, one or two, but that is partly to do with . . . learning difficulties, as well as the language. (B3)

This teacher prioritizes second-language learning over content-learning. Or, at least, s/he sees the way to learning curriculum language as through the process of second-language learning. Indeed, this is in keeping with policy documents. The non-bilingual EAL teacher presents the dilemma as: to teach subject curriculum through the first language or to teach it through the second. Obviously each route requires different skills. However, both routes require collaboration and agreement with the ST concerning language- and curriculum-learning aims. The problem is that of those subject teachers involved in my research, with the exception of those teachers working in partnerships, did not see it as their responsibility to pay attention to both sets of aims simultaneously.

Before we turn to look at the ST's view of using the first language, let us look at two more EAL teacher transcripts and the views expressed regarding the use of community languages. In the first, we see the EAL teacher make the important link between identity and learning and the role of community languages and bilingual EAL teachers in this process. In the second, we see the importance assigned to community languages in making the transition to learning fully in English:

142 I think actually in all the schools I've worked I hear more of other languages than I've heard in other schools, which is quite amazing. I think there is tolerance here of other people's languages. I think there is more tolerance between the children of each other's languages and ethnic differences and similarities. There seems to be a bigger sense of community here than in other schools where I've worked, but there isn't among the staff, and I think part of the problem is the staff don't reflect the population of the children that we've got. We've got very few staff who came to Britain from overseas. [I] mean, the relief when Ayşe came to work for us last year. The relief of the students was enormous, absolutely enormous. They were just thrilled to pieces. She got a gaggle of little ducklings all waddling behind her. (A1)

143 I think it is invaluable for the teacher at stage one because when you are in a classroom there is so much misconception that it is difficult to put across, it is difficult to put across your instructions in a classroom with lots of other things going on because it cuts across, therefore, if simple instructions could be given in the mother tongue (MT) I would do it if I could. The use of the MT raises the learner's confidence. At the early stages it is productive (for the students), but it can be used counterproductively by students who know

that you don't wish to forbid them to talk in the MT but they can introduce disruptive strategies such as calling across the classroom in their MT, creates a situation whereby if the MT were not being used you would reprimand the children, but of course you don't want to say to them don't use your own language. I mean I have seen that done with the older girls and the answer for that I suppose is to say, well don't shout across the classroom in any language. To go back to the staff and student interactions using the MT, I think if it can be done, it should be done. The difficulty is not just getting your bilingual staff but difficulty you face is when your learners do not share the language and then I suppose you would have to use English as the medium of instruction of the target language as the medium of instruction. (B4)

In these transcripts (Quotes 140–3), from a deputy head and from non-bilingual EAL teachers, we see a variety of views expressed concerning the use of community languages in the classroom. Three of the four teachers support community languages predominantly for their use in helping students in theor transition from learning in their MT to learning subject content in English. One transcript (Quote 142) makes the important point that identity and learning are linked, and that community languages can serve an important role in helping children to feel a sense of belonging within their school (see also Chapter 10).

Now we will turn to look at the views of STs towards the use of community languages in the mainstream classroom. From my data 7 of the 14 subject teachers in open ethnographic interviews spoke of the importance of first languages for subject teaching in a similar way. A flavour of this is given in the extracts below:

144 I don't discourage the use of the first language if people need to communicate in it. I am quite happy if it clarifies. I mean I can't use it myself because I have no idea. **But if somebody said, yes we could understand this if we translated it then yes. Because as I said my aim is to get them to understand. I don't care if they understand in English, Turkish or whatever ... it might give them some positive things like they understand what all the others do but in their own language.** (History teacher, Sinchester)

145 [non-bilingual EAL] Support is like having another teacher in the room, and it means they can sit with one person and you know that person is getting attention, but having Nur here is a different sort of thing. I know the children will understand what I am saying. I mean I definitely couldn't do it without Nur. (Information Technology teacher, Soldingstoke)

146 Well, I would be really supportive of having more mother tongue but the problem is time and resources. We (laughs) we have got one girl that we sit with and we work out a glossary and she gives as a translation (laughs) which we then photocopy for others, but it is very difficult, because of

time and resources and because neither of us speak Turkish, and not just Turkish, all the Asian kids as well. Having so many different languages in the school is a real problem. (Humanities teacher, Soldingstoke)

Such endorsement by subject teachers for the use of the first language for the transmission of subject curriculum is an indication of what the subject teachers see as the primary purpose of secondary school teaching and the pedagogy which delivers this. It supports a particular view of pedagogy as built upon subject knowledge and its efficient transmission to pedagogic subjects. However, some STs also commented on the importance of other languages in the classroom in terms of cultural enrichment. Quote 147 is taken from one of the teachers involved in partnership teaching who is also bilingual. He presents some very interesting and fairly radical ideas for English secondary schools. His transcript is very much focused on the benefits of being bilingual. The two extracts which follow this (Quotes 148 and 149) also comment on the school's role in viewing linguistic and ethnic differences as a resource. Quote 148 calls upon the school to respond to minority needs by prioritizing the needs of large minority groups within the school. Quote 149 shows an ST's recognition of the struggle teachers face in trying to avoid stereotyping by gender, ethnicity and language, and the importance of constantly revisiting these conceptions so that such stereotypes do not become entrenched in a school community:

147 I don't think it comes into the equation, bilingual children, enough and I feel we do not do enough for them. We do not do enough about different cultures, about their cultures, getting them involved, bringing their culture into the classroom. I would love to do teaching technology in another language, things like that. I would love to make it more cultural because it tends to be very, very, white, middle-class teaching that happens, certainly within the food area I've noticed. Perhaps you could come in, you could have a technology lesson, look at [it] in another language, look at it in another culture. I mean obviously I'm half Spanish – I could go in there, we could look at Spanish history, architecture, we could do a project on something based on that, we could look at the language involved, look at where the language comes from. We could do the same with Greek. We could look at technology within Greece. We could look at language because a lot of technological language comes from ancient Greek. You could have a lesson perhaps in Spanish and I would teach the class in Spanish and I'd teach technology. Something like that would be very interesting. (A6)

148 They [bilingual students] play such an important part in this school you know and I was even talking to another support teacher today. We were talking about this tendency to pander to a kind of semi-middle-class group and pander to the parents and pander to, you know, people down below. This is something that the previous head didn't do. He was somebody

that was into the kids in a really big way. You know there are a lot of people outside who now perceive this as a good school and a lot of them are the middle-class trendies who will send their kids there. But they also want a big say in what is happening. They are the people who turn up at the parents' evenings. I mean if you go to any of those parents' evenings. I was president of the staff association here last year, you know there wasn't one Afro-Caribbean person at the meeting. On the whole committee I think there was one Turkish woman. . . . And as I say it does pander to a small group and I think that is a problem. If I were head here I would employ a few more Turkish teachers without a doubt and I would have them in the class. You know, in different classes. . . . I think first and foremost support and I would have a very clear programme of what I wanted to do. You know I'd maybe attach a Turkish teacher to every big department and have them working with that department. You know something like that could be real and it could work. But I don't think there is any urgency, I don't think they see that . . . I mean this is all to do with money . . . definitions of success are dictated by league table[s] and I mean Turkish kids are not going to show well in the league tables no matter what you do, so you know they are going to take a back seat. (C6)

149 You do tend to hear conversations, oh you know, '9 N all the Turkish boys in it' where they are lumped together. But one of the reasons why I think that is because they also, they do tend to clump together and I've noticed with my own Turkish group that I've got five Turkish boys in there and they started off mixing and then they kind of formed this little clique, which I try and sort of integrate them more but I think it is quite a negative thing because anything then that a Turkish boy does that is bad, is then 'oh well, you know, the Turkish kids are like this' and so I think it is bad thing. You don't see, the Turkish girls tend to stick together but you don't seem to get that same kind of [reputation]. It is almost like a bad boy culture or that is how it is perceived, and it is not necessarily a bad boy culture but it is perceived as being like that. So yeah, they are seen as being a kind of group and they sort of hang around together . . . in the play ground and that sort of thing. . . . I don't think there is antagonism about it but subconsciously they do club together, they do think, 'oh well Turkish kids are like this' and they make generalizations about [them] and I am guilty of this myself. But they do think Turkish boys tend to XYZ and that everyone gets lumped into that. . . . Boys and girls. Yeah you've got . . . we have got an awful lot of very dedicated very able, very intelligent and very motivated Turkish girls and they stay well clear of it um but there are a lot of Turkish girls who are involved in it and a lot of black girls as well. (C7)

Subject teachers, like EAL teachers, express a variety of attitudes to the use of community languages in the classroom. Many of these are innovative and far-reaching.

Ironically, subject teachers' endorsement of community languages for curriculum-learning appears to stem from policy documents endorsement of curriculum teaching over other educational functions. Such is the pressure on subject teachers to deliver examination results which show curriculum-learning that these teachers express a willingness to have the curriculum taught in any language as long as subject-learning takes place. Subject teachers, in endorsing the use of bilingual explanation, interpretation and translation, are therefore playing their part in expanding the role of other languages in the mainstream beyond the rhetorically safe 'language as resource' position which keeps other languages 'outside and incidental to the learning process' (Bourne, 2001: 251).

There is little in the way of bilingual education in English secondary schools. It has not been supported in either policy documents or found to exist in any sustainable way in empirical work that has investigated the use of other languages in English classrooms. Work on other languages in English secondary schools has mostly described its pastoral and transitional role. This chapter has attempted to show other languages' teaching and learning role in the mainstream and the support it receives from subject curriculum teachers. My argument has been that bilingual teachers choose to endorse dominant educational discourses and, in doing so, include bilingual children in the same endeavours as other non-bilingual children.

Chapter Summary

This chapter has attempted to illustrate the importance of bilingual discourse in English secondary school classrooms for subject-learning. Bilingual EAL teachers do not use support work in the same way as their non-bilingual EAL colleagues: they use first languages to engage directly in subject teaching, thus their focus is on subject content first. In this way, bilingual EAL teachers share similar aims to STs. However, this chapter leaves many questions unanswered and may debates unheard. Some of these questions include: Where are the boundaries and overlaps in translating and explaining in the use of first and community languages for subject teaching?; How much do bilingual teachers 'borrow' and/or transform the words of others in their teaching of subject curriculum?; What impact does the use of other languages have on the construction of teacher knowledge in secondary schools?; What constitutes teacher professional knowledge in co-taught classrooms?; How do these classroom discourses impact on issues of discourse and power in the construction of different pedagogic players? In addition to these questions, one of the debates unheard in this chapter is whether this transmission approach to pedagogy offers only a limited solution to the needs of all students in schools and whether more radical pedagogies offer more scope for students' learning (Edwards, 2000; Kress, 1999; Scardamalia & Bereiter, 1999). Discussions on bilingual education and EAL support need to retain a front seat for such mainstream pedagogic debates.

Notes

1. A version of this chapter has appeared in the *International Journal of Bilingual Education and Bilingualism*. See Creese (2004).
2. Community/heritage languages can be taught on the secondary school timetable as a modern foreign language.
3. In order to increase the profile of language-learning in England there have been some recent moves to pilot content- and language-integration projects (CLIP, 2003). However, the emphasis is on the use of modern European foreign languages rather than community languages (http://www.cilt/org.uk/clip/index.htm, accessed February 2003). The primary aim appears to be providing more opportunities for the majority monolingual population to become better language learners rather than increasing the use of community languages for the teaching of mainstream curriculum in secondary schools. Moreover, the importance of language-learning and bilingualism has been heightened in recent years. The Nuffield Inquiry on Languages (Nuffield, 2000) recommended that there should be a nationally coordinated programme of bilingual learning in the UK and argued that, 'An early start to language learning also enhances literacy, citizenship and intercultural tolerance' (Nuffield, 2000, see http://www.wmin.ac.uk/sshl/nuffield/findings.htm, accessed May 2004).
4. General Certificate of Secondary Education: national school-leaving qualification usually taken at age 16.

Chapter 10

Mediating Allegations of Racism: Bilingual EAL Teachers in Action[1]

Introduction

This chapter illustrates how bilingual EAL teachers, employed in one of the three London schools in this study, dealt with one particular event which disrupted the school over several days. This chapter differs from the previous chapters in that it draws on data from one school only. It offers an account of a particular incident to illustrate the kinds of work bilingual EAL teachers do in mediating between participants in and beyond the school. It shows how important other languages and bilingual staff are to the school.

The incident involves an accusation of racism made by one group of Turkish-speaking Kurdish-background students against the school. The students accused the school of treating its students from different ethnicities differently and unjustly. This chapter will look at how different languages are used in the school by the head teacher to refute these accusations and also the role the Turkish-speaking bilingual EAL teachers played in mediating the school's message.

Skonnington School and its Turkish-speaking Students

Skonnington school is a lively mixture of colours, cultures, languages and difference housed in an old and rather bleak Victorian building on the side of a busy road. The school is a single-sex girls school. Over 90% of the students are listed as having English as an additional language (EAL). The largest linguistic minority during the period of data collection was Turkish-speaking.

The Turkish-speaking minority at the school consist of an older, more-established, Turkish Cypriot community and newer Turkish/Kurdish-speaking refugees. Both have settled in the same areas of London. The more recent group came to Britain as political refugees, having been caught in the crossfire of the Turkish government's battle with the separatist Kurdistan Workers' Party (PKK), a left-wing Kurdish revolutionary group fighting for an independent Kurdistan. Those seen as promoting or even supporting any form of Kurdish autonomy or rights within Turkey are dealt with extremely harshly by the Turkish state (see Amnesty International, 1995a, 1995b; Refugee Council, 1995). Since the late 1980s, and increasingly so in the 1990s, large numbers of Turks and Turkish/Kurdish-speaking Kurds from mainland Turkey have arrived in Britain. The group tends to be highly politicized (Campbell, 1994). However, very little research exists on the Turkish-speaking communities in London (IOE, 1999; Ladbury, 1977; Mehmet Ali, 1991).

We now move to look at how a particular incident in the school impacted on its community. This case study consists of two student-produced texts distributed to passers-by and visitors to the school, and ethnographic field notes written up as analytic vignettes of the two-day event (Erickson, 1990). After the information has been presented, I use an ecological model of linguistic diversity to consider how Turkish was used and its speakers constructed during the incident.

Institutional Racism or Equal Opportunities?

On 12 October 1994, at 8.45 a.m. I entered Skonnington school as I had done for the previous five weeks to collect data for the ethnographic study I was conducting on the relationships, roles and talk of English as an additional language (EAL) teachers and the mainstream subject curriculum teachers with whom they worked. However, this day was immediately different. It started with a demonstration of 20 to 25 bilingual (Kurdish) Turkish/English-speaking girls from the school who were standing outside the gates with banners and a loud hailer saying 'black and white unite against racism' and 'beep your horn if you are against racism'. The girls were also distributing the following text to passers-by and to teachers who had gone outside to speak to them.

Text 1

WE WANT TEACHERS NOT TO DIVIDE US BUT TO GIVE BETTER EDUCATION

On 11 October a group of students started arguing with the other groups of Turkish and Kurdish students.[2]

They all forced them to get into a room and blackmailed, so that they don't tell the teachers about this. There wasn't a good reason for this. But only prejudice. That is not the first time its happened, it continues for years and years in our school. Also we are aware of that the students in schools of Borough X are facing the same problems. And attacks on the students is not the only problem in our school. Briefly the problems we are facing are;

1. When there is a complain about the foods we get, what staff tell is if the food is cleaner in your country then go back to your own country.
2. Some of our teachers e.g. the English teacher Miss X is insulting the students especially refugees.

---

3. The teachers in Skonnington school and other schools are treating to the students depending on their nationalities. While the other students get rid of everything, some students especially Turkish and Kurdish students are being blame.
4. By this they are trying to divide the students into aparts. We know that all the problems that we are facing can be solved. The teachers and the management of the school do not want to solve the problems deliberately.

The students have nothing to attack each other. We only want to study and be educated in better methods. Students should be united against all other problems we are facing in our school. But the school management is avoiding this by dividing the students in spite of their nationalities. We don't want our teachers to divide us, we just want better education. We don't want racism in our schools, we want to unite with all black and white students. That is why we are having the boycout in our school and our demands are as follows.

1. We don't want any racist teachers in our school, especially, Mrs X.
2. We don't want teachers and managements to divide students by their nationalities.
3. We want them to consider all the complaints that we have e.g. foods, bullying.
4. Our only demand is to have friendly and equal education for all students

(Spelling and punctuation as in the original.)

Later in the day, this was followed by a second text, written by a different group of girls (African-Caribbean), who were contesting the account of the writers of the first text. This second text was distributed to students and teachers within the school community, and also to the local BBC network who had arrived at lunchtime.

Text 2

STOP FOOLING AROUND

Due to recent letters that have been received by the students outside of Skonnington that are against your silly boycott we feel that you are making a mockery out of yourselves.

Nothing will be resolved if you carry on acting like immature little 5 year olds. This is only to make you see what fools you are. Some of us think that you are right to appeal against your rights but not in this manner. By holding up banners and posters saying that **'black and white unite'** has no meaning because most of the people or students like each other and have no means for racism so we all think by what you are doing is wrong.

You are making our school reputation go down and you are hurting alot of peoples feelings by what you are doing although you might have already noticed. Maybe what you are doing is right but you have no feelings and consideration of what other people think of you. Many turkish and kurdish people are not protesting because they feel that nothing will not be resolved and that they also think it is wrong.

We gather that some people are racist but a fact is that everybody in a way is racist and that includes all of the kurdish and turkish people. Fair enough we admit some of the students can be rascist but that does not allow you to bring any of the teachers into it and by doing that you have made things worse. STUDENTS THAT CARE !!!

(Spelling, bold and punctuation as in the original.)

It is clear from just an initial reading that the writers of Texts 1 and 2 present the school community and teachers very differently in their two accounts. Text 1 constructs the teachers as racists and divisive, saying that the teachers:

- insult refugees;
- treat students differently depending on their national backgrounds;
- single out Turkish and Kurdish pupils for blame;
- divide students against one another;
- let problems go unsolved and do not follow up complaints.

While Text 2 constructs the teachers as victims, saying they:

- have been hurt;
- are having their reputation damaged;
- are the same as anyone else.

In Text 1 the writers present themselves as united with the rest of the student community. Students:

- should not attack one another;
- are united in their need for a better and fairer education.

Whereas in Text 2 the student writers' of Text 1 are presented as different from the rest of the student community. They are seen as:

- silly;
- immature;
- like 5-year-olds;
- fools;
- wrong;
- hurtful;

- not supported by other Turkish/Kurdish-speaking students;
- have no feelings and show no consideration.

What is apparent in Text 1 from the beginning are claims of ethnic difference and how different groups of students are treated differently within the school. The girls are fighting against the 'establishment'. In the text there are clear elements of intertextuality (Fairclough, 1995; Gee, 1999). One idea of Bakhtin's work (1986) is the notion of 'appropriation'. Text 1 reads as a political manifesto in which the unfair treatment of different ethnic groups is central. However, there is also reference to the students' more recent experiences and discourse at the school, with a mention in the last line of the text of equal opportunities and their expectations that all 'nationalities' be treated the same. As newly arrived political refugees from rural south-east Turkey, where their families might have been involved in political struggle, these students may have had first-hand experience of fighting for their political and human rights. It is this history that they bring to their school, where it meets a common educational discourse of equal opportunities. However, the writers of Text 1 do not yet 'own' this discourse (Cameron, 1997) and the ones they do own, as we will see, are rendered too difficult for the school to consider.

The writers of Text 2, on the other hand, do 'own' the equal opportunities discourse and see their message as being taken up and endorsed by the school. This group of students builds upon the notion of a school community, to which both teachers and students belong: 'You are making our school reputation go down and you are hurting alot of peoples feelings by what you are doing although you might have already noticed.' The writers of Text 2 position the majority of students and teachers as being within the same community. For them, it is the writers of Text 1 who are now outside this community. The writers of Text 2 are attempting to isolate these students, not only from their ethnic group, who they aspire to represent, but also from the rest of the school community.

Like the writers of Text 1, this second text is a map of the writers' previous social experiences and histories. This piece of text endorses the school's discourse of equal opportunities and wider societal attitudes towards equality, and distances itself from the discourse of challenge put forth in Text 1. The student writers of Text 2 use a discourse very unlike the political manifesto of Text 1; rather they appear more to be writing a letter to a media editor of some kind. Indeed the BBC was one of their intended audiences because at the time of writing the girls knew they would be visiting the school. Moreover, little is made of difference of any kind within the school. Ethnicity is played down, as are differences between teachers and students. Ethnicity is mentioned in as much as to claim that the dissonant party does not represent the Turkish/Kurdish group as a whole. Shared agendas have been constructed here, with racism attributed to everyone rather than any particular group.

My next step in this analysis is to consider how different participants within the school took up positions around the demonstration. I ask two questions to achieve this:

(1) What interpretations and identifications do different participants take up in the school around the student demonstration of Text 1 (in varying degrees I had access to the head teacher, teachers and students)?
(2) How do these interpretations impact on the roles Turkish and English played in the school and on their speakers?

Legitimate and Non-legitimate Protests

In the production of Text 2, the school had a clearly preferable message for the outside world. This message presented the school as a community in which all its participants were treated equally around issues of learning, discipline, procedure, ethnicity and race. It was this message, via Text 2, which was handed to the local BBC network when the camera crew turned up just after lunch. The head teacher was advised by the local educational officers not to speak to the BBC film crew herself. However, she did arrange for the writers of Text 2 to speak with the press. I was not present at this meeting. In the end, however, the local BBC current affairs programme did not run this news. Despite the fact that the head had avoided a direct commentary with the media, she had gone some way to effectively managing the kind of messages which the outside world would hear about the school, given the rather uncomfortable accusations made by the student writers of Text 1.

The work that went into producing a united community discourse was thus partially orchestrated by the head teacher and senior managers, but this is only partly true. Their position was not simply 'imposed' from above on the rest of the school community, but also emerged from the teachers and the students them-selves to differing degrees. The writers of Text 2, many of the teachers and, indeed, even the writers of Text 1 recognized the discourse of equal opportunities as being an important ideology in the school community. I wish to argue that it was particip-ation in this discourse, rather than expertise, allegiance or heritage of a particular language (Leung *et al.*, 1997; Rampton, 1990), which determined the students of Text 1 as (temporarily at least) outside the school 'community'. That is, the discourse of equal opportunities held more allegiance than whether students or staff spoke Turkish or not. We will now look at two further instances of data that shows the complexity of participants' differing identification positionings throughout the event. The first example is taken from field notes of a year 10 geography class. The second is a vignette of a staff meeting held the day after the demonstration.

In the year 10 geography classroom

During the first morning of the demonstration I attended, as usual, the year 10 geography class. This class was in the unusual position of being supported by both a bilingual teacher, Mr Hakan, and another EAL teacher, Mr Noble, during different timetable periods. This was because of the high number of EAL/bilingual students in the class needing support. Some of the girls from this class were taking part in the demonstration. Below are my written-up field notes from that morning.

Vignette 13

Geography, year 10, 12 October 1994 – 9.40 a.m.

I go to the geography class but there are no teachers there and very few students. Mr Hakan is contacting parents of the demonstrating girls while the geography teacher, Mr Scott, has gone outside to talk to the girls and is trying to persuade them to come back in. I listen to one student speaking Turkish with Ayşe, a newly arrived and early stage bilingual Turkish–Cypriot-speaking girl. This is the first time I have heard Ayşe's interactant, Jasmine, speak Turkish. She is not known to the EAL staff as she is fully proficient in English and does not need their learning and language support. She usually sits at the front of the class away from the other EAL students. She and Ayşe are talking about the demonstrators. In Turkish they ask each other if the girls outside had told them about the demonstration. It appears they were not told anything. They both say 'it has nothing to do with them' and 'they don't want anything to do with it'. The class is very much changed. The few students in there are not doing any work and there is a lot of discussion about what is going on outside.

At 9.40 two of the girls who have been demonstrating outside return to class along with the two teachers, Mr Scott and Mr Hakan. The teachers get the class started on their work. Mr Hakan tries to settle the two returnees and help them with their work. However, they are angry with him and do not want his help. They respond much more warmly to me. He is seen as the enemy. However, they are slow to work and spend a lot of time arguing with the Ayşe and Jasmine. Their exchanges are angry.

After class, I hear that the police were called in to frighten the demonstrators, but the policeman turned up on his bike and this didn't have the intended effect!

I wish to make three points from this vignette. The first is that the event itself brought out a speaker of Turkish in this class not known to the school. Moreover, it allowed this bilingual speaker of Turkish and English to use her Turkish in ways beyond the usual 'language support' for curriculum-learning and all the deficit associations that often, and unfairly, go with this function. The second point is that it appears that the Turkish–Cypriot-speaking girls were not involved in the organization or implementation of the demonstration, which appeared to be under the ownership of one particular group of Turkish-speaking Kurdish girls. The third point to be made is that using Turkish with the Turkish-speaking bilingual teacher for learning purposes in this class was rejected by the two girls who had returned to the class from the demonstration. There are a number of possible reasons for this. Mr Hakan was clearly engaged in doing the work of the school in phoning their parents and, therefore, was acting against the demonstrators' objectives.

Moreover, like the Cypriot girls they were arguing with, Mr Hakan was from a similar background and did not have the same inheritance of Turkish that these girls had. This may have been particularly relevant as throughout the class Turkish was being used by different Turkish heritages to either endorse or reject the primary message put out by the girls demonstrating.

We shall now go on to look at how the event was perceived by another set of participants in the school community: the head teacher and teaching staff.

At the staff meeting

During and following the demonstration, the head teacher held a series of ad hoc and emergency staff meetings. One of these is reported in detail taken from my field notes below.

Vignette 14
Staff meeting, 13 October 1994

The whole staff is assembled and school is to start late. The head teacher narrates the incident. A lot is made about the reputation of the school. She talks about the successes of the school: names some 'Turkish' girls who have been successful, and what a good reputation the school has for integrating all races. She explains there have been racist incidents in other schools in the borough but not in this school.

She thanks the staff repeatedly for their support and says she does not want to see staff turn against one another. After she has finished speaking several teachers are selected to give their opinions. She starts with Mr Hakan and Miss Zengin. Both bilingual teachers support the head's arguments that the group of girls were organized by outside groups; that there is a girl who has been trouble ever since she arrived, agitating the others. Both the bilingual teachers support the school's line that the girls, even if they have grievances, should have gone through the regular channels. The majority of teachers who speak say that girls should be disciplined, that they were lying if they say they did not know about the anti-racist policy.

The teachers react angrily to the girls' accusation that the teachers treat the Afro-Caribbean girls differently from the Turkish girls because, they the teachers, are afraid of confrontation. The physical education teacher is really angry and says, 'that's a load of rubbish'.

In the main it is those who are taking the same line as the head teacher who speak out. Only one teacher offers an alternative view when he says that 'we' the teachers should admire the girls for demonstrating, because we have all done this in our lives, 'After all they wouldn't be able to do this in Turkey'. While he is speaking, the teacher accused of racism gets up and walks out. He continues saying that we must look into the comment that the girls don't know about the anti-racist statement. He is the only teacher to take a different line. Following his comment there is an uncomfortable silence. The meeting is drawing to a close and the head teacher tells her teachers she will keep them fully informed.

This vignette makes salient some of the interpretations made by the head and her teaching staff towards the accusations made in Text 1. The head teacher develops three main arguments against the girls' behaviour. One theme which the students of Text 1 had raised was the lack of follow-up by staff of their grievances when racist incidents occurred. The head teacher does not address this directly, but she (and her teachers) are adamant that the students themselves have not followed the correct procedures. This was central to the head teacher as it allowed her to show the school as having equal measures for all when dealing with racism. There seems to be little awareness that the students might not have followed normal procedure because of their frustrations in the past or that the school had not been successful in making its procedures known.

Related to the discussion of procedures is the second theme the head develops, which is the description of the girls as rude and heavily influenced by outsiders. This interpretation of the girls behaviour is similar to that made by the students in Text 2. The demonstrators are presented as foolish and easily influenced by others. They are stripped of their intentions to make claims and demands. The girls are presented as outside of the school community because of their rudeness and lack of willingness to play by the school's rules.

A third theme apparent in the field notes is the reaction to accusations of racism and the argument that teachers treat various ethnic groups differently within the school. Teachers are outraged by this suggestion and a discussion about the feasibility of this cannot even be developed in the staff meeting, such is the anger it creates. The general consensus is that all groups are treated equally and in the same way within the school.

The interpretations the head teacher and the majority of teachers choose to take-up around the event are parallel to those developed by the student writers of Text 2. Both the staff meeting and Text 2 develop a position of shared and equal agendas. Diversity is celebrated in the same way, with each 'multi' culture treated as if it were equal and the same. Only those teachers who are seen to be central in supporting this discourse are recruited to help in its endorsement. Some teachers are silenced, either because their views are considered to be too dangerous or because they are not seen to be relevant. The two bilingual teachers were seen as central to supporting the school's message and were actively recruited during the staff meeting to lend their voices to the head teacher's.

Recognizing and Endorsing Difference

During and in the aftermath of the demonstration, the two bilingual Turkish-speaking teachers were called out of the classroom to help the head teacher contact and meet parents of the girls who had been demonstrating. From my field notes, I have the following extract:

> 12 October 1994
> Mr Hakan is frantically translating letters, being called to phone parents and talk to them when they arrive. Miss Zengin is also taken out of the science class that she has been covering. She is also talking to parents.

The two teachers were exhausted by the time the weekend arrived. The school had made extensive use of their linguistic and knowledge resources, which no other teachers in the school were able to offer. During this incident, knowledge of Turkish and English within the school was extremely important. That is, linguistic knowledge of a community language rose over other, more usually, dominant knowledge and temporarily changed the knowledge hierarchy in the school (Luke & Luke, 1999; Martin-Jones & Heller, 1996). For the head teacher, it was the bilingual EAL teachers' expertise in Turkish that was the single most important knowledge in helping the school deal with the demonstration and disseminate the equal opportunities message. This linguistic expertise was unproblematically used by the head. As long as the bilingual teachers spoke Turkish, she had access to a group of parents she would not normally have been able to reach. For her, the differences in cultural, political, social, economic, historic, age and knowledge backgrounds between the bilingual EAL teachers and the student demonstrators were immaterial – language as a resource to communicate the school's agenda was paramount. However, these complexities *were* apparent to the bilingual teachers, the students and their parents.

The two bilingual EAL teachers did not share the same inheritance of Turkish as the demonstrating students. As mentioned earlier, the girls were a group of refugees from Turkey whose recent and family histories involved a struggle against the Turkish state for linguistic rights and demands for greater Kurdish independence. This history meant a very different affiliation towards Turkish than Unal Hakan and Dilek Zengin had, coming themselves from Turkish–Cypriot backgrounds. However, despite these differences, the bilingual teachers and students also shared similarities in their awareness of linguistic and cultural differences. The teachers' own ethnic and linguistic complexities meant they understood the dangers of simplifying all Turkish speakers into an unproblematic 'idealized Turkish native speaker' category (Leung *et al.*, 1997; Rampton, 1990). Whereas the intricacies of this knowledge did not seem to feature in the schools' use of the bilingual teachers, it did with the bilingual teachers themselves who used this awareness in the day-to-day teaching of their bilingual pupils.

The two bilingual teachers chose to endorse certain issues relating to the school's collective response to dealing with a potentially explosive issue. In doing so, they stood alongside other teachers in the school to legitimate the central response to the girls' demonstration. For example, they endorsed the head's account of the students' rudeness and lack of following procedures. They were vocal in the staff meeting and throughout the two-day incident in arguing that the girls should be treated the same as everyone else in enforcing school rules and disciplinary matters. However, they were silent in the staffroom when the discussion turned to differential treatment of ethnic groups within the school by teachers. It is hard to know what they thought. It is certainly clear that within the atmosphere of the staff meeting reported (see Vignette 14), it would have been difficult for a any teacher to argue that teachers did treat the students from various ethnic groups differently around behaviour issues. It would have been difficult also to argue against a discourse of equal opportunity and in favour of the differential treatment of different minority linguistic and ethnic groups within the school. In the section that follows I shall take-up some of these possibilities. I do this using a model of language ecology offered by Haugen (1972).

Turkish in the Mainstream

In his book, *The Ecology of Language*, Haugen (1972: 337) presents ten questions to be asked when considering how languages interrelate with their environment. Four of these are helpful in considering how Turkish was used by its speakers and non-speakers during this incident in the school:

- Who are the users of the language?
- What are its domains of use?
- What kind of institutional support has the language won?
- What are the attitudes of its users towards the language in terms of intimacy and status, leading to personal identification?

These questions are used heuristically to consider how different languages and their speakers are held in complex relations with one another as events unfolded. They are useful tools in an analysis that attempts to show not only how a shifting context allows participants multiple identification positionings, but also how societal and institutional discourses impact on whichever of these identifications comes to dominate discursively. I use Haugen's questions to show the complexity of the context in capturing how languages and their speakers interact during one particular event within the school.

Who are the users of the language?

There are many different languages in use within this school. Of the minority languages, Turkish has the highest profile, not only because it is used by the largest minority but also because the school has employed two Turkish-speaking bilingual teachers. One of these has a middle management position within the school. It is usual, therefore, to hear Turkish being used around the school. However, of particular interest during this event was how speakers of Turkish not known to the EAL staff, because they did not need language support, emerged as bilingual speakers of both Turkish and English. The event itself created opportunities for some speakers of Turkish to use their bilingualism in the school in new ways. Whereas it appears to be the case that minority languages are used predominantly by the school as a means to learning the curriculum in English, this event provided students with the possibility to use Turkish to express opinions beyond curriculum-learning. Moreover, Turkish was not only used to endorse what the girls demonstrating were doing; it was also used to articulate against it. Similarly, the use of English took on the same flexibility and was used both to articulate against and lend support to the demonstrators. We have seen how in one class English was preferred to Turkish by the two returning demonstrators as a means of distancing themselves from the help the Turkish-speaking teacher usually gave them who, because of his role in assisting the school, appeared to be positioned as a traitor to their cause.

What are its domains of use?

During the event, Turkish certainly expanded its use within the school. It continued to be used in the classroom for support in curriculum-learning and it also continued to be used for pastoral purposes as students were inducted into the school. As events unfolded, however, the head teacher made extensive use of it, through her bilingual teachers. She required the bilingual EAL teachers to write to parents requesting they attend the school for meetings, and when these parents arrived, to narrate the school's version of events. As such, Turkish had grown beyond its usual support role. A minority language usually restricted to certain domains and uses, Turkish expanded its scope considerably during the two-day event.

What kind of institutional support has the language won?

Although Turkish expanded its function within the school, this was only in the short term. The institution gave support to Turkish as a means to extend the school's central message. Moreover, those who did not take up this line, either in English or Turkish, were temporarily seen as outside the school's ideological community. Turkish was recruited by the school to implement wider educational discourses within and beyond the school.

What are the attitudes of its users towards the language in terms of intimacy and status, leading to personal identification?

Haugen uses 'status' to mean association with power and influence in the social group and intimacy in the sense of being associated with solidarity, shared values, friendship, love; that is, those contacts established through common family and group life (1972: 327). The incident at Skonnington shows how complex the participants' identification positionings were with regard to ethnicity, linguistic affiliations, and what it meant to be a member of the school community. The teachers and students all took up positions around 'the Turkish language' during the event. We can see that student expertise and heritage previously unknown to the bilingual staff emerged. We can also see that the Turkish speakers affiliated themselves to the language in different ways as the events unfolded. Moreover, we see that the non-bilingual Turkish-speaking staff and students also took up positions about and around Turkish and its users. One view of Turkish which continued to dominate within the school was of the language stripped of its cultural and historical roots. This meant that the school showed little understanding of differences within and between the Turkish-speaking communities. The head teacher's main concern was to use Turkish to convey the school message. There appeared to be a real danger that all Turkish-speaking students would be perceived as a single homogenous group. This meant that Turkish mainlanders, Turkish/Kurdish refugees and Turkish–Cypriot islanders were all being grouped together as one Turkish-speaking whole. One danger of this simplification is that the school would never understand why and how this particular group of girls chose to demonstrate in this way.

The writers of Text 1 accused the school of treating certain groups of students differently and unfairly. However, could it not also be argued that the girls were not treated differently enough? The pursuit of equity in education has been guided and enhanced by a discussion of equality of opportunity. But this movement has often produced analyses of educational practices that consider only one category of inequality at a time (Daniels *et al.*, 2001). The question becomes one of how we should recognize and respond to difference in an equitable manner. It may well be that we should seek to establish new forms of difference rather than impose sameness. Daniels *et al.* (2001) suggest that to treat people equally is not necessary to treat them in exactly the same manner. On the contrary, to treat people as equals may require that they are not treated the same way. However, it is essential that they are treated fairly. Perhaps it is equity that is the starting point rather than equality. Solstad (1994, in Daniels *et al.*, 2001) argues that rather than dealing with equity from a centralised position, the principle of equity may be referenced to diversity, and realized in particular settings, regions and localities.

Inclusive education is based on 'difference' as a usual part of any classroom environment (Ballard, 1995; Norwich, 1996). If this is so, we must beware of 'off-the-peg' approaches to pedagogy and learning that are supposedly suitable for all students. We need to continue our empirical and ethnographic work into local school communities and cultures to understand what kind of situated responses might serve each school's participants most usefully so that all students, even those most 'different', can be included.

Chapter Summary

This chapter has shown how community languages and their speakers were managed by a school around one particular event. The school wished to project a message of equal opportunities, which it attempted to unite its community members around. Turkish and English were both put to use in order to project this message to students, staff, parents and the media. The bilingual EAL teachers' positioning as events unfolded was crucial to the head teacher. The chapter has described how bilingual EAL teachers became engaged in mediating their different roles within the school: as representatives of the children, linguistic and ethnic communities; and as teachers themselves within a school.

Notes

1. A version of this paper has appeared in the *International Journal of Bilingual Education and Bilingualism*. See Creese (2003).
2. According to the girls demonstrating outside, the 'group of students' with whom they were arguing were African-Caribbean, and it was also this group that the demonstrating girls felt were being given preferential treatment by the teachers.

Chapter 11
Conclusions

This book has investigated how an education/language policy which aims at inclusion and pluralism is played out in secondary school classrooms. This has been done by describing and analysing the various voices of the secondary school classroom. Some voices have been louder than others. My main focus has been on teachers and their relationships, and how these influence language use and pedagogies in classroom contexts. My own voice as part of this interpretive process has also been evident. I have described multiple and intertwining views of policy and practice using the language of the participants themselves and, of course, my own. Behind the use of observational vignettes, interviews and classroom transcripts is the belief that language indexes our social world. To this end, I have attempted to apply a theoretical framework which takes a social semiotic and linguistic ethnographic approach to the analysis of language and society. I have looked at how language functions within a speech community and described the patterned speech events of the classroom. However, I have also looked at how participants create meanings contingent on their local circumstances. The purpose of this chapter is to offer the reader a short summary of the main findings reported throughout the whole of this book. Towards the end of this chapter, I also look at the implications of this research for future developments in EAL.

Marginalization of EAL Across the Three Schools

EAL was marginalized across the three schools despite the best efforts of the EAL staff. Marginalization of EAL occurs because not much has been done over the years to support this subject area of the teaching profession. Little thought has been given to what happens when two teachers work together in one classroom. One finding of this research is that having two teachers in the classroom impacts on how knowledge is perceived within the class and, ultimately, how the bilingual children are seen there as well. STs and EAL teachers become linked to different pedagogies, which within the local and situated context of two-teacher classrooms are differentially valued. Currently, in secondary schools a professional knowledge based on facilitation, access and awareness of language in the absence of a curriculum subject seems to hold little currency, despite the very sound educational rationale behind such work.

I have suggested that the two kinds of teachers' different professional pressures lead them to interact differently in the classroom. EAL and subject teachers' discourses with students are qualitatively different, both in whole-class and small-group teaching. This is because teachers are balancing the dilemma of meeting both students' common and individual needs. EAL teachers engaged in more negotiation in their interactions with individual students. They were more responsive to students' utterances and guided students through the use of finely tuned questions. STs tended to move much more quickly to providing students with an answer. When teaching the whole class, the two teachers' discourses again differed. There was evidence of quantitative and qualitative differences in discursive routines. STs used a certain pattern of discourse to link themselves to the students' actions and the curriculum. EAL teachers tended not to engage in so much whole-class teaching, and when they did it was to collect answers rather than to evaluate them or to discuss study skills rather than subject content. There was also evidence of EAL teachers needing to use 'I' to define a place for themselves in the mainstream, whereas STs used 'I' to secure the relationship between themselves, their students and the curriculum. These discursive variations, along with others, such as ownership of a task, reference to the examination system and higher authorities, positioned the teachers very differently in the classroom.

In this book, I have argued for the importance of facilitative work around subject teaching. It creates learning opportunities for the bilingual student that would not otherwise exist to the same extent in the subject-focused classroom. EAL teacher-led individual and small group work is also important to the ST. This is because it keeps the class grouped together in terms of curriculum aims. In this way EAL expertise adds to class coherence and inclusion.

Language-learning as a Problem in the Mainstream

Educational policy requires STs to take full responsibility for bilingual children. The inclusive policy of mainstreaming views the classroom as providing the best environment for an input rich and motivating context for language-learning. This means that teachers need an understanding of the possibilities of how English can be learned there. I found very little evidence of this indeed. Teachers did not plan a syllabus which brought together language and subject content. STs generally placed responsibility on the students themselves for developing second-language proficiency. There was very little evidence of STs feeling a sense of responsibility for providing opportunities for second-language development. Despite the rhetoric, linguistic diversity was not seen as a resource in the mainstream setting. More often than not, it was seen as a problem (Ruiz, 1984).

EAL teachers did attempt to bring a language focus into the mainstream classroom. At times they succeeded with this. However, there were also examples of students resisting a language focus. This is not surprising when it was clear that neither the ST nor the monolingual children considered this aim as primary. Bilingual students understood this and would often reject a focus on language, however tied to subject context it was.

A reason for this appears to be the lack of understanding or agreement on what a 'focus on language' might mean in this context. As mentioned previously, there is no clear evidence of any thought having gone into how a curriculum syllabus might interact with a language syllabus, as is the case in other English-speaking countries (Mohan *et al.*, 2001). Nor was there evidence of placing language awareness at the heart of any learning. A view of knowledge and learning persists which sees subject content as fixed and superior to the processes of meaning-making, dialogue and negotiation in the construction of knowledge.

Without such a clear rationale, EAL work which focused on language form in the message-orientated context of curriculum teaching is likely to confuse bilingual students further. Moreover, opportunities were missed by all teachers to look at the role language plays in the construction of knowledge, and how students might use this knowledge within and across school contexts and, indeed, beyond the school.

Bilingual EAL Teachers: Using Community Languages in the Mainstream

An interesting finding of my research was that bilingual EAL teachers were not marginalized in the same way as non-bilingual EAL teachers were in support mode. Bilingual EAL teachers were seen by STs as providing a short cut to the transmission of subject knowledge. STs argued for a greater use of community languages for curriculum teaching. Such is the importance of this function of education, that as one ST said, 'My aim is to get them to understand. I don't care if they understand in English, Turkish or whatever'. The status given to community languages by STs is an interesting finding. It endorses the earlier point that STs see their main aim as the teaching of the curriculum rather than English-language development. Bilingual EAL teachers allow them to pursue this aim.

Bilingual EAL teachers weighed up their role in schools rather differently. The balance of language-learning and curriculum-learning aims was different. They used their skills as bilingual speakers themselves to explain subject discipline concepts in similar ways to the ST. In many ways, their pedagogies were similar to the ST. They used their knowledge of community languages to help students make connections between concepts in different languages.

However, there was a great deal of ambiguity around the use of community languages in the three schools. There was resistance by senior management to using community languages other than minimally and only until a full transition to English had been made. In line with policy statements, senior managers spoke of the necessity of support in English rather than through other languages. However, the same managers were very keen to use community languages to communicate the school's agenda to minority linguistic communities. I have illustrated how Turkish was used by one school in order to put forward its own interpretation of a particular event (see Chapter 10). Bilingual teacher identities and languages were crucial to the school in this regard.

Difficulties of Partnership Teaching in Mainstream Settings

Cooperative fully fledged teaching partnerships between subject teachers and EAL teachers in secondary schools were rare. It appears very difficult for secondary schools to support them and for teachers to organize them. However, despite these difficulties, there were real differences in the way EAL was seen in classroom where teachers worked in partnership. It was through partnerships that EAL teachers mediated their position in the school and made language and diversity more central to the school's agenda. Only in these partnerships did I observe subject teachers willing to take on roles which foregrounded language issues and some of the pedagogies associated with teaching and learning (through) them. In teaching partnerships, the EAL teacher engaged in more whole-class teaching and planned the syllabus with the ST. Discursively, teachers used 'we' to present their aims. There was mutual development and shared agendas. This included a continuity in the materials used and knowledge of students' development. There was joint responsibility for a wider set of classroom activities.

The partnerships researched in this study were formed between an experienced EAL teacher and a newly qualified subject teacher. In these secondary schools, partnerships were an oasis of collegial goodwill. However, they were not unproblematic. They received little institutional support and despite the very clear efforts that teachers made to present their work as equal, this was never completely successful. Institutional structures mediated against them, as did wider societal discourses on education. One example of an institutional discourse was the notion of 'support work' which has become attached to EAL. Language support teachers are conceptually different from language specialists and were constructed as the former in the three schools involved in this study.

Inclusion Needs to be Understood Locally

My argument has been that a language policy founded on inclusivity will achieve little if it does not consider how micro contexts of classroom life interact with larger discussions, discourses, debates and conversations on education policy. Mainstreaming as education policy and practice seeks to transform the secondary school subject-based classroom. It matters, therefore, what teachers working together do and say in class to create a new environment or sustain old ones.

Currently the policy is not working as envisaged. I have tried to show that this is not the 'fault' of the teachers themselves. Teachers are easy targets for policy failure. Rather, it is the discourses underpinned by ideologies at institutional and societal level which come to endorse certain pedagogies and sideline others. A finding of my research is that a policy of inclusivity for bilingual students does not consider linguistic diversity in any practical way. If the mainstream secondary school classroom is to be inclusive of bilingual students then managers and teachers need a clear understanding of what can be done for bilingual students and their linguistic resources. That is, multilingualism needs to be more carefully considered within ideologies of multiculturalism and inclusion. Teachers need training on the role of language in the classroom. Language needs to be considered in several ways. Teachers need a knowledge of how language(s) functions in teaching and learning for bilingual students and the skills to apply this knowledge through their pedagogies. Teachers also need training in how to make their subject curriculum available for English-language-learning.

Professional Discourses, Power and Teacher Status

A consideration of power in discourse is central when teaching linguistically diverse students. As Blommaert and Verschueren (1998: 4) have argued 'the "problem" exists to a large extent in the way in which it is put into words. The discourse on diversity is an instrument for the reproduction of social problems, forms of inequality and majority power.' In our schools, diversity is at once celebrated while also being qualified in practice as difficult and problematic. Underneath the rhetoric of the celebration of linguistic diversity is a concern with what to do about it in the classroom. Many teachers involved in this research supported the ideology of inclusion but in practice seemed not to know how to respond and work with it. The inclusion of bilingual students presented a dilemma for them. The response of many STs was to hope that EAL teachers would respond to the individual needs of bilingual students in ways that they described as not being able to. Unfortunately, working with individual students in 'support' mode positioned the EAL teachers as marginalized, despite the great importance of this work. The positioning of EAL teachers on the periphery of the school only marginalizes the needs of linguistic and ethnic minority students further. Those teachers in partnership were more able (although not without difficulty) to negotiate a place for language and diversity in the mainstream than those working in support mode. In placing language-learning and the promotion of diversity alongside curriculum aims, teachers working in partnership mode and the six bilingual EAL teachers were more able to create a discourse of 'multilingualism' as 'usual' rather than as a problem.

Some Implications

This chapter concludes with some brief suggestions for ways forward in EAL education policy. These are practical suggestions rather than theoretical and methodological ones.

(1) There is a need for teachers to receive professional development in their initial teacher training in the role language plays in teaching and learning processes. This kind of language awareness should be tied into an understanding of how the pedagogies of transmission and facilitation are discursively different. Teachers need an understanding of how different pedagogies impact on learning possibilities for their students.

(2) Education policy needs to endorse the facilitation work done by EAL teachers. Policy documents should move toward constructing this work as involving 'expertise' rather than 'support'. Notions of support position EAL work negatively within the classroom. EAL as a profession needs to be underpinned by a clearly stated professional and skills-related knowledge base (see ongoing work by NALDIC, http://www.naldic.org.uk). EAL teachers could be described as language specialists rather than language support teachers. EAL should be seen as a specialized discipline within the teaching profession.

(3) There is a need for a renewed debate on the underuse of *bilingual* EAL teachers and community languages for curriculum teaching/learning in secondary school classrooms. There is great potential to develop bilingual pedagogies within the mainstream for subject knowledge teaching. At present there is ambiguity surrounding the use of community languages for subject teaching. Policy documents need to give clear guidance to schools about using community languages for curriculum teaching, and not just in the short term.

(4) If mainstreaming is to be more than a submersion 'sink or swim' policy, it needs a coherent language and content syllabus. A clear indication of what a language focus might mean in the subject-based classroom is required and a rationale for explaining how students' English language will develop in the classroom. We need to be able to describe how students are developing their second-language learning abilities and to reward this. We need to understand how teachers are to work together to fulfil language- and subject-focused aims.

(5) A view of inclusion and multiculturalsim ought to be developed that addresses the common and individual needs of bilingual students. Specific bilingual pedagogies should be introduced and developed. Much greater thought is required on our understanding of linguistic diversity. We need to move beyond the rhetoric of celebration to an application of other languages in the mainstream for curriculum-learning. Mainstream schools can be encouraged to look at other kinds of schooling, particularly mother tongue language complementary schools, international schools, and, where possible, bilingual schools in other countries. The interface between these different kinds of schools offers opportunities for teachers to bring other languages into their classrooms for teaching and learning the curriculum.

Bibliography

Adamson, H. (1993) *Academic Competence: Theory and Classroom Practice: Preparing ESL Students for Content Courses*. New York: Longman.

Amnesty International (1995a) *Turkey: Families of 'Disappeared' Subjected to Brutal Treatment*. September. AI: EUR 44/80/95.

Amnesty International (1995b) *Turkey: Unfulfilled Promise of Reform*. September. AI Index: EUR 44/87/95.

Arkoudis, S. (1994) Changing the role relationship between classroom teacher and ESL teacher. *Prospect* 9 (3), 47–53.

Arkoudis, S. (2000) 'I have linguistic aims and linguistic content': ESL and science teachers planning together. *Prospect* 15, 61–71.

Arkoudis, S. (2003) Teaching English as a second language in science classes: Incommensurate epistemologies? *Language and Education* 17 (3), 161–73.

Atkinson, D. (1999) TESOL and culture. *TESOL Quarterly* 33 (4), 625–54.

Baetens Beardsmore, H. (2003) Who is afraid of bilingualism? In J.-M. Dewaele, A. Housen and Li Wei (eds) *Bilingualism: Beyond Basic Principles* (pp. 10–27). Clevedon: Multilingual Matters.

Bakhtin, M.M. (1973) *Problems of Dostoevsky's Poetics* (R.W. Rotsel, trans.). Ann Arbor, MI: Ardis.

Bakhtin, M.M. (1986) *Speech Genres and Other Late Essays* (V.W. McGee, trans.; C. Emerson and M. Holquist, eds). Austin, TX: University of Texas Press.

Ball, S.J. (1997) Policy sociology and critical social research: A personal review of recent education policy and policy research. *British Educational Research Journal* 23 (3), 257–74.

Baker, C. (2001) *Foundations of Bilingual Education and Bilingualism* (3rd edn). Clevedon: Multilingual Matters.

Ballard, K. (1995) Inclusion, paradigms, power and participation. In C. Clark, A. Dyson and A. Millward (eds) *Towards Inclusive Schools?* (pp. 1–15). London: David Fulton Publishers.

Barwell, R. (2004) Teaching learners of English as an additional language: A review of official guidance. *NALDIC Working Paper* 7. York: NALDIC Publications.

Benjamin, S. (2002) *The Micropolitics of Special Educational Needs: An Ethnography*. Buckingham: Open University Press.

Benson, C. (2004) Do we expect too much of bilingual teachers? Bilingual teaching in developing countries. *Bilingual Education and Bilingualism* 7 (2/3), 204–21.

Bereiter, C. and Scardamalia, M. (1981) From conversation to composition: The role of instruction in developmental process. In R. Glasser (ed.) *Advances in Instructional Psychology* (Vol. 2) Hillsdale, NJ: Erlbaum.

Billig, M., Condor, S., Edwards, D., Gane, M., Middleton, D. and Radley, A. (1988) *Ideological Dilemmas: A Social Psychology of Everyday Thinking*. London: Sage Publications.

Biott, C. (ed.) (1991) *Semi-Detached Teachers: Building Support and Advisory Relationships in Classrooms*. London: The Falmer Press.

Blackledge, A. (2001) Literacy, schooling, and ideology in a multilingual state. *The Curriculum Journal* 12 (3), 291–312.

Blackledge, A. (in press) *Discourse and Power in a Multilingual World*. London: Sage Publications.

Blommaert, J. and Verschueren, J. (1998) *Debating Diversity: Analysing the Discourse of Tolerance*. London: Routledge.

Bourdieu, P. (1977) The economics of linguistic exchanges. *Social Science Information* 16, 645–68.

Bourne, J. (1989) *Moving into the Mainstream: LEA Provision for Bilingual Pupils*. Windsor: NFER–Nelson.

Bourne, J. (1997) The continuing revolution: Teaching as learning in the mainstream multilingual classroom. In C. Leung and C. Cable (eds) *English as an Additional Language* (pp. 77–88). York: NALDIC Publications.

Bourne, J. (2001) Doing 'what comes naturally': How the discourses and routines of teachers' practice constrain opportunities for bilingual support in UK primary schools. *Language and Education* 15 (4), 250–68.

Bourne, J. and McPake, J. (1991) *Partnership Teaching: Co-operative Teaching Strategies for English Language Support in Multilingual Classrooms*. London: HMSO.

Brinton, D.M., Snow, A.M. and Bingham-Wesche, M. (1989) *Content-based Second Language Instruction*. Boston, MA: Heinle & Heinle.

Brown, G. and Wragg, E.C. (1993) *Questioning*. London: Routledge.

Bruner, J. (1975) Language as an instrument of thought. In A. Davies (ed) *Problems of Language and Learning*. London: Heinemann.

Bruner, J. (1990) *Acts of Meaning*. Cambridge, MA: Harvard University Press.

Brutt-Griffler, J. and Varghese, M. (eds) (2004) *Bilingualism and Language Pedagogy*. Clevedon: Multilingual Matters.

Bunch, G.C., Abram, P.L., Lotan, R.A. and Valdés, G. (2001) Beyond sheltered instruction: Rethinking conditions for academic language development. *TESOL Journal* 10 (2/3), 28–33.

Cameron, D. (1997) Performing gender identity: Young men's talk and the construction of heterosexual masculinity. In S. Johnson and U.H. Meinhoff (eds) *Language and Masculinity* (pp. 47–64). Oxford: Blackwell.

Campbell, D. (1994) Kurds campaigner escapes shooting. *The Guardian* 31 December, 3.

Carrasquillo, A.L. and Rodriguez, V. (1995) *Language Minority Students in the Mainstream Classroom*. Clevedon: Multilingual Matters.

Chaudron, C. (1988) *Second Language Classrooms*. Cambridge: Cambridge University Press.

Clark, R. and Ivanič, R. (1997) *The Politics of Writing*. London: Routledge.

Clark, C., Dyson, A., Millward, A. and Skidmore, D. (1995) Dialectical analysis, special needs and schools as organisations. In C. Clark, A. Dyson and A. Millward (eds) *Towards Inclusive Schools?* (pp. 78–95). London: David Fulton Publishers.

CLIP (2003) Centre for English language teaching website. On WWW at http://www.cilt/org. uk/clip/index.htm. Accessed February 2003.

Cochran-Smith, M. and Lytle, S.L. (1993) *Inside Outside: Teacher Research and Knowledge*. New York: Teachers College, Columbia University.

Coelho, E. (1998) *Teaching and Learning in Multicultural Schools*. Clevedon: Multilingual Matters.

Cohen, E. (1981) Sociology looks at team teaching. *Research in Sociology of Education and Socialization* 2, 163–93.

Corder, S.P. (1967) The significance of learners' errors. *International Review of Applied Linguistics* 4, 161–9.

Creese, A. (2000) The role of language specialists in disciplinary teaching: In search of a subject? *Journal of Multilingual and Multicultural Development* 21 (6), 451–70.

Creese, A. (2002a) EAL and ethnicity issues in teacher, professional and institutional discourses. In C. Leung (ed.) *Language and Additional/Second Language Issues For School Education: A Reader for Teachers* (pp. 14–24). York: NALDIC Publications.

Creese, A. (2002b) The discursive construction of power in teacher partnerships: Language and subject specialists in mainstream schools. *TESOL Quarterly* 36 (4), 597–616.

Creese, A. (2003) Language, ethnicity and the mediation of allegations of racism: Negotiating diversity and sameness in multilingual school discourses. *International Journal of Bilingual Education and Bilingualism* 6 (3/4), 221–36.

Creese, A. (2004) Bilingual teachers in mainstream secondary school classrooms: Using Turkish for curriculum learning. *International Journal of Bilingual Education and Bilingualism* 7 (2/3), 189–203.

Creese, A. (in press) Mediating allegations of racism in a multi-ethnic London school: What speech communities and communities of practice can tell us about discourse and power. In D. Barton and K. Tusting (eds) *Communities of Practice and New Literacy Studies.* Cambridge: Cambridge University Press.

Creese, A. (in press) Supporting talk? Partnership teachers in classroom interaction. *International Journal of Bilingual Education and Bilingualism.*

Creese, A. and Leung, C. (2003) Teachers' discursive constructions of ethno-linguistic difference: Working with inclusive policy. *Prospect* 18 (2), 3–19.

Creese, A. and Martin, P. (2003) Multilingual classroom ecologies: Inter-relationships, interactions and ideologies. *International Journal of Bilingual Education and Bilingualism* 6 (3/4), 161–7.

Creese, A., Norwich, B. and Daniels, H. (2000) Evaluating teacher support teams in secondary schools: Supporting teachers for SEN and other needs. *Research Papers in Education* 15 (3), 307–24.

Cummins, J. (1988) From multicultural to anti-racist education: An analysis of programmes and policies in Ontario. In T. Skutnabb-Kangas and J. Cummins (eds) *Minority Education* (pp. 79–102). Clevedon: Multilingual Matters.

Cummins, J. (1991) Interdependence of first- and second-language proficiency in bilingual children. In E. Bialystok (ed.) *Language Processing in Bilingual Children* (pp. 70–89). Cambridge: Cambridge University Press.

Cummins, J. (2000) *Language, Power and Pedagogy: Bilingual Children in the Crossfire.* Clevedon: Multilingual Matters.

Cummins, J. (2001) *Negotiating Identities: Education for Empowerment in a Diverse Society* (2nd edn). Ontario, CA: California Association of Bilingual Education.

Daniels, H., Creese, A., Hey, L.D. and Smith, M. (2001) Gender and learning: Equity, equality and pedagogy. *Support for Learning* 16 (3), 112–16.

Davison, C. and Williams, A. (2001) Integrating language and content: Unresolved issues. In B. Mohan, C. Leung and C. Davison (eds) *English as a Second Language in the Mainstream: Teaching, Learning and Identity* (pp. 51–71). Harlow: Longman.

Department of Education and Science (DES) (1975) *A Language for Life* (The Bullock Report). London: HMSO.

Department of Education and Science (DES) (1985) *Education for All: The Report of the Committee of Inquiry into the Education of Children from Ethnic Minority Groups* (The Swann Report). London: HMSO.

Department of Education and Science (DES) (1989) *English for Ages 5–16* (The Cox Report). London: HMSO.

Department for Education and Skills (DfES) (2003) *Aiming High: Raising the Achievement of Minority Ethnic Pupils.* London: DfES Publications.

Dewaele, J.-M., Housen, A. and Li Wei (eds) (2003) *Bilingualism: Beyond Basic Principles.* Clevedon: Multilingual Matters.

Donaldson, M. (1978) *Children's Minds.* Glasgow: Collins.

Eckert, P. and McConnel-Ginnet, S. (1998) Communities of practice: Where language, gender and power all live. In J. Coates (ed.) *Language and Gender: A Reader*. Oxford: Blackledge.

Edwards, A. (2000) Researching pedagogy: A socio-cultural agenda. Inaugural Lecture, University of Birmingham. On WWW at http://www.edu.bham.ac.uk/SAT/Edwards1.html. Accessed August 2001.

Edwards, V. and Redfern, A. (1992) *The World in a Classroom*. Clevedon: Multilingual Matters.

Erickson, F. (1975) Gatekeeping and the melting pot: Interaction in counseling encounters. *Harvard Educational Review* 45 (1), 44–70.

Erickson, F. (1990) Qualitative Methods. In R.L. Linn and F. Erickson *Research in Teaching and Learning* (Vol. 2). New York: Macmillan.

Erickson, F. (1996) Ethnographic microanalysis. In S.L. McKay and N.H. Hornberger (eds) *Sociolinguistics and Language Teaching* (pp. 283–306). New York: Cambridge University Press.

Erickson, F. and Shultz, J. (1982) *The Counselor as Gatekeeper: Social Interaction in Interviews*. New York: Academic Press.

Fairclough, N. (1989) *Language and Power*. London: Longman.

Fairclough, N. (1995) *Critical Discourse Analysis: The Critical Study of Language*. London: Longman.

Fairclough, N. (1997) Discourse across disciplines: Discourse analysis in researching social change. *AILA Review* 12 (3), 17.

Fairclough, N. (2000) Dialogue in the public sphere. In S. Sarangi and M. Coulthard (eds) *Discourse and Social Life* (pp. 170–84). Harlow: Longman.

Feinberg, W. (1996) *The Goals of Multicultural Education: A Critical Re-evaluation*. On WWW at http://www.ed.uiuc.edu/EPS/PES-yearbook/96_docs/feinberg.html. Accessed July 2004.

Freeman, Y.S. and Freeman, D.E. (1992) *Whole Language for Second Language Learners*. Portsmouth, NH: Heinemann.

Fujimoto-Adamson, N. (2003) Policy and practice of the partnership in team-teaching classrooms: Ideology and reality. *Bulletin of Shinshu Honan Junior College* 20.

Fullan, M. and Hargreaves, A. (1992) *What's Worth Fighting For In Your School?* Buckingham: OUP/OPSTF.

Gal, S. and Woolard, K. (1995) Constructing languages and publics: Authority and representation. *Pragmatics* 5 (2), 129–38.

Gardner, S. (in press) Centre-stage in the instructional register: Partnership talk in primary EAL. To appear in *International Journal of Bilingual Education and Bilingualism*.

Gee, J.P. (1999) *An Introduction to Discourse Analysis*. London: Routledge.

Geertz, C. (1988) *Works and Lives: The Anthropologist as Author*. Cambridge: Polity Press.

Gerber, M.M. and Semmel, M.I. (1985) The microeconomics of referral and reintegration: A paradigm for evaluation of special education. *Studies in Educational Evaluation* 11, 13–29.

Gibbons, P. (1993) *Learning to Learn in a Second Language*. Portsmouth, NH: Heinemann.

Gibbons, P. (2002) *Scaffolding Language, Scaffolding Learning: Teaching Second Language Learners in the Mainstream Classroom*. Portsmouth, NH: Heinemann.

Giddens, A. (1993) In P. Cassell (ed.) *The Giddens Reader*. Basingstoke: Macmillan.

Gravelle, M. (1996) *Supporting Bilingual Learners in Schools*. Stoke-on-Trent: Trentham Books.

GTC (General Teaching Council for England) (2003) On WWW at http://www.gtce.org.uk/news/newsDetail.asp?NewsId=482. Accessed January 2004.

Guerra, J. (1997) The place of intercultural literacy in the writing classroom. In C. Severino, J.C. Guerra and J.E. Butler (eds) *Writing in Multicultural Settings* (pp. 248–60). New York: Modern Languages Association.

Gumperz, J.J. (1972) Sociolinguistics and communication in small groups. In J.B. Pride and J. Holmes (eds) *Sociolinguistics* (pp. 203–24). Harmondsworth: Penguin.

Gumperz, J.J. (1982) *Discourse Strategies*. Cambridge: Cambridge University Press.

Gumperz, J.J. (1999) On interactional sociolinguistic method. In S. Sarangi and C. Roberts (eds) *Talk, Work and Institutional Order: Discourse in Medical, Mediation and Management Settings* (pp. 453–71). New York: Mouton de Gruyter.

Halliday, M.A.K. and Martin, J.R. (1993) *Writing Science.* London: Falmer. (US edn: University of Pittsburg Press.)

Hammersley, M. (ed.) (1984) The paradigmatic mentality: A diagnosis. In L. Barton and S. Walker (eds) *Social Crisis and Educational Research.* London: Croon Helm.

Hanko, G. (1999) *Increasing Competence Through Collaborative Problem-solving.* London: David Fulton Publishers.

Hanks, W.F. (1996) *Language and Communicative Practices.* Boulder, CO: Westview.

Hargreaves, A. (1994) *Changing Teachers, Changing Times.* London: Cassell.

Harley, B. (1993) Instructional strategies and SLA in early French immersion. *Studies in Second Language Acquisition* 15, 245–59.

Haugen, E. (1972) The ecology of language. In A.S. Dill (ed.) *Essays by Einar Haugen* (pp. 325–37). Stanford, CA: Stanford University Press.

Heller, M. (1999) *Linguistic Minorities and Modernity: A Sociolinguistic Ethnography.* London: Longman.

Heller, M. and Martin-Jones, M. (eds) (2001) *Voices of Authority: Education and Linguistic Difference* (pp. 1–28). Westport, CT: Ablex.

Hoey, M. (1991) *Patterns of Lexis in Text.* Oxford: Oxford University Press.

Holliday, A. (1999) Small cultures. *Applied Linguistics* 20 (2), 239–64.

Hornberger, N. (1989) Trámites and transportes: The acquisition of second language communicative competence for one speech event in Puno, Peru. *Applied Linguistics* 10 (2), 214–22.

Hornberger, N. (1993) Ethnography in linguistic perspective: Understanding school processes. Paper presented at the Annual Meeting of the American Anthropological Association, Washington DC.

Hornberger, N. (1996) Language and education. In S.L. McKay and N.H. Hornberger (eds) *Sociolinguistics and Language Teaching* (pp. 449–73). New York: Cambridge University Press.

Hornberger, N. (2002) Multilingual language policies and the continua of biliteracy: An ecological approach. *Language policy* 1 (1), 27–51.

Hornberger, N. (2003) Linguistic anthropology of education (LAE) in context. In S. Wortham and B. Rymes (eds) *Linguistic Anthropology of Education* (pp. 245–70). Westport CT: Praeger Press.

Hornberger, N. (2004) The continua of biliteracy and the bilingual educator: Educational linguistics in practice. *Bilingual Education and Bilingualism* 7 (2/3), 155–71.

Hornberger, N. and Skilton-Sylvester, E. (2000) Revisiting the continua of biliteracy: International and critical perspective. *Language and Education* 14, 96–122.

Hymes, D. (1968) The ethnography of speaking. In J. Fishman (ed.) *Readings in the Sociology of Language* (pp. 99–138). The Hague: Moulton.

Hymes, D. (1972) On communicative competence. In J.B. Pride and J. Holmes (eds) *Sociolinguistics* (pp. 269–93). Harmondsworth: Penguin.

Hymes, D. (1974) *Foundations in Sociolinguistics: An Ethnographic Approach.* Philadelphia, PA: University of Pennsylvania Press.

Hymes, D. (1980) Language in education: Forward to fundamentals. *Language in Education: Ethnolinguistic Essays.* Washington, DC: Center for Applied Linguistics.

IOE (Institute of Education) (1999) Turkish Cypriot children in London schools: A report for the Turkish Cypriot Forum by the International Centre for Intercultural Studies and the Culture, Communication and Societies Group. London: Institute of Education, University of London.

Ivanič, R. (1998) *Writing and Identity: The Discoursal Construction of Identity in Academic Writing.* Amsterdam: John Benjamins.

Ivanič, R. (2004) Discourses of writing and learning to write. *Language and Education* 18 (3), 220–45.

Jakobson, R. (1960) Linguistics and Poetics. *Selected Writings II*. The Hague: Mouton.

Jakobson, R. (1971) Shifters, verbal categories, and the Russian verb. *Selected Writings II*. The Hague: Mouton.

Jarvis, J. and Robinson, M. (1997) Analysing educational discourse: An exploratory study of teacher response and support to pupils' learning. *Applied Linguistics* 18 (2), 212–28.

Johnson, K.E. (1995) *Understanding Communication in Second Language Classrooms*. Cambridge: Cambridge University Press.

Johnson, S. (1997) Theorizing language and masculinity. In S. Johnson and U.H. Meinhoff (eds) *Language and Masculinity*. Oxford: Blackwell.

Kessler, C. (ed.) (1992) *Cooperative Language Learning*. Englewood Cliffs, NJ: Prentice Hall Regents.

Kottak, C.P. and Kozaitis, K.A. (1999) *On Being Different: Diversity and Multiculturalism in the North American Mainstream*. New York: McGraw-Hill.

Kramsch, C. (1998) The privilege of the intercultural speaker. In M. Byram and M. Fleming (eds) *Language and Learning in Intercultural Perspective* (pp. 16–31). Cambridge: Cambridge University Press.

Kress, G. (1999) English at the crossroads: Rethinking curricula of communication in the context of the turn to the visual. In G.E. Hawisher and C.L. Selfe (eds) *Passions Pedagogies and 21st Century Technologies* (pp. 66–88). Logan, UT: Utah University Press and NCTE.

Ladbury, S. (1977) The Turkish Cypriots: Ethnic relations in London and Cyprus. *Between Two Cultures*. Oxford: Basil Blackwell.

Lee, A. (1997) Working together? Academic literacies, co-production and professional partnerships. *Literacy and Numeracy Studies* 7, 65–82.

Lemke, J. (1990) *Talking Science: Language, Learning and Values*. Norwood, NJ: Ablex.

Lemke, J. (2002) Becoming the village: Education across lives. In G. Wells and G. Claxton (eds) *Learning for Life in the 21st Century*. Oxford: Blackwell Publishing.

Leont'ev, A.N. (1981) *Problems of the Development of Mind*. Moscow: Progress Publishers.

Leung, C. (2001) English as an additional language: Distinct language focus or diffused curriculum concerns. *Language and Education* 15 (1), 33–55.

Leung, C. and Franson, C. (2001a) Curriculum identity and professional development: System-wide questions. In B. Mohan, C. Leung and C. Davison (eds) *English as a Second Language in the Mainstream: Teaching, Learning and Identity* (pp. 153–64). Harlow: Longman.

Leung, C. and Franson, C. (2001b) England: ESL in the early days. In B. Mohan, C. Leung and C. Davison (eds) *English as a Second Language in the Mainstream: Teaching, Learning and Identity* (pp. 199–214). Harlow: Longman.

Leung, C., Harris, R. and Rampton, B. (1997) The idealized native speaker, reified ethnicities and classroom realities. *TESOL Quarterly* 31, 543–56.

Levine, J. (ed.) (1990) *Bilingual Learners and the Mainstream Curriculum*. London: Falmer.

Long, M. (1983) Native speaker/non-native speaker conversation and the negotiation of comprehensible input. *Applied Linguistics* 4, 126–41.

Long, M. (1991) Focus on form: A design feature in language teaching methodology. In D. Kees de Bot, R.G. Coste and C. Kramsch (eds) *Foreign Language Research in Cross-Cultural Perspective* (pp. 39–52). Amsterdam: John Benjamins.

Long, M. and Sato, C. (1983) Classroom foreigner talk discourse: Forms and functions of teachers' questions. In H.W. Seliger and M.H. Long (eds) *Classroom Oriented Research in Second Language Acquisition*. Rowley, MA: Newbury House Publishers.

Lucy, J.A. (1991) Empirical research and linguistic relativity. Paper prepared for symposium No. 112 'Rethinking linguistic relativity', 3–11 May. Ocho Rios, Jamaica.

Lucy, J.A. (1993) *Reflexive Language*. Cambridge: Cambridge University Press.

Luke, A. and Luke, C. (1999) Pedagogy. In Bernard Spolsky (ed.) *Concise Encyclopaedia of Educational Linguistics* (pp. 332–6). Amsterdam: Elsevier.

Lynch, T. (1996) *Communication in the Language Classroom*. Oxford: Oxford University Press.

Mackey, A., Gass, S. and McDonough, K. (2000) How do learners perceive interactional feedback? *Studies in Second Language Acquisition* 22 (4), 471–97.

MacLure, M. (2003) *Discourse in Educational and Social Research*. Buckingham: Open University Press.

Martin, P., Bhatt, A., Bhohani, N. and Creese, A. (2004) Final report on complimentary schools and their communities in Leicester. University of Leicester/University of Birmingham (ESRC R000223949). On WWW at: http://www.le.ac.uk/education/research/complementaryschools.index.html.

Martin, P., Bhatt, A., Bhohani, N. and Creese, A. (in press) Managing bilingual interaction in a Gujarati complementary school in Leicester. To appear in *Language and Education*.

Martin-Jones, M. and Heller, M. (1996) Introduction to the special issues on education in multilingual settings: Discourse, identities, and power. *Linguistics and Education* 8, 3–16.

Martin-Jones, M. and Saxena, M. (1989) Developing a partnership with bilingual classroom assistants. Working Paper No. 16, Centre for Language in Social Life, Lancaster University.

Martin-Jones, M. and Saxena, M. (1996) Turn-taking, power asymmetries and the positioning of bilingual participants in classroom discourse. *Linguistics and Education* 8, 105–23.

Martin-Jones, M. and Saxena, M. (2003) Bilingual resources and 'funds of knowledge' for teaching and learning in multi-ethnic classrooms in Britain. *International Journal of Bilingual Education and Bilingualism* 6 (2/3), 267–82.

May, S. (2001) *Language and Minority Rights: Ethnicity, Nationalism and the Politics of Language*. London: Longman.

Mehmet Ali, A. (1991) The Turkish speech community. *Multilingualism in the British Isles* (Vol. 1) (pp. 202–13). London: Longman.

Mercer, N. (1994) Neo-Vygotskian theory and classroom education. In J. Maybin (ed.) *Language, Literacy and Learning in Educational Practice*. Clevedon: Multilingual Matters/Open University.

Mercer, N. (1995) *The Guided Construction of Knowledge: Talk Amongst Teachers and Learners*. Clevedon: Multilingual Matters.

Mohan, B.A. (1986) *Language and Content*. Reading: Addison-Wesley Publishing Company.

Mohan, B., Leung, C. and Davison, C. (2001) *English as a Second Language in the Mainstream: Teaching, Learning and Identity*. Harlow: Longman.

Morgan, B. (2004) Teacher identity as pedagogy: Towards a field-internal conceptualisation in bilingual and second language education. *Bilingual Education and Bilingualism* 7 (2/3), 172–88.

Musumeci, D. (1996) Teacher-learner negotiation in content-based instruction: Communication at cross purposes. *Applied Linguistics* 17 (3), 286–325.

NALDIC (National Association for Language Development in the Curriculum) (1999) *Working Paper 5. The Distinctivenss of English as an Additional Language: A Cross-curriculum Discipline*. Watford: NALDIC.

National Curriculum Council (NCC) (1991) *Circular Number 11: Linguistic Diversity and the National Curriculum*. York: NCC.

Nias, J. (1989) *Primary Teachers Talking*. London: Routledge.

Nias, J. (1993a) Changing times, changing identities: Grieving for a lost self. In R. Burgess (ed.) *Educational Research and Evaluation* (pp. 139–56). London: The Falmer Press.

Nias, J. (ed.) (1993b) *The Human Nature of Learning: Selection from the Work of M. L. J. Abercrombie*. Buckingham: Open University Press.

Norwich, B. (1994) Differentiation: From the perspective of resolving tensions between basic social values and assumptions about individual differences. *Curriculum Studies* 2 (3), 289–308.

Norwich, B. (1996) *Special Needs Education, Inclusive Education or Just Education for All?* Inaugural lecture, Institute of Education, University of London.

Nuffield Languages Inquiry (2000) *Languages: The Next Generation.* The final report and recommendations of the Nuffield Langauges Inquiry. London: Nuffield Foundation.

Ochs, E. (1996) Linguistics resources for socializing humanity. In J.J. Gumperz and S. Levinson (eds) *Rethinking Linguistic Relativity* (pp. 407–37). Cambridge: Cambridge University Press.

Office for Standards in Education (Ofsted) (1993) *Report of the Inspection of X School.* London: HMSO.

Office for Standards in Education (1994) *Report of the Inspection of X School.* London: HMSO.

Office for Standards in Education (2001) *Inspecting English as an Additional Language: 11–16 with Guidance on Self-evaluation.* London: Ofsted.

Pavlenko, A. and Blackledge, A. (eds) (2004) *Negotiation of Identities in Multilingual Settings.* Clevedon: Multilingual Matters.

Peirce, C. (1955) *Collected Papers II. Philosophical writings of Peirce* (J. Buchler, ed.). New York: Dover (originally published in 1940 as *The Philosophy of Peirce: Selected Writings.* London: Routledge and Kegan Paul).

Pica, T. (1991) Classroom interaction, participation and comprehension: Redefining relationships. *System* 19, 437–45.

Pica, T. (1995) Teaching language and teaching language learners: The expanding roles and expectations of language teachers in communicative, content-based classrooms. In J.E. Alatis, C.A. Straehle, B. Gallenberger and M. Ronkin (eds) *Linguistics and the Education of Language Teachers: Ethnolinguistic, Psycholinguistic, and Sociolinguistic Aspects* (pp. 379–97). Washington, DC: Georgetown University Press.

Pica, T. (2000) Tradition and transition in English language teaching methodology. *System* 28, 1–18.

Qualifications and Curriculum Authority (QCA) (2000) *A Language in Common: Assessing English as an Additional Language.* London: QCA.

Rampton, B. (1990) Displacing the 'native speaker': Expertise, affiliation and inheritance. *ELT Journal* 449, 503–27.

Rampton, B. (1995) *Crossing: Language and Ethnicity Among Adolescents.* London: Longman.

Rampton, B. (1998) Speech community. In J. Verschueren, J.-O. Ostman, J. Blommaert and C. Bulcan (eds) *Handbook of Pragmatics.* Amsterdam/Philadelphia, PA: John Benjamins.

Rampton, B., Harris, R. and Leung, C. (1999) Multilingualism in England: A review of research in A. Tosi and C. Leung (eds) *Rethinking Language Education: From a Monolingual to Multilingual Perspective.* London: Royal Holloway, University of London and CiLT.

Refugee Council (1995) Kurds: Turkish Kurdish refugees in the UK/Kurds in Turkey. *Refugee Council Factsheet.* January.

Reid, E. (1988) Linguistic minorities and language education: The English experience. *Journal of Multilingual and Multicultural Development* 9 (1/2), 181–92.

Ricento, T. (1998) National language policy in the United States. In T. Ricento and B. Burnaby (eds) *Language and Politics in the United States and Canada: Myths and Realities* (pp. 85–112). Mahwah, NJ: Lawrence Erlbaum.

Ricento, T. (2000a) Historical and theoretical perspectives in language policy and planning. *Journal of Sociolinguistics* 4 (2), 196–213.

Ricento, T. (2000b) *Ideology, Politics and Language Policies: Focus on English.* Amsterdam: John Benjamins.

Richard-Amato, P.A. and Snow, M.A. (1992) *The Multicultural Classroom.* London: Longman.

Roberts, C. and Sarangi, S. (1999) Hybridity in gatekeeping discourse: Issues of practical relevance for the researcher. In S. Sarangi and C. Roberts (eds) *Discourse in Medical, Mediation and Management Settings.* Berlin: Mouton de Gruyter.

Rosenholtz, S. (1989) *Teachers' Workplace: The Social Organization of Schools.* White Plains, NY: Longman.

Ruiz, R. (1984) Orientations in language planning. *NABE Journal* 2, 15–34.

Ruiz, R. (1992) Critical research issues in bilingual secondary education. Third national research symposium on limited English proficient student issues: Focus on middle and high school issues. On WWW at http://www.ncela.gwu.edu/ncbepubs/symposia/thir/ruiz.htm. Accessed 24 January 2003.

Sapir, E. (1921) *Language: An Introduction to the Study of Speech.* London: Hart-Davies.

Sapir. E. (1949) *Culture, Language and Personality: Selected Essays* (D.G. Mandelbaum, ed.). Berkeley, CA: University of California Press.

Sarangi, S. and Coulthard, M. (eds) (2000) *Discourse and Social Life.* Harlow: Longman.

Sarangi, S. and Roberts, C. (2002) Discoursal (mis)alignments in professional gatekeeping encounters. In C. Kramsch (ed.) *Language Acquisition and Language Socialisation: An Ecological Perspective.* London: Continuum.

Scardamalia, M. and Bereiter, C. (1999) Schools as knowledge building organizations. On WWW at http://csile.oise.utoronto.ca/abstract/ciar-understanding.html. Accessd August 2000.

Schegloff, E. and Sacks, H. (1973) Opening up closings. *Semiotica* 8, 289–327 (reprinted in R. Turner (ed.) *Ethnomethodology: Selected Readings.* Baltimore, MD: Penguin).

Schmidt, R. (1990) The role of consciousness in second language acquisition. *Applied Linguistics* 11 (2), 17–46.

Schmidt, R. and Frota, S. (1986) Developing basic conversational ability in a second language: A case study of an adult learner of Portuguese. In R. Day (ed.) *Talking to Learn* (pp. 237–326). Rowley, MA: Newbury House Publishers.

School Curriculum and Assessment Authority (SCAA) (1996) *Teaching English as an Additional Language: A Framework for Policy.* London: SCAA.

Scribner, S. and Cole, M. (1973) Cognitive consequences of formal and informal education. *Science* 182, 553–9.

Silverstein, M. (2003) Indexical order and the dialectics of sociolinguistic life. *Language and Communication* 23, 193–229.

Silverstein, M. and Urban, G. (eds) (1996) *The Natural History of Discourse.* Chicago, IL: University of Chicago Press.

Sinclair, J.M. and Coulthard, M. (1975) *Towards an Analysis of Discourse.* London: Oxford University Press.

Snow, C.E., Cancino, H., De Temple, J. and Schley, S. (1991) Giving formal definitions: A linguistic or metalinguistic skill? In E. Bialystock (ed.) *Language Processing Bilingual Children* (pp. 90–112). Cambridge: Cambridge University Press.

Street, B. (1999) New literacies in theory and practice: What are the implications for language in education? *Linguistics and Education* 19 (1), 1–24.

Swain, M. (1995) Three functions of output in second language learning. In G. Cook and B. Seidhofer (eds) *Principle and Practice in Applied Linguistics: Studies in Honour of H.G. Widdowson* (pp. 125–44). Oxford: Oxford University Press.

Tsui, A.B.-M. (1985) Analyzing input and interaction in second language classrooms. *RELC Journal* 16, 8–32.

Tsui, A.B.-M. (1995) *Introducing Classroom Interaction.* London: Penguin.

UKLEF (UK Linguistic Ethnography Forum) (2004) On WWW at http://www.ling-ethnog.org.uk. Accessed January 2004.

Valdés, G. (1997) Dual-language immersion programmes: A cautionary note concerning the education of language-minority students. *Harvard Educational Review* 67 (6), 391–429.

Valdés, G. (1998) The world outside and inside schools: Language and immigrant children. *Educational Researcher* 27 (6), 4–18.

Valdés, G. (2004) Between support and marginalisation: The development of academic language in linguistic minority children. *Bilingual Education and Bilingualism* 7 (2/3), 102–32.

Van Dijk, T. (1993) Principles of critical discourse analysis. *Discourse & Society* 4, 249–83.

Varghese, M. (2004) Professional development for bilingual teachers in the United States: A site of articulating and contesting professional roles. *Bilingual Education and Bilingualism* 7 (2/3), 222–37.

Vislie, L. (1995) Integration policies, school reforms and organsation of schooling for handicapped pupils in western societies. In C. Clark, A. Dyson and A. Millward (eds) *Towards Inclusve Schools?* (pp. 42–53). London: David Fulton Publishers.

Vygotsky, L.S. (1978) *Mind in Society*. Cambridge, MA: Harvard University Press.

Vygotsky, L.S. (1986) *Thought and Language* (A. Kozulin, trans. and ed.). Cambridge, MA: MIT Press.

Wells, G. (1986) *The Meaning Makers*. London: Hodder and Stoughton.

White, J. (1999) The development of EAL methodology in UK schools. Teaching materials, Institute of Education.

White, L. (1987) Against comprehensible input: The input hypothesis and the development of second-language competence. *Applied Linguistics* 8 (1), 95–110.

Wodak, R. (2000) Recontextualization and the transformation of meanings: A critical discourse analysis of decision making in EU meetings about employment policies. In S. Sarangi and M. Coulthard (eds) *Discourse and Social Life* (pp. 185–206). Harlow: Longman.

Wolfson, N. (1981) Compliments in cross-cultural perspective. *TESOL Quarterly* 15 (2), 117–24.

Wolfson, N. (1989) *Perspectives: Sociolinguistics and TESOL*. Cambridge, MA: Newbury House Publishers.

Wong-Fillmore, L. (1991) Second-language learning in children: A model of language learning social context. In E. Bialystok (ed.) *Language Processing in Bilingual Children* (pp. 49–69). Cambridge: Cambridge University Press.

Woods, P. (1993) *Critical Events in Teaching and Learning*. London: The Falmer Press.

Woollacott, M. (1995) All dazed and confused. *The Guardian* 14 October, 26.

Wortham, S. (2003) An introduction. In D. Wiliam and B. Rymes (eds) *Linguistic Anthropolgy of Education* (pp. 1–30). Westport, CT: Praeger Press.

Yanow, D. (1996) *How Does a Policy Mean? Interpreting Policy and Organizational Actions*. Washington, DC: Georgetown University Press.

Index